FOREWORD

The task I set myself in this book was to give some account of every 'significant' brand of whisky made and bottled in Scotland. I defined 'significant' as: a) every available single malt and single grain whisky; b) every brand of whisky blended in Scotland with a reasonable market-share, anywhere in the world; and c) every blended whisky with a story to tell. And the stories are abundant: generally, I have been uncritical in my inclusion of myth as well as dry fact, although I have cheerfully laid a few ghosts!

My original intention was to write a comprehensive Directory of Scotch whisky brands. At an early stage in the research it was discovered that there have been in the region of 10,000 brands around at one time or another, and that merchants' lists even from ten years ago offer over 2,000 brands and expressions. So I have limited myself to brands which are currently available.

The huge majority of these brands are no longer being made, or were one-off bottlings, or are bottled exclusively for clubs, companies or hotels, so it is unlikely that you will encounter them. However, there may be some interesting or 'significant' brands I have missed – I apologize in advance, and hope readers and brand owners will alert me to them. For future editions I shall also be grateful for any additional information about the brands included in this book. The information I have managed to obtain from owners and from published sources is patchy: the whisky industry has never been assiduous in preserving its historical records – in some cases, little or nothing is known about an individual brand; in other cases marketing departments choose to be discrete, or to supply unedifying information.... The length and detail of the entries which follow to a large extent reflects the help I have had from brand owners.

Space does not allow me to acknowledge everyone who has contributed towards the making of this book. However, I should especially like to thank the following:

First my Editorial Assistant, Philip Woyka, who kept abreast of an awesome research programme – we commenced with over a thousand brands to investigate – and who made sure the book continued to progress even through periods of frustration. Second, my wife, Sheila, who detests the taste of whisky yet has endured endless whisky talk and tasting into the small hours. Third, my editors at Mitchell Beazley, Anne Ryland and Stephanie Horner, whose painstaking attention to detail has ensured focus and accuracy. Fourth, I should like to thank the following individual members of the industry, for help and advice which went beyond duty: Sheila Birtles and Dr Jim Swan (Pentlands Scotch Whisky Research, Ltd), Trevor Cowan (The Invergordon Distillers, Ltd), Campbell Evans (The Scotch Whisky Association), Wynn Fanshaw (United Distillers plc), Matthew Gloag (Highland Distillers plc), Richard Gordon (Macdonald Martin Distillers plc), Robin Lambie (Macallan-Glenlivet, plc), Colin Lidell (and his assistant, Janice Mack, United Distillers, plc), Denise Neilson (Scotch Malt Whisky Society) and Ian Urquhart (Gordon & MacPhail Ltd).

Finally, this book would not have been possible without the support of the companies whose brands are included, to all of whom I am profoundly grateful.

HOW TO USE THIS BOOK

The purpose of this book is simple: to encourage the enjoyment and appreciation of Scotch – both single malts (the *grands crus* of whiskies) and blended whiskies (which account for over 96% of the Scotch drunk, and which have proved their world-wide appeal).

The main sections of the book are accordingly laid out alphabetically as a Directory of brands, first Malt and Grain Whiskies (there are only two of the latter), then Blended Whiskies (including Liqueur Whiskies and Vatted Malts). Names in bold type within the entries refer readers to other entries in the directory.

To understand fully some of the references in the individual entries, I have prefaced the Directory with an Introduction, comprising a brief history of Scotch and of the whisky industry, an account of the salient features of production of the three kinds of whisky – malt, grain and blended – and some observations on whisky tasting and appreciation.

The Appendices provide what I hope will be useful 'support' information: a glossary; a 'whisky flavour checklist', (this might be photocopied and used for practical research purposes!); a list of distilleries which welcome visitors; details of a handful of whisky societies; some curious statistics about the major markets for Scotch and the best-selling brands; something about collecting whiskies, and a bibliography.

If this little book adds to your enjoyment of the dram in your glass, to your pleasure in the bottle you have just purchased, it will have succeeded. But my hope is that you might be sufficiently intrigued to foray forth and try whiskies with which you are unfamiliar. Then the book will have introduced you to the most pleasurable pursuit in the world.

A NOTE ON 'PROOF SPIRIT'

Proof spirit means alcohol of tried (i.e. proved strength), and in early times the test of 100° proof was that strength of alcohol which, when mixed with water and gunpowder, would still allow the gunpowder to ignite.

The invention of the hydrometer allowed for more precise definition: British proof spirit is that which, at 51°F (10.5° C) weighs twelve-thirteenths of an equal volume of water at the same temperature (i.e. spirit which contains 57.1% alcohol by volume).

American proof is calculated differently, and the standard is 50% alcohol at 60°F (15.5° C). So British proof spirit (i.e. at 100° proof) is equal to 114.2° proof in the US (or 14.2° over proof). American 100° proof is the same as British 87.7° proof.

NB: Throughout the book I have followed imperial/metric units of measurement as appropriate.

INTRODUCTION

A BRIEF HISTORY OF SCOTCH WHISKY

A Sublime Remedy

There is a tradition that St Patrick introduced distilling to Ireland in the 5th century AD, and that the Dalriadic Scots brought the secret with them when they arrived in Kintyre around 500. This quaint legend may hold a grain of truth, since it is certain that St Patrick brought his adoptive country into contact with Continental culture, and possible that the art of distilling was known in Spain and France at that time.

Taliesin, the 6th-century British poet, who lived in present-day Cumbria (where St Patrick hailed from, forby) praises distilled mead, but this may be a mis-translation, and it is more likely that the secrets of distilling were perfected, if not discovered, by the Arabs and brought to Europe by the Moors in the 10th century.

The process was originally applied to perfume, then to wine, and finally adapted to fermented mashes of cereals in countries where grapes were not abundant. The spirit was universally termed *aquavitae* ('water of life'; in Gaelic, *uisge beatha*) and was commonly made in monasteries, used chiefly for medicinal purposes. There were monastic distilleries in Ireland by the late 12th century.

Scotland's great Renaissance king, James IV (1488–1513), was fond of 'ardent spirits'. The earliest written reference to distilling in Scotland dates from the Exchequer Rolls for 1494 where an entry records the sale of eight bolls of malt (i.e. 1,120 lb (508 kg)) to one Friar John Corr, wherewith 'to make *aquavitae*', and twelve years later, when the King visited Dundee, the Treasury Accounts record a payment to a local barber for the supply of *aquavitae* for the King's pleasure. The reference to a barber is not surprising. In 1505 the Guild of Surgeon Barbers in Edinburgh was granted a monopoly over the manufacture of *aquavitae* – a fact which reflects the spirit's perceived medicinal properties.

James IV also supported the alchemical researches into distilling of John Damien, an Italian whom the King made Abbot of Tongland in Kirkudbrightshire, who unsuccessfully attempted to fly from the walls of Sterling Castle with wings of his own invention, in the presence of the King. (He explained his failure by the fact that he had used some hen's feathers in his flying machine, and that 'hens aspire more to the midden than to the heavens'!)

During the course of the 15th century, better still design combined with the dissolution of the monasteries to spread the practice of distilling throughout Scotland.

By the 1570s it is safe to assume that distilling was endemic: crop failure in 1579 led to the Scottish Parliament banning it for a year (exempting only 'lords and gentlemen, for their own use'), on the grounds that the amount of barley being used for distilling was having an adverse effect on food supplies.

The first tax on spirits was imposed by the Scottish Parliament in 1644 to help finance the Royalist army; this was reduced by Cromwell, abandoned after the Restoration of Charles II and reimposed in the 1690s.

Throughout the 17th century distilling remained small-scale, mostly done in private houses, as a sideline to farming (see **Haig's**). But whisky drinking was widespread: during the funeral wake for Sir Donald Campbell of Ardnamurchan in 1651 the largest item on the bill was for "*5 gallons and one quart of uisge beatha*"; later in the century recruits to the Earl of Argyll's regiment were allowed a gill of whisky a day (about half a pint at 40% alcohol). The first reference to a distillery was in an Act of 1690. Duncan Forbes of Culloden had supported the Protestant succession, and had had his lands sacked by Jacobites for his pains. Following the success of his cause, the Scottish Parliament granted him and his successors the right to distil free of duty in perpetuity (the privilege was only withdrawn in the 1780s).

Whisky Wars

The Act of Union (1707) provided that the English duties on excisable liquors should be levied in Scotland, and in 1713 this clause was applied in the form of a malt tax, despite fierce opposition. When the tax was increased in 1725 for political reasons (Walpole wanted to assert his authority in Scotland), there were riots in Glasgow. The tax led to a decline in the production of ale, which was the universal drink of the commonalty, and to an increase in the production of spirits (which tripled in a year).

It should be explained that most whisky – this phonetic abbreviation of *uisge beatha* (usually written as *usky*) began to be widely used in the 1720s – was made on farms during the winter months, in the Highlands especially, where its production was a natural extension of the farming year and an essential part of the local economy. This was perfectly legal, provided the spirit was not offered for sale. During the 1740s and 50s there was a dramatic increase in the number of small malt and (particularly in the Lowlands) grain distilleries, encouraged by the Gin Act of 1736 which imposed heavy duty on gin manufacture, but exempted *aquavitae*.

In 1757 distilling was prohibited throughout the United Kingdom for three years, as a result of crop failures. This ban did not extend to private stills, whose owners suddenly found they had a huge and eager English market for their product, although they could not legally sell it. Smuggling began on a vast scale, and even after the ban on distilling was lifted in the 1760s it was estimated that private distillers were making ten times more whisky than licensed distillers. Many licensed distillers were forced out of business, or had to resort to fraud to survive, producing spirit and not declaring it to the Excise. In 1777, while there were only eight licensed distilleries in Edinburgh, there were over 400 illegal stills.

During the late 1770s the licensed distillers began to band together to defeat the smugglers, flooding the market with cheap grain whisky. They obtained the support of Parliament, which summarily banned the private production of spirits in 1781 and authorized the Excise to seize stills and equipment. In 1783 these powers were extended to include the seizure of horses and vehicles used to transport illicit whisky.

There then began an all-out war, which lasted until the 1820s. Private distilling was considered an inalienable right by the huge majority of Scots, including many landowners and magistrates, who were not inclined to enforce the increasingly severe penalties imposed by the Government, especially since the money their tenants made from smuggling guaranteed their rents. Furthermore, contraband spirits were universally considered superior in flavour to legally produced whisky.

The legal distillers prospered under the protection of the monopoly. By the 1780s the powerful Haig and Stein families (see **Haig's**) were joined by a number of others who established large-scale distilleries in the Lowlands, quickly becoming crucial to the economy of these parts. Export of spirit to England (much of it for rectification into gin) rose from 2,000 gallons (9,000 litres) in 1770 to over 450,000 gallons (over 2 million litres) in 1784.

Famine ravaged much of Scotland, especially the Highlands, in 1782–83. Some Lowland distilleries were mobbed, since it was thought they were using up food supplies, and in 1784 the Wash Act sought to encourage legal distilling in the Highlands by allowing lower duties on whisky made in small stills from locally grown barley. It also gave impetus to Lowland distilling by reducing duty and simplifying the regulations under which whisky was made.

Within a year Lowland production doubled (to over 800,000 gallons – over 3.6 million litres). London was awash with whisky, to the annoyance of the powerful London grain distillers, who first instigated a price war then used their influence to raise duty on Scotch spirits so high that it amounted to prohibition (1786). In 1788 further legislation required Scottish distillers to give a year's notice of intention to export to England – an impossible state of affairs which drove many into bankruptcy; five years later duty was tripled to help pay for the war with France.

Distillers in the Highlands had not been included in the legislation before 1793, but the tripling of duty again encouraged widespread illegal distilling. By the end of the century huge amounts of illicit Highland whisky was pouring into the Lowlands, further exacerbating the difficulties faced by Lowland distillers.

The Highlanders had little alternative. Distilling was the only outlet for barley, so landowners encouraged it, raised the price of barley and increased rents for inferior land. Unable to afford the increased duties, tenants were caught in a vicious circle.

At the turn of the century there was another sequence of bad harvests. Distilling was banned in 1801, 1802, and again in 1809 and 1811; duty was again doubled, then trebled (1800 and 1803) and the Excise service in the Highlands strengthened. Smuggling was widespread and the authorities openly flouted: much more whisky was being produced illegally than in licensed stills.

Further enactments were made in 1814, 1816 and 1818 but these did little to check the flow of smuggled spirit from the Highlands, which was universally considered to be of better quality than that produced legally. Clashes with the Excise sometimes amounted to pitched battles. Improved roads in the Highlands made southern markets more accessible and encouraged more landowners to become involved in (legal) distilling, but they found their profits badly eroded by the illicit trade. In 1820 their influential spokesman, the Duke of Gordon, who owned huge estates in Aberdeenshire (including part of Speyside), drew the attention of the House of Lords to the chaotic condition of the licensing laws and promised the landowners' support against smuggling in return for a more reasonable fiscal approach. A Royal Commission was set up under Lord Wallace, and the resulting Excise Act of 1823 cut duty dramatically, sanctioned the weak washes which made smuggled whisky more palatable and permitted export to England. This, together with the Illicit Distillation (Scotland) Act of the previous year, which had imposed very severe penalties on illicit distillers, encouraged distillers to take out licences (see **The Glenlivet**).

How the World was Won

Many of the distilleries listed in this book trace their histories to the mid-1820s. Landlords throughout Scotland supported the construction of new distilleries, mostly relying on the knowledge of former smugglers to run the new enterprises: the number of licensed distilleries tripled in three years (from 108 to 329, yet by 1835 the number had declined to 230); 37 distilleries opened in Campbeltown alone between 1823 and 1837. Smuggling declined dramatically: 14,000 cases were awaiting trial in 1823 – by 1830 the number of prosecutions had fallen to less than 400.

Apart from a handful of large Lowland distilleries, production remained small-scale and continued to be a seasonal extension of the farming year, providing employment for farm workers during the winter months. Then, in 1827, the leading Lowland distiller, Robert Stein, developed a method which permitted continuous distillation (until now whisky making in pot stills was a batch process (see Grain Whisky Production, p. 19), and by 1830 this had been perfected by a former Inspector General of Excise in Dublin, Aeneas Coffey, who patented his invention in 1831.

The vast increase in the capacity of the Lowland distilleries made possible by these inventions led to over-production and increased concern about over-consumption and drunkenness. Temperance Societies began to appear in the late 1820s, and in 1830 Parliament yielded to pressure from these groups, abolishing the duty on beer and raising that on spirits. This measure, combined with poor harvests during the 1840s caused many distilleries to close, especially in the Highlands, where the rural economy was so closely linked to whisky production.

The Lowland distilleries were better off. The coalfields of the Central Belt were being developed, providing a cheap source of fuel. The new railways brought supplies of grain from all over the UK, and from abroad. Reliable steamboat services to English ports were emerging. The repeal of the Navigation Acts in 1845 freed trade to the colonies and within a decade grain whisky was being exported to the USA, India, Canada, Australia and South Africa. The bland patent-still whisky suited these markets, where it was used in mixed drinks and cordials, or rectified and compounded.

In 1853 Andrew Usher, Edinburgh agent for the well-known Glenlivet Distillery (see **The Glenlivet**), produced the first proprietary 'vatted' malt (i.e. a blend of whiskies of different ages). He named it Usher's Old Vatted Glenlivet (see **Usher's**). Blends had been made before: during the 'whisky wars' legal distillers sometimes blended their own inferior product with more flavoursome illicit whiskies, and after 1823 older malts were often vatted with new spirit. Also, public houses, spirits merchants and grocers often diluted malt whisky with grain – but it was all done in a random fashion. Usher was the first to set out to achieve a consistent product, and immediately began to win markets in London and India.

The Spirits Act of 1860 turned Usher's innovation into a revolution for the Scotch whisky industry. The Act raised duty substantially and at the same time permitted whiskies from different distilleries to be blended without paying duty (until then, only whiskies from the same distillery could be vatted in bond). In an effort to reduce the price at which he sold his whiskies, Andrew Usher immediately applied his experience to blending malt and (cheaper) grain whiskies to a fixed (repeatable) recipe. The result was a drink which combined the flavour of the former with the lightness of the latter, and which could be sold at a competitive price. The confection had a very broad appeal: a drink which has since won the enthusiastic support of the entire world.

Many firms immediately followed Usher's example, and some of their names are still familiar (**Bell's**, **Dewar's**, **Haig's**, **Lowrie's**, **Johnnie Walker**, etc.). The early blenders were often wine and provisions merchants – known as 'Italian warehousemen' – but dedicated blending firms soon began to appear, selling their products to hotels and public houses, and applying themselves to winning markets in England and abroad.

The nascent industry was encouraged by the general boom that accompanied the Franco-Prussian War (1870–71). Strong-flavoured Islay and Speyside malts (the latter known generically as 'Glenlivets') were in demand since they could 'cover' as much as 90% grain whisky in a blend, and at the same time the large-scale marketing of soda water, particularly in the colonies, increased demand for fiery whiskies which lent themselves to dilution. Until the 1880s this was sold in bulk, by the cask or stone jar, and bottled by the purchaser. Whisky and soda remained the most popular way to drink whisky until at least the turn of the century.

In 1877 the Distillers Company Limited (DCL) was formed by the amalgamation of the six leading grain distillers, in order to protect their interests, reduce expenditure and increase profits in the boom market. In the years to come DCL was to become the major player in the industry, and it remains so to this day under its new name, United Distillers plc.

Perhaps the most significant factor in the development of the market for Scotch whisky, however, was an insect – phylloxera – which ravaged the vineyards of France from the late 1860s until well into the 1890s. Brandy – the favourite spirit of the English middle classes (also drunk with soda) – became almost unavailable, and Scotch filled the vacuum, now sold by the branded bottle and energetically promoted by a number of extremely able Scots (see **Bell's**, **Johnnie Walker**, **Buchanan's**, **Dewar's**).

During the last decade of the century blended whisky enjoyed an unprecedented boom. Two new grain distilleries and thirty-three new malt distilleries were built – several of them on Speyside (see Glenfiddich, Tomatin, Tamdhu, Dalwhinnie, Aberfeldy, Ardmore, *et al.*). The huge majority of the product of the malt distilleries went for blending, but there was still a significant market for 'selfs', as single malts were called, notably **The Glenlivet**, **Glenmorangie**, **Highland Park** and **Talisker**.

The boom came to a sudden end in 1900, and this was presaged by the collapse into bankruptcy of Pattison's Ltd of Leith, one of the major and most flamboyant blending firms, whose credit networks throughout the industry caused widespread difficulties.

Unremitting Adversity
The high level of public spending on war materials with which to wage the Boer War came to an end in 1900. This and other factors brought on a recession which lasted for more or less ten years. At home whisky consumption slumped, although exports stayed buoyant (mainly to the USA, Canada and South Africa). Many companies amalgamated, and DCL began to acquire Lowland distilleries to prevent price cutting. The smaller malt distilleries in the Highlands felt threatened by the stronger Lowland interests, and mounted a campaign to prevent grain whisky – and by implication, blended whisky also – being referred to as 'whisky', since the product of the pot still was 'the real stuff'. A decision in an English court supported their cause, then DCL entered the dispute and a Royal Commission was set up in 1908. It reported that the products of both styles of still could be named Scotch whisky – a bitter blow for the Highland malt distillers. Interestingly, for a decade or so after the advent of blended whisky, pure malt whisky was referred to in England as 'Irish whiskey' – with an 'e' – which must have been doubly galling for its producers.

With the death of Queen Victoria in 1901, drinking fashions changed. On the one hand, following the example of King

Edward, champagne and dry wines became fashionable in England: on the other there was a marked growth in the anti-drinking lobby. Lloyd George, the teetotal Chancellor of the Exchequer, shared these views, and increased duty by one-third in his People's Budget of 1909.

The effect of this was not as dramatic as was first expected, since the overall economy began to improve after 1911, but the outbreak of the First World War provided Lloyd George with further opportunities to cut consumption. He stated that strong drink 'was doing more damage in the war than all the German submarines put together', and proposed total prohibition and, when this failed, the doubling of duty on spirits. This measure was also dropped owing to protests from the Irish Members of Parliament, who held the balance of power in the House of Commons, and instead the Central Control Board (Liquor Traffic) was introduced in 1915.

The Board took action wherever it could through an incomprehensible maze of regulations, and in the face of such difficulties – compounded by wartime grain shortages – many distilleries and blending houses were sold (a number of them to DCL, including John Begg, John Hopkins and J. & G. Stewart); some of the larger companies merged (most importantly Buchanan-Dewar).

In 1916 the Central Control Board cut production by 30%, then banned pot-still production altogether; then set about reducing the strength at which whisky could be sold. At the time it was bottled at 60% alcohol which the board wanted reduced to 28.6% (i.e. 50° under proof). A compromise was reached at 37.2% (35° under proof), which has remained more or less the norm ever since. By 1918 all whisky exports had been prohibited and duty doubled (to £1.50 a gallon; at the end of the war this was raised to £2.50, with provisions that the increased duty must not be passed on to the consumer).

Many blenders merged with or sold out to DCL (notably Haig's and Usher's (in 1920), Buchanan-Dewar and John Walker (1925), and White Horse (1927)), and by 1927 DCL controlled nearly all the major Scotch whisky brands and about one-third of the distilleries.

A brief economic recovery, lasting only a year, was followed by the second recession of the century. This time it was presaged by the Prohibition in the USA (January 1920) – a major setback for the Scotch whisky industry, since the US was one of its most important export markets.

Domestic sales declined throughout the 1920s, but production remained high and towards the end of the decade there was a widespread price war, which significantly reduced profitability and further damaged the whole industry.

The General Strike (1926) was followed by the collapse of the US stock market (1929), and the Great Depression: whisky output plummeted by 60%, and by 1933 only two malt distilleries were in production. Still the government did nothing to stimulate home demand by reducing duty.

At last Prohibition was lifted (1933), but for two years the American government imposed a heavy import duty. By 1935 the whole economy was picking up, and the prospects for the whisky industry looked better than at any time since 1900.

Alas the hopes were short-lived. Upon the outbreak of the World War in 1939, the industry was again called upon to help pay for the coming conflict: duty was immediately raised by 10/- (i.e. 50p ; by 1943 duty was over twice what it had been in 1939, at £7.87 per gallon). During the first two years of the war, exports to America were maintained in order to earn dollars and pay for armaments, while restrictions were placed upon sales in the home market. In 1942 supplies of grain to the industry were cut altogether and all distilleries were closed. It was not until victory was clearly in prospect, in August 1944, that supplies were again made available by the Ministry of Food and after VE Day – following the personal intervention of the Prime Minister, Winston Churchill, who was very aware of whisky's export potential – a large allocation for the coming season★ was promised.

Good Times, Bad Times

It quickly became apparent that the amount of cereals estimated by the Ministry of Food was over-optimistic, and the election of a Labour Government in 1946 committed to the slogan 'Food before Whisky' limited production to less than half the pre-war output. Demand was rising, stocks were falling; supplies to the home market were rationed to a quarter of the pre-war figure (later 20%), and a keen black market sprang up. The sterling crisis of 1946–47 obliged the Government to release more grain for distilling, provided the industry would concentrate on exports.

By 1949 the situation was easing, and the Government abandoned control of home barley sales, leaving distillers free to buy on the open market. From 1953 output recovered sharply. Distilleries were enlarged, and the first new ones built since the 19th century (Glen Keith in 1957; Tormore in 1958). The worldwide demand for whisky soared, especially in North America, but until stocks recovered (in 1959) the Scotch Whisky Association administered a voluntary rationing scheme.

By 1960 four brands commanded half the world sales of Scotch: **Johnnie Walker**, **Dewar's**, **Cutty Sark** and **J&B Rare**. The largest market was the USA, followed by the UK – where the most popular brands were **Haig's**, **Johnnie Walker**, **Black & White** and **White Horse** (all DCL brands). Towards the end of the decade, **Teacher's**, **Bell's** and **Chivas Regal** began to threaten DCL's ascendancy: the giant reacted by cutting prices and offering discounts, attempting to use its size and power to crush the opposition, in direct contravention of undertakings given to the industry in 1925.

Production was geared to cater for an export market which was increasing by 10% per annum. Between 1959 and 1966 grain whisky production doubled (to 90 million gallons – to over 400 million litres) and new distilleries were built at Airdrie, Girvan and Invergordon. Malt whisky production in the same period increased from 16 million to 51 million gallons (from 72 million to 230 million litres). Old distilleries were reopened and refurbished (Glenglassaugh, Glenturret, Isle of Jura, Caperdonich) and new ones built (Tomintoul, Tamnavulin, Glenallachie, Inchmurrin).

The high prices fetched by mature whiskies in the late 1950s and early 1960s encouraged investment from speculators from outside the industry. By 1968 large quantities of mature grain whisky were available, and the bottom fell out of the market. The experience of malt sales was similar, although not as dramatic.

The world demand for Scotch whisky seemed insatiable, however, and this small slump only halted the optimistic mood temporarily. Between 1970 and 1975 many distilleries were increased in size, most of them substantially (Mannochmore, Glendullan,

★ *The fact that whisky production is still thought of as being seasonal recollects the time when it was part of the farming year, a winter occupation. Nowadays 'the silent season' (when the distillery is closed) extends for only about a month: it used to last from May to September.*

Teaninich, Linkwood, Aberfeldy, Caol Ila, Tamdhu, Tormore, Aberlour, Glengarioch, Glen Grant, Glenfiddich, Tomatin, Tomintoul, Ardmore, Tullibardine, Miltonduff – all rebuilt or extended). New malt distilleries were built at Allt a Bhainne, Braes of Glenlivet, Pittyvaich and Auchroisk.

By the late 1970s, economic conditions were less stable and the huge US market had begun to contract. Moreover, in both the USA and the UK there was a shift in consumer taste towards blander spirits (white rum and vodka), drunk with mixers, and towards white wine. Younger drinkers were especially targeted and vigorously marketed with 'lifestyle' advertising. Whisky companies responded by exploring the potential of other markets – particularly South America, Japan, Hong Kong and Europe.

At the end of the decade, the world economy went into recession. Output of both grain and malt whisky declined sharply (by 1983 it was at its lowest level since 1959). Many distilleries were placed on part-time production, and some closed permanently.

THE MAKING OF SCOTCH WHISKY

Scotch whisky is an elemental elixir. Its constituents are the earth, the water, the fire and the air of Scotland. Its only ingredients are barley, the quintessential harvest of the earth, pure water, imbued with the fugitive minerals of the land itself, and a dash of yeast to ferment the brew. Fire malts the barley and raises the ethereal spirit in the still, and the fresh northern air, often damp and chill, permeates the casks while the spirit matures and works a magic which is still not yet fully understood by chemists.

Distilling developed as a branch of alchemy, and in truth the transmutation of the base elements of barley into the golden liquid which has won the enthusiastic support of the entire world might still be accurately considered to be an alchemical process. More so since, despite deploying the very latest chemical and technological knowledge, nobody has been able to make whisky with the same flavour characteristics as Scotch furth of Scotland.

It is not within the scope of a pocket book to dwell at length upon how whisky is made, but a short account of the processes and procedures will help the reader understand the notes which comprise the body of the book.

Distilling is the process by which elements in a liquid are separated by vaporization and condensation. The creation of potable spirits requires that the liquid to be distilled contains alcohol and water, and the process involves separating the two. This is achieved by heating the liquid so that the alcohol vaporizes and is then liquefied again by means of cooling.

The base liquid from which Scotch is made is not unlike thin beer – a mash of cereals and water fermented with yeast. Two basic kinds are made in Scotland: malt whisky and grain whisky. Malt whisky is made from a mash of only malted barley; grain whisky makes use of maize or wheat as well as (a relatively small amount of) malted barley. Mixed together they become blended whisky. Further mixed with herbs and sugars they become whisky-based liqueurs. The vast majority of whisky made is blended: 96.4% of the malt whisky sold in 1992 went for blending.

However, the main area of market growth in recent years has been for single malts (the bottled product of individual distilleries), and there are more examples of these, the original and most distinctive expressions of Scotch whisky, available today than ever.

In 1993 there are 91 operating malt whisky distilleries, and a further twelve which are currently 'mothballed'. There are 7 grain distilleries. In 1980 there were 114 malt and 11 grain distilleries, although five years later the number of distilleries in production had shrunk to 81 and 10 respectively. The differences between the processes employed by the two different kinds of distillery are considered below.

Malt Whisky Production

Malting

First the barley must be malted – in other words, germinated to convert the starches in each grain into a simple sugar. Distillers look for plump, ripe barley with plenty of starch and not too much nitrogen. Barley varieties are not important so long as they meet these requirements. Nor is it important where the barley comes from: good Scottish barley is generally considered to be best (on account of climatic and soil conditions), but there is not enough of it to supply the industry, so barley is imported from England and abroad.

Originally, the barley was grown locally and malted at the distillery – the familiar pagoda-shaped roofs of the malt kilns are a feature of whisky distilleries. Today, only a handful of distilleries have their own maltings – in several places the old maltings have been converted into visitor centres (see Appendix) – since specialist maltsters can supply them with malt made to their own detailed specification at a lower price.

Traditionally*, the barley was first steeped in water for two or three days, then drained and spread out on a stone or cement floor to a depth of about a foot (30 cm) and encouraged to germinate. Germination generates heat, and the malt had to be turned frequently with wooden shovels, ploughs and rakes to maintain an even temperature, and to ensure that the rootlets and sprouts are uniform, and do not become entangled.

After about a week, when the sprouts have reached a certain length, the grain is termed 'green malt' and transferred to a kiln for drying. It is spread out on the perforated iron sheets of the floor, through which heat rises from a fire below. Formerly this was a peat fire and imparted a strong flavour to the malt and to the whisky itself. Peat is still used in the early stages of drying the malt, but kilning is now done by indirect heat, like an oven.

When the malt has been dried, the remains of the stalks and rootlets are cleaned off in a dressing machine, and it is ground – coarsely or finely depending on the distillery's mashing equipment (fine milling is thought to have an adverse affect on flavour where the equipment is traditional). Many distilleries had their own water-driven meal mill, but since the 1880s most milling has been done by machines with steel rollers.

Mashing

The milled malt, known as grist, is mixed with hot water. The nature of the water has a major influence on the final product – some still maintain that it is the key element in dictating the distinctive quality of individual whiskies, though chemists now reckon it accounts for only a tiny part of the flavour of mature

* *The process described is 'Floor Malting'. Some distilleries still use it, but in the early 1960s, it began to be replaced by a method which employed a long concrete trough with a perforated floor and mechanical rakes, called a Saladin box.. In the 1970s a further variant was introduced: Drum Malting, which makes use of large, slowly turning drums cooled by blown air, and capable of producing large quantities of malt in an almost continuous process.*

whisky. Soft peaty water, such as that used in Islay and Campbeltown, contributes to making heavier whiskies, while the harder water of Speyside and some northern distilleries (like Glenmorangie, whose water is the hardest of all) is one of the factors which make for lighter styles. A distillery jealously guards its water source, both as to quality and quantity. Some use springs, some wells, others streams or rivers.

In the mash room, the water is heated (to between 63°C/145°F and 68°C/154°F) and mixed with the grist into a thin porridge in a mashing machine. It then flows into a cylindrical vessel holding upwards of 5,000 gallons (nearly 23,000 litres), called a mash tun, where it is stirred by revolving paddles for several hours. Mashing causes the starches in the liquor to be converted into sugars; the resulting sweet liquid – called 'wort' – is filtered out, and the mash tun refilled with water a further three times, each time at a higher temperature. The first two refills pass to the next stage; the third becomes the first water of the next mash. The residue of husks and spent grains makes excellent cattle feed, and has always been an important part of the rural economy of the Highlands. Whisky production literally provided the meat and drink of Scotland!

Fermenting

The wort is chilled to 22–24°C (71–75°F), then pumped into fermenting vessels called 'washbacks', large tubs, holding about 7,000 gallons (31,000 litres), made from Oregon pine or larch, or (increasingly) from stainless steel, which is easier to keep clean.

Here yeast is added – distilleries have their own favourites – and fermentation takes place, causing the liquid (now called 'wash') to bubble and froth up the washback, sometimes requiring the use of mechanical switches to keep it from foaming out of the tub. In the old days, when yeasts were less stable, fermentation could be extremely violent – the whole washback would rock: the sound has been compared to a ship in a stormy sea. Small boys were employed to fight back the foam with heather brooms.

After two days the fermentation subsides: the wash is now at 5–10% alcohol, and is pumped into the wash charger ready to be distilled. Once discharged, the washbacks must be scrupulously cleaned to prevent bacterial infection of subsequent fillings.

Distilling

Distilling takes place in pairs of copper pot stills with tall 'swannecks'. One is larger than the other, but otherwise their exact shape, capacity and height vary from distillery to distillery. The life

The malt whisky production process

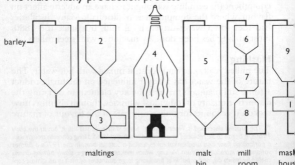

barley— | 1 | 2 | 4 | 5 | 6 | 7 | 8 | 9 | 3

maltings   malt   mill   mash
                  bin   room   hous

of a still is between 15 and 30 years, depending on how hard it has been used; new stills copy old ones faithfully – sometimes with superstitious fervour, reproducing every dent and patch.

The wash is pumped into the larger of the two stills, called the wash still, where it is gradually brought to the boil. Stills are either directly heated from below (by gas, oil or coke) or, since the 1880s, from within by steam-heated coils, not unlike an electric kettle. The temperature has to be carefully controlled to prevent the foaming wash rising up the swan-neck and into the condenser. A little window in the neck tells the distiller how far up it has risen.

The vapours that are given off pass over the neck of the still into the 'worm' or other style of condenser – essentially, a coiled pipe encased in a cold-water jacket (sometimes located outside the still room to help keep it cool) where the vapours condense. The distillate from the wash still is known as 'low wines' and flows through the spirit safe (a brass-bound, glass-fronted box, padlocked to prevent access to the new whisky) to the 'low wines charger' ready to fill the second or spirit still.

The same process is repeated in the second distillation, but this time the still-man watches the spirit carefully as it flows through the spirit safe. The early part of the run – called 'foreshots' – is pungent and impure. He tests the spirit by adding water (which turns it cloudy), measuring its specific gravity and watching the clock, and until the foreshots run clear, he directs them back to the low wines charger to be redistilled. This takes between 15 and 45 minutes, depending on the size of the still.

When he is certain the run is clear, the still-man re-directs the spout and begins to collect the spirit for maturing. This is 'new make' whisky, and will run for between two and four hours (again, depending on the size of the still), commencing at about 70–75% alcohol and decreasing steadily down to 63%. The still-man begins to save spirit at about 74% alcohol and cuts off at about 64%, but the precise strengths, the heat at which he operates his still and the length of time he saves spirit – in short the amount of spirit col-

1 grain silo	9 grist hopper	17 spirit safe
2 steep	10 water	18 low wines charger
3 Saladin box	11 mash tun	19 spirit still
4 kiln	12 yeast store	20 spirit receiver
5 malt bin	13 washback	21 spirit store
6 screen	14 wash charger	22 barrels
7 hopper	15 wash still	
8 mill	16 condenser	

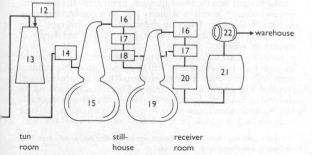

tun room / still-house / receiver room

lected, known as the 'cut' – is part of his art, which influences the flavour and quality of the product. It varies from distillery to distillery, but may be as low as one-third of the spirit distilled.

Only part of the run is collected because about half way through the second distillation various oily compounds, called 'feints', begin to vaporize. They are mild and pleasant at first – and lend character and flavour to the whisky – but in time their intensity increases to such a degree that to continue to collect the spirit would spoil the whole batch. The still-man will again direct the distillate to the low wines charger. Distilling continues until all that is left is 'spent lees' (more or less water). Distillation of 1,500 gallons (6,800 litres) of low wines and feints normally takes about six hours.

Maturation

The new make whisky is pumped to a spirit vat in the filling store, where it is reduced with the same water with which it has been mashed to 63.5% alcohol and filled into oak barrels of different sizes. This strength (111° proof) was long ago discovered to be the best at which to mature spirit. Experiments in the mid-1960s with maturing at higher strengths were unsuccessful.

By law, the casks used for maturing Scotch must be made of oak. Most commonly they are: '*re-made*' *hogsheads* (of 250 litres capacity), made from a mixture of new American oak staves and staves from casks which have been used once for maturing bourbon (for four years), *bourbon barrels* (barrels of approx. 200 litres that have been previously used for bourbon, but are not 're-made') and *sherry wood* (butts or puncheons of about 500 litres capacity, made from Spanish oak, which have been previously used for maturing fino, amontillado or oloroso sherries, typically for at least four years). New wood (i.e. previously unused), port pipes, wine barrels and rum puncheons are also used experimentally.

Currently, 96% of cask imports are hogsheads or barrels: only about 4% of whisky is matured in sherry wood. The Macallan Distillery is the only one to use sherry-wood exclusively for its single malt fillings; some others mature in bourbon-wood, then transfer to sherry casks for about 18 months to complete maturation (known as 'sherry finishing'). Most use bourbon-wood exclusively, believing that sherry masks the subtle flavour of the whisky.

Much depends on the character of the individual 'new make' whisky, but what is certain is that the casks in which the whisky matures are much more than storage vessels. Wood makes a vital contribution – perhaps 'the' vital contribution – to the character and flavour of the final product.

The inside walls of the casks are first charred (merely toasted in the case of sherry), in order to facilitate the release of vanillin (a vanilla flavour) into the first-fill liquor. In turn, the flavour of the first incumbent – bourbon or sherry (the latter considerably more so than the former) – lingers in the wood, and re-emerges, along with compounds in the wood itself, in the aroma and flavour of the mature whisky.

Casks are used until their qualities are deemed to be exhausted by their owners – a few casks, still in service, are over a hundred years old. After each maturation period they are checked and repaired, and sometimes re-charred and or 'reconditioned' with a sherry derivative called paxarete*. In truth, after two or three fillings the vital contribution made by the cask is negligible, so single malt bottlings are usually made from first- or second-fill casks.

* Paxarete, also called Paxarette and Pajarete, was named after the Spanish village, Torre de Pajarete, once famous for its vino de color.

Older barrels are used for maturing grain whisky or 'marrying' blends. Whisky must be matured for three years before it can legally be called 'Scotch', but it is not by any means mature after so short a time and most single malts are bottled after 10 or 12 years in cask. The rate at which the whisky matures depends upon the size of the cask (the larger, the longer maturation will take) and how often they have been filled. It is said that some whiskies peak twice, with a dull middle period, and very old whisky can become undesirably woody.

The rate of maturation also depends to a large extent upon the conditions in which the spirit is matured. Traditional warehouses are low, stone-built and earth-floored. The atmosphere is damp and cool, and the casks are stacked three high. Modern warehouses are like aircraft hangars, with casks stacked as many as 20 high, and the rate of maturation may vary according to where the cask is positioned in the warehouse. In traditional warehouses, evaporation is low, but the strength of the spirit drops by 3%–4% in ten years; in high-rise warehouses, strength remains high, but evaporation is greater. The Customs and Excise expects and allows for 2% volume loss per annum – nearly 10 gallons (over 45 litres) of spirit in ten years. This is known as the 'Angels' Share'.

Climate also plays a part: the rate of maturation is affected by seasonal changes in temperature, so warehouses on the coast, where there is less seasonal variation than inland, tend to mature their precious contents at a steadier rate.

It is said that, while it slumbers, whisky does not like to be shocked by wild swings in temperature. Scotland's climate – temperate and oceanic – is perfectly adapted to maturing whisky, just as the end product is so suited to cheering the heart during long northern winters and damp Scottish summers.

Grain Whisky Production

As noted in the History section large quantities of grain whisky were made in pot stills from at least the 17th century until the First World War, sold generically as 'Irish Whiskey' in England. However, the perfection of the patent still by Aeneas Coffey in 1831 (see **Haig's**, **Cameron Brig**) enabled production by a continuous process, and this is how all grain whisky is made in Scotland today.

The fact that it is a continuous process is significant. It means that vastly more spirit can be produced – about 8 million gallons (40 million litres) of pure alcohol per distillery per annum (a typical malt distillery annually produces under 500,000 gallons, or about 2.5 million litres). Not all the output goes into blended whisky – much of the base spirit for gin and vodka manufacture comes from the same stills. Malt whisky production is a batch process, and the equipment (mash tun, washbacks, pot stills) must be scrupulously cleaned after each round of distilling, while patent stills may be run continuously for seven days before they require cleaning. Since the bulk of the raw materials (i.e. any cereal which yields fermentable sugars, usually wheat and maize) is cheaper than malted barley, grain whisky is far cheaper to produce.★

Mashing and Fermenting

The mash from which grain whisky is made is unmalted wheat or maize, (so distilleries are free to buy in at the best price) and a small proportion of either 'green' malt (see p. 15) or malted barley

★ *In 1992 a tonne of malted barley cost £310 (producing new malt spirit @ £1.72 per litre of pure alcohol), while a tonne of maize cost £155 and a tonne of wheat £128 (both producing Scotch grain spirit @ 68p per litre of pure alcohol, since more wheat is required).*

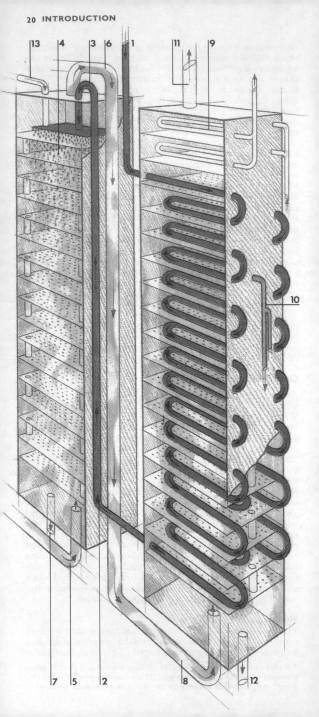

Left: The patent still has two columns. The cool wash enters at **1** and passes down the coil in the rectifier, the right-hand column, being heated by hot vapour rising from **8**. The now hot wash leaves the rectifier at the bottom and rises up to the top of the second column, the analyser, at **2**. It falls onto perforated plates in the analyser. Hot steam enters at **5** and rises, causing volatile elements to rise. They escape as vapour via **6**. The water contents boils at a higher temperature, so it falls down the analyser to escape via **7**. The spirit vapour from **6** enters the rectifier at **8**, rises, and is condensed by the incoming pipe of cool wash. Less volatile elements (feints) condense and escape as liquid via **12**, to be pumped back to the top of the analyser at **13** to repeat the process. The spirit alone reaches the top of the rectifier as vapour. It is cooled by a cold radiator at **9** and flows out of the still at **10**. Very volatile elements emerge as vapour at **11**.

(about 16%, it varies from distillery to distillery). Instead of malting, the unmalted cereals are milled fine, then cooked at a high temperature in a pressure cooker to release the starch into a slurry solution, and added to the malted barley in the mash tun, where the mixture is mashed, in the same way as for malt whisky.

The wort, complete with any solids it contains, is then cooled and pumped to the washbacks, where yeast is added to induce fermentation. In two days the wash will be ready to be distilled. All very similar to malt whisky manufacture.

Distilling

Patent stills are utterly different to pot stills. They consist of two interconnected copper-lined columns, each about 50 feet (15 m) tall, the 'analyser' and the 'rectifier'. Copper lining has been found essential to achieve the flavour profile of grain whisky, although may be dispensed with in producing plain spirit for English gin or vodka.

The (cool) wash passes down the rectifier column in a long, serpent-like pipe. During its passage it is heated by hot vapour rising up the column. The (now hot) wash then rises to the head of the analyser where it flows onto a series of perforated plate. On the way down it meets ascending steam, which causes the volatile (i.e. alcoholic) elements to rise. The balance of the wash (water and grains) is drawn off at the bottom and converted into animal feed.

The alcoholic vapour now starts its return journey. From the top of the analyser it passes to the foot of the rectifier, through which it rises, gradually being condensed by the incoming pipe of (cool) wash, which is in its turn heated by the hot vapour. The ascending vapour increases in alcoholic strength as it rises, until it reaches the 'spirit plate' where it is drawn off. Less volatile elements (the feints) condense and fall to the bottom of the rectifier as liquid, and are then pumped back to the top of the analyser to go through the process again.

Maturation

The spirit is drawn off the still at a strength not higher than 94.8% alcohol. This is then reduced to 68.5% and filled into oak casks for a minimum of three years before it can be called Scotch whisky – as with malt whisky. Being lighter-bodied than malt whisky, grain whisky matures more rapidly. Some grain whisky is matured for similar long periods to malt whisky, to be used in de luxe blends or bottled as single grains. If a blend makes an age statement – 15, 21 Years Old, etc. – its component grain whiskies must be at least of that age, as well as its component malts. In most instances, though, there will be malt whiskies in the blend that are older than its age statement.

Blended Whisky Production

David Macdonald, chairman of Macdonald Martin Distillers, has defined blending as: "The art of combining meticulously selected, mature, high quality whiskies, each with its own flavour and other characteristics, with such skill that the whole is better than the sum of its parts, so that each makes its own contribution to the finished blend without any one predominating."

When the selected whiskies are all malts the result is called a 'vatted malt' rather than a 'blend'. Some vatted brands are described as 'pure malt', or simply as 'malt whisky' – this is as opposed to 'single malt' which is the product of one distillery.

Blended whisky is therefore a mix of malt and grain whiskies. Perhaps surprisingly, given the eminence of malt whisky promotion and quality, this style of Scotch accounts for just over 96% of sales world-wide (1992 figure: in 1980 it accounted for 99%).

The first true blend (in the sense that it was carefully produced and marketed with a view to consistency of flavour, and repeatability) was created by Andrew Usher in the early 1860s. Prior to this date blends – and vattings of malt whiskies especially – had been made and offered for sale, mainly by grocers and wine shops, but little science was applied to their creation.

Selection

Typically, a blend will include between 15 and 40 different malt whiskies and 2 to 3 grains. Although grain whisky is comparatively light in flavour, attempts to use only one grain in a blend have not been successful. The proportion of malt to grain is between 20% and 40% – the cost price of the end product will reflect this and the ages of the constituent malts.

The malts used in any blend are categorized as 'base malts' (the 'heart' of the blend – commonly, fillings from distilleries owned by the blender – around which the blend is constructed), 'flavouring malts' (sometimes called 'top dressings' – a handful of malts have long been famous among blenders for their flavouring properties) and 'packers' (these whiskies are not inferior: they simply have low aroma intensities and their contribution to the flavour of the blend is minimal).

Every malt whisky is different, and each has a different 'flavour profile' – its discernible (sometimes dominant) aromatic characteristics (see p. 26). The blender sets out to balance the characteristics of one whisky with those of another (in fact many others) so that the individual aromas are so well integrated that they are unidentifiable. The combined aromas each make their contribution to a 'flavour complex' which is more than the sum of its parts. For this reason I have not attempted to provide tasting notes for the blended whiskies listed in this book.

Method

Each blend is made to a formula, but the formula itself is not slavishly adhered to – it cannot be: some fillings may not be available or may be prohibitively expensive. The blender's task is to produce a product which tastes the same from batch to batch over many years. The familiar claims that an individual blend is identical (in constituents and/or flavour) to that produced 20 or 50 or 100 years ago should be taken with a pinch of salt: distilleries cease production and others are built.

With the formula to guide him and a deep familiarity with the flavour characteristics of the blend he wants to re-create, the blender noses samples of every constituent malt and grain whisky that will go into his creation, at the ages he wishes to use them. Samples are drawn from the individual casks which will be used in that batch, since there are variations from cask to cask. He must be aware that slight changes in flavour may occur over time – the peaty dryness of some Highland or Island malts might increase, so additional sweet and floral Speyside fillings may be required to redress the balance. On the other hand, blends which employ a large amount of Speyside malt may have to be 'dried out', by adding individual malts known for their dry flavour.

Once he is satisfied that the marriage of the ingredients will create what he is searching for, the individual casks are transported from the warehouses in which they have been maturing to the blending hall. Here the blender will check them (by nosing) – he will have spent years committing the individual characteristics of each whisky to memory, and is assisted by an extensive library of samples. Once he has approved their quality they are 'disgorged' into a trough, whence they flow into a large blending vat.

Some blenders prefer to vat the malt fillings separate to the grains. In the blending vat the mixture is roused by stirring or by blowing air through it, to thoroughly mingle the ingredients. Then it is either rested for a short while and bottled, or, traditionally, run off into casks to be allowed to 'marry' for a period (typically between 1 and 6 months (and see **Edradour**)).

It is often remarked that while distilling is a science, blending is an art. I hope it will be clear from the foregoing summary of how whisky is made, that the there is a high level of artistry – judgement, tradition, skill, magic – in both.

REGIONAL DIFFERENCES

The whisky regions of Scotland are not as clearly defined as the wine regions of France or Germany. The traditional division is into Highland, Islay, Campbeltown and Lowland (sometimes with the middle two lumped together, and some early writers referred simply to Eastern and Western malts!). Then Speyside – which has been described as the *Grande Champagne* region – was added as a division of Highland, and 'Island' was made a separate category.

Some contemporary experts, notably Michael Jackson and the Scotch Malt Whisky Society, break the Highland category down into districts – North, South, East, West and Midlands (or Perthshire) – and use the names of 'Greater' Speyside's rivers to sub-categorize the region. I have followed the sub-categorization Lossie, Upper Spey, Lower Spey, Dufftown and Strathisla.

It is difficult to generalize about the regional flavour of malt whiskies – every one is different and bottling can vary (especially at cask strength – when the nature of the cask in which the whisky has been matured is most apparent – or when it is done by independent bottlers). However, there are certain broad characteristics:

Lowland: Pale in colour, light-bodied; a nose which is hay-like or grassy, often with malty or cereal notes; the flavour tends towards dryness, or finishes dry. These whiskies are often drunk as *digestifs*, and have been compared to fino sherries.

Islay: These are the strongest smelling and tasting whiskies. They tend to be medium-bodied, dry and phenolic (i.e. redolent of peat, smoke, iodine, carbolic). Much of the Isle of Islay is peat and this taints the water. Some distilleries draw their water from springs to avoid this and produce a lighter-flavoured whisky; some use heavily peated malt to reinforce it.

Campbeltown: Although there are today only two distilleries in Campbeltown, there were once 32, and the category is still recognized. Campbeltown whiskies are medium bodied, and have a slightly smoky or misty taste, with a trace of salt on the palate.

Highland:

a) North Highland malts vary considerably. They tend to be medium bodied, sweetish (often with a dry finish) and fresh-flavoured, with heathery, nutty, spicy or citric notes.

b) West Highland and Island malts are lighter bodied, with some

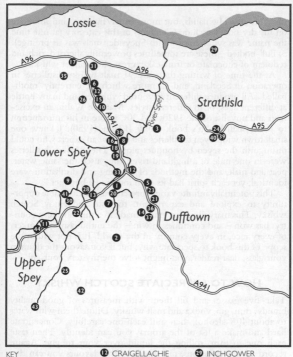

Lossie

A96

Strathisla

A96

River Spey

A95

Lower Spey

A941

Dufftown

Upper Spey

A941

KEY

• OBAN   Distillery in production in 1993

• Glenugie   Other distillery

DISTILLERIES
1 ABERLOUR
2 ALLT A'BHAINNE
3 AUCHROISK
4 AULTMORE
5 BALVENIE
6 BENRIACH
7 BENRINNES
8 CAPERDONICH
9 CARDHU
10 COLEBURN
11 CRAGGANMORE
12 CRAIGELLACHIE
13 DAILUAINE
14 DUFFTOWN
15 GLEN ELGIN
16 GLEN GRANT
17 GLEN MORAY
18 GLEN ROTHES
19 GLEN SPEY
20 GLENALLACHIE
21 GLENDULLAN
22 GLENFARCLAS
23 GLENFIDDICH
24 GLENKEITH
25 GLENLIVET
26 GLENLOSSIE
27 GLENTAUCHERS
28 IMPERIAL
29 INCHGOWER
30 KNOCKANDO
31 LINKWOOD
32 LONGMORN
33 MACALLAN
34 MANNOCHMORE
35 MILTONDUFF
36 MORTLACH
37 PITTYVAICH-GLENLIVET
38 SPEYBURN
39 STRATHISLA
40 STRATHMILL
41 TAMDHU
42 TAMNAVULIN
43 TOMINTOUL
44 TORMORE

peaty or phenolic characteristics, and some spice.
c) South and East Highland malts (Perthshire and Aberdeenshire mainly) can be light, medium or full bodied; they often have flowery or herbal notes, sometimes with a trace of peat.
Speyside: Geographically, this is part of the Highlands. It is also the heartland of whisky production, and its whiskies have long been esteemed for their complexity and diversity.

There are three styles: 1) Light-bodied – tending to be estery and floral scented, with some cereal-notes;. 2) Medium-bodied –

these are like Highlands, but more fruity/fragrant, and some are on the dry side. I include Glenlivets in this category (at one time the name was synonymous with Speyside, such was its prestige). 3) Full-bodied – these are sometimes powerfully sherried, rich and redolent of chocolate or fruit-cake: great after-dinner whiskies.

At the time of writing there are 91 malt whisky distilleries in operation in Scotland, and 12 more which are currently 'mothballed'. All produce different flavoured whiskies, and many bottle at different ages, or in different styles. Maurice Walsh, an exciseman and novelist of the 1920s and 30s, wrote in his introduction to J. Marshall Robb's book *Scotch Whisky* (1950):"I knew one small town with seven distilleries and I knew an expert who could distinguish the seven by bouquet alone. These seven distilleries were in one mile of a highland river; they used the same water, peat and malt, and the methods of brewing and distillation were identical, yet each spirit had its own individual bouquet."

This potentially infinite variety presents an inexhaustible opportunity to explore and experiment, to taste and enjoy Scotch whisky. This marvellous beverage, made in a tiny northern country, has won – and continues to win – the enthusiasm of drinkers of every race, in every country in the world. It is not within the scope of this book to speculate why; but if you savour the dram in your glass, dear reader, you might solve the mystery yourself!

HOW TO APPRECIATE SCOTCH WHISKY

Take five glasses and fill them with measures of good-quality brandy, rum, gin, vodka and malt whisky. Dilute them with water to about 40% alcohol, then sniff each one carefully. Concentrate hard and make a list of the aromas you can identify. Then taste each one in turn, rolling the liquid over your tongue. Again, record your impressions, put words to the flavours you can discern. I will bet that of the five lists, the one pertaining to the malt whisky is the longest and the most varied.

Malt whisky is the most complex of all spirits. With a little application and concentration a vast range of aromas and flavours may be identified. With a blend, the aromas are more difficult to identify, since part of the blender's task is to integrate the flavour characteristics of the individual malt and grain whiskies so well that no particular aroma or flavour predominates. For this reason the notes which follow relate principally to malt whisky, although the techniques and vocabulary may equally be applied to blended whisky.

Aroma and Flavour

The latest techniques of chemical and sensory analysis have identified some 300 constituents in malt whisky, and chemists estimate that there is likely to be as many more which have yet to be isolated and described.

Yet the flavour elements in an average bottle of Scotch at 40% alcohol must be sought in 0.2% of the bottle's content: the remaining 59.8% is water, and apart from the essential warming effect of alcohol, both it and water are relatively neutral in smell and taste.

The word 'smell' is used advisedly. The 'tasting' of whisky and other spirits is mainly done with the nose, compared to which the tongue could be said to be a relatively crude organ. While there are only four primary tastes – sweet, sour, salty, bitter (just as there are only four primary colours) – it has been estimated that there are some 32 'primary' aromas. These combine to provide the infinite variety of aromas detectable by the nose. What is more, the average human nose is capable of detecting aromatics at concentrations as low as one part in a million!

Flavour is a combination of smell and taste, and although the former sense is often less consciously used, one only has to hold one's nose to remind oneself of the vital contribution it makes to the appreciation of what one is eating or drinking.

The nose records pungency (i.e. sharpness, nose-prickle, nose-drying, even pain – often noted when sniffing undiluted or immature whisky samples) and aroma – in the case of whisky these are the many volatile aromatics (esters, aldehydes, feints) which give rise to characteristics such as fruitiness, smokiness or cereal-like. With continued sniffing, pungency increases and intensity of aroma decreases rapidly. From a practical point of view, this means it is pointless to nose a whisky sample for too long: if the first impression is lost, move on to another sample or take a rest.

The tongue and palate record 'mouth-feel' (i.e. body, viscosity, drying effects, texture) as well as primary tastes. Sweetness is detected on the tip of the tongue, saltiness and sourness (also astringency and acidity) at the sides and bitterness at the back.

Response to primary tastes deteriorates with age, but, perhaps surprisingly, is not affected by smoking. At least one of today's leading noses is a heavy smoker, as are many great French wine-tasters. It goes without saying that smoking while tasting ruins not only the smoker's palate, but those of everyone in the vicinity.

Tasting

Tasting – more properly termed 'sensory evaluation' – can be either 'analytical' (i.e. objective) or 'hedonic' (i.e. subjective).

The first is the methodology employed by professional tasters, and describes a procedure in which biases are minimized and which can be verified by repetition. The goal is 'to describe what is there' and to exclude personal preferences. Professional tasters are screened to determine any particular areas of sensitivity or insensitivity, biases or gaps in their flavour spectrum. Statistical analysis may be used to prove 'significance' in the findings. Then they are thoroughly trained.

Hedonic evaluation – I need hardly say that the word derives from the Greek for pleasure and refers to personal preference – is the kind of tasting pursued by consumers and allows for greater latitude and subjective assessment. The tasting notes included in this book are generally in this category.

Preparation

The evaluation of a whisky is bound to be affected by a variety of factors, not least mood and situation. I have heard a second-rate supermarket blend described as excellent by experienced tasters in a fishing hut on the Tweed, after a successful day's salmon fishing!

Other factors have a bearing on one's ability to assess accurately. Wearing perfume, aftershave and even using strongly scented hand-soap can have a surprisingly powerful and distracting influence on the taste of a sample. The room itself should be as free from smells as possible – such as cooking, fresh paint, smoke, etc. Tasters should, ideally, not just have eaten a heavy meal; smokers should not smoke for half an hour before tasting.

Perhaps the most important influence on the sensory evaluation of whisky is the glass in which it is sampled. What is required is a clear, tulip-shaped glass – ideally a large sherry copita, even a wine glass. Classic, cut crystal whisky tumblers are fine for long swigging drinks – whisky and soda, whisky and lemonade, whisky high balls – but they are hopeless as tasting glasses, since they do not collect and concentrate the aromas. The flavour of the whisky changes rapidly as it 'breathes' in an open glass (and generally deteriorates, in my view, although others would say it improves) so for 'serious' tastings, cover the sample with a watch glass or lid.

Procedure

Stage 1: *Appearance*

As with wine tasting, note the colour, depth and clarity. New spirit, fresh from the still, is colourless; whisky which has been matured for 20 years in a first-fill oloroso cask may be the colour of treacle. The spectrum between runs from pale straw, sunlight, fino sherry and pale gold; through old gold, amber, amontillado sherry and red gold; to bronze, oloroso and palo cortado sherry.

The spirit's appearance should give an indication of how it has been matured, and for how long. Whisky obtains its natural colour from the cask in which it is matured, but the colour will depend not only upon how long it has lain in wood, but also on whether the barrel is on its first, second or third filling.

To further confuse matters, it has long been the practice of the industry to add colouring (in the form of caramel) prior to bottling, in order to a) to make for colour uniformity in a batch or brand, and b) for historic marketing purposes (North America prefers pale whisky; the Far East likes it to be rich amber). It is maintained that this additive is tasteless, but this depends how robust and flavourful the individual whisky is. In my view it is a useful practice in relation to blends, but unforgivable for malts. It certainly means that one cannot judge age, etc., by appearance alone.

Stage 2: *Aroma (Straight)*

Swirl the neat whisky in the glass, and nose it gingerly. A deep sniff of cask strength spirit may anaesthetize your sense of smell for a time (known as 'palate fade'). You may note 'nose prickle' or 'nose drying' – even 'nose burn' – which indicates the strength of the whisky. How 'forward' or 'shy' is it? You should also note the key aromas: they will be somewhat subdued, spirity and vaporous.

Stage 3: *Aroma (Dilute)*

For tasting purposes whisky should be diluted to 20% alcohol. The strength at which it is presented will be marked on the bottle, usually 40-43% in the UK and 46% in the USA, but there are variations. 'Cask' strength – unreduced spirit – is normally about 60%.

Here an aside. How you enjoy whisky – straight, on the rocks, with water, soda, ginger, Coca-cola – is a personal preference. It will vary, both according to the nature of the whisky – a venerable sherry-finished malt is best savoured neat, like brandy and sipped in small quantities (your saliva acts as the dilutant!), and according to the occasion (serious drinkers on the West Coast of Scotland favour dilution with lemonade). For 'sensory evaluation', however, it is diluted to a uniform 20% alcohol. This agitates and 'awakens' the spirit – you will see the oils eddying, unlocking aromatics.

Swirl the glass again and sniff, first over the top of the glass (the bouquet) then deep within it (the aroma). Note your immediate impressions; try to put words to the scents which first strike you. Then, perhaps after a couple of deep sniffs of fresh air, repeat the performance. Now more subtle nuances may become apparent – elusive fragrances and 'notes'.

It may be useful to run through a checklist of characteristics (see Appendices).

Stage 4: *Mouth Feel*

Take a large enough sip to fill your mouth and roll it over your tongue. What is your first impression of the intensity of flavour?

Then, consider the 'texture' of the whisky, the feeling as it slides across your palate.

Malt whiskies can usually be grouped into three different textures: 'mouth coating' (i.e. viscous), 'mouth warming' (i.e. spirity) and 'mouth furring' (i.e. slightly astringent and dry).

Stage 5: *Primary Taste*

What are the initial flavours you pick up? Is it sweet on the tip of your tongue? Is there any saltiness, sourness or acidity? Does the flavour change (it does with most whiskies) as it reaches the back of your tongue, becoming dryer or more bitter?

Stage 6: *Overall Taste*

As you swallow, is the back palate flavour consistent with that promised by the bouquet and first taste? Or is it changing, beginning to play a different tune? It has been said that taste is like a golf ball – it rarely travels in a straight line: it bends, loops and curves. As you go through the tasting process it can take several different directions, and you will also notice that even over a brief time the flavour of the whisky will change slightly.

Stage 7: *Finish*

What can you taste, if anything, about a minute after swallowing? Did the taste fade rapidly, or did it linger like a northern sunset? Are there any echoes of earlier flavours or aromas, which return, for good or bad?

One might add a final stage, when you lay down your pencil and pad, suspend your super-critical judgement and abandon yourself to inarticulate enjoyment. Pure hedonism!

THE INDUSTRY TODAY

Whisky consumption in the UK between 1970 and 1979 held in line with general consumer consumption, then the recession of the early 1980s began to bite and consumption declined, exacerbated by substantial increases in excise duty in 1979 and 1980.

Following a 1977 European Commission ruling concerning 'parallel exports' (see **John Barr**), DCL was obliged to withdraw a number of its leading brands from the UK market, including **Johnnie Walker** Red Label (which commanded about 10% of the market) and Haig **Dimple**, in order to protect its export trade. The company increased domestic prices on other major brands, introduced a number of new brands, with mixed success (see **John Barr**, **Buchanan Blend**, **The Claymore**) and sold the UK rights of others to Whyte & Mackay (see **Haig's**). DCL's market share slumped from 37% to just under 18% in 1985, and although the company won a relaxation of the EC edict in 1983, which permitted the return of Red Label to the UK market, the brand never recovered, and the company's morale was badly affected.

So badly, that the mighty DCL became vulnerable to takeover. In December 1985 the Argyll Group, a UK food-retailing chain, made a bid to buy the company. This was rejected outright, but the management were shaken by the equivocation of shareholders and Government and recommended the acceptance of an offer by Guinness plc, the brewing giant which had acquired Arthur Bell & Sons the year before (see **Bell's**). There followed the most acrimonious take-over battle of modern times, and the greatest change in the whisky industry this century.

Guinness was ultimately successful (May 1986) and became the largest drinks group in the world (with a market capitalization in excess of £10 billion; Scotch whisky interests, which are looked after by its subsidiary, United Distillers plc, account for some 60% of group profits). The Scotch whisky industry was initially nervous, but United Distillers has won back its confidence with a statesman-like approach and effective leadership.

Led by United Distillers, the industry resolved to reverse the cut-price/low-quality policy of the 1960s and 70s, and set about restoring Scotch whisky's reputation as a natural product of infinite variety and to restore its high-quality image.

In 1988 United Distillers launched a selection of six of its previously little known malt whiskies – 'The Classic Malts' – with a massive re-packaging and promotional campaign. Other companies followed suit, bottling and promoting their malt whiskies, repositioning their blended brands, re-designing labels and packaging, and introducing new up-market expressions. So successful was this move that the market for malt whisky grew dramatically; in 1992 United Distillers began to bottle small amounts of the single product all its malt distilleries, and to present them in attractive wooden boxes. Never in the history of the industry has so many malts been widely available.

At the same time, the 1980s was a decade of increased concentration of distillery and brand ownership in the hands of a few large international companies, many of which had interests beyond that of Scotch. At the opening of the decade, ownership was generally by companies whose main interests were in whisky – Seagram was the exception, and DCL had major interests in gin and cognac.

By the end of the 1980s major diversified conglomerates – including Guinness, Allied Lyons (with Allied Distillers as its whisky subsidiary) and Grand Metropolitan/International Distillers and Vintners (the main whisky subsidiary is Justerini & Brooks) – had bought distilleries and brands and joined the industry's principal players. Many distilleries followed the example which had been set during the 1970s by Glenfarclas, Glenfiddich, Glenlivet and Glenturret to open or re-vamp visitor centres – distillery visits are now a well-established feature of any holiday in Scotland, and the facilities are generally excellent (see Appendices).

Prior to the current world recession which began about 1989, export sales began to improve. The Japanese have relaxed trade restrictions designed to protect their own distilling industry; the Chinese are making similar moves; the former Eastern bloc countries are well disposed towards Scotch whisky; European sales continue to grow. The only shadows looming are the decline in whisky's two leading markets: the USA and the UK. In the USA market share declined by 35.3% between 1981 and 1991. The swing towards white spirits, particularly vodka, has continued, accompanied by a 10% fall in overall spirits consumption. The leading Scotch whisky brand, **Dewar's**, currently stands at 19 on the All Spirits League Table.

The fashion for white spirits is paralleled in the UK, but here the main reason for the decline in Scotch whisky drinking is fiscal. The 1984 budget increased duty on spirits by only 2%, but that on wine was reduced by 20% to comply with EC regulations, and this disparity was increased by a 10% increase in spirits duty in 1990 (compared to 7.6% increase for beer and wine).

Whisky sales, which had faltered throughout the decade began to drop steadily, but the Government continued to raise duty – by 9.3% in 1991 (on all alcoholic drinks), which together with a 2.5% increase in VAT raised the price of a bottle from £9.50 to £10.27.

The Scotch Whisky Association described the increases as "disappointing, unnecessary, inflationary, illogical and against the national interest". With the highest levels of tax as a proportion of retail price of all the major whisky markets, the Government was effectively discriminating against a UK product. Indeed, since 1979, when the Conservatives were first elected, home whisky consumption has declined by 30%, while the consumption of imported wine has increased by 60%.

Norman Lamont, in his time as Chancellor, was deaf to entreaties and again increased duty on alcoholic drinks, including whisky, by 4.5% in 1992; a year later, however, in the March 1993 budget, whisky was excluded from the familiar round of tax increases. Perhaps this is a sign that the Government is at last beginning to listen to reason, and to recognize the immense value of Scotch whisky both as an ambassador and as an export earner.

About 85% of Scotch whisky is sold overseas – 39% of that within the EC, representing a 19% increase since 1973. This performance has been achieved in the teeth of discriminatory taxation, whose basis is protectionist – wine-producing countries in the EC have sales taxes which favour wine; beer producers protect beer. The UK is unique: it is the leading producer and exporter of spirits, but it discriminates against spirits in favour of imported wine.

Logical arguments in favour of the harmonization of duties – the often-proclaimed 'level playing field' on which alcoholic drinks compete on an equal basis – cannot be made convincingly by the UK government so long as its own taxation of spirits is so ludicrously high in relation to that of other member states: it is two and a half times the European average!

CONCLUSION

The year 1994 will mark the 500th anniversary of the first written record of whisky-making in Scotland. The past five centuries have seen a cottage industry grow into a world industry, without altering the essentials of the way in which whisky is produced. They have witnessed the fortunes of an industry characterized by periods of great growth, followed by dramatic down-swings. They have seen the product itself win world-wide acceptance. And at the end of this era, it is pleasant to report that the appreciation of Scotch whisky reaches broader and deeper than ever before in the spirit's history.

When he visited Edinburgh in 1822, King George IV was able to savour some Glenlivet which was "*long in wood, mild as milk, and with the real contraband* goût *in it*" (see **Glenlivet**). A hundred years later, Aeneas Macdonald (*Whisky*, 1930) bemoaned the decline of whisky as a civilized pleasure, properly understood by only "a handful of Scottish lairds, farmers, gamekeepers and bailies, relics of a vanished age of gold when the vintages of the north had their students and lovers", and promoted by its makers as "a mere brute stimulant...to the swillers, the drinkers-to-get-drunk who have not organs of taste and smell in them but only gauges of alcoholic content ...[for whom] there are no whiskies but only one whisky – and, of course, soda".

Today there are more single malts available to the general market than ever before. Bottlings of single malts from individual casks, at full strength and without chill-filtration, have proliferated. A genus of 'Super-De Luxe' whiskies has emerged – blends which make use of very old fillings and which amply demonstrate the contention that a blend is greater than the sum of its parts. As many books about whisky were published over the past ten years as appeared in the previous eighty.

Only punitive taxation prevents widespread celebration.

DIRECTORY

SINGLE MALT and SINGLE GRAIN WHISKIES

Key

Category: This listing divides Scotland into Lowland; Campbeltown; Island (Islay, Mull, Jura, Orkney); Highland (North, South, East, West and Perthshire (Midland)); and Speyside. Sub-regions, or districts, are also provided. See also p. 23, Regional Differences.

Distiller: In many cases the owning company will have licensed the distillery to another company.

Owner: About one-third of the distilleries in Scotland are owned by United Distillers, the successors to the Distillers Company Ltd. UD is a subsidiary of Guinness plc and is the largest spirits company in the world.

Expressions: This lists the age/vintages at which the whisky is available. Unless otherwise stated, each malt or grain is bottled by its owner at between 40 and 43% alcohol. Sometimes casks are bottled and sold by 'independent bottlers' – the main ones being Gordon & MacPhail of Elgin (abbreviated to G&M – see **MacPhail's** for history) or Cadenhead's of Edinburgh (abbreviated to C) – and sometimes the whisky is bottled at higher strength: I have mentioned where this is the case.

Tasting Notes: Professional tasters, or 'noses', attempt to be as objective as possible in their definition of a whisky's characteristics and flavour profile. I have allowed myself a little more latitude. Sensory evaluation is bound to have a subjective content – one's mood, health, appetite (or lack of it), circumstances, even the time of day, all have a bearing on what one will perceive in the whisky. I approach the task as a consumer, eager to get the most out of the dram before me. So these notes should be read as 'one (or more) person's impression at a particular moment in time'. Unless otherwise stated, comments apply to the proprietary bottling.

Where possible, the notes have come from several people (it would be too grand to call them 'panel tastings'); in other cases I have augmented my impressions with published notes, particularly those of Michael Jackson, Wallace Milroy and the Scotch Malt Whisky Society (SMWS). I am beholden to these experts, and their notes are acknowledged wherever I have consulted them.

ABERFELDY

Category: Highland (Perthshire)
Distiller: John Dewar & Sons Ltd, Perth
Owner: United Distillers
Expressions: 15 Years Old; G&M 1974

Aberfeldy Distillery was built in 1896 on a small area of land bought by Dewar's from the Marquis of Breadalbane, on the outskirts of the spa town of the same name, and close to Taymouth Castle, the Marquis' seat. It was an ideal site for a distillery, having the main railway line at its door, which provided a direct link to Dewar's blending and bottling operations in Perth, being close to the Pitlie Burn which had supplied a previous distillery on the site with abundant water.

The distillery opened in 1898 and apart from the war years it has remained in production ever since. In 1925 when Dewar's, Buchanan's and Walker's joined the Distillers Company Ltd, Aberfeldy was taken over by Scottish Malt Distillers, the subsidiary responsible for the business of DCL's malt distilleries.

Tasting Notes: Perfumed aroma – pear-drops; violets; some peppermint – lightly peated – trace of biscuits. Flavour is pleasant but plain, somewhat syrupy, well rounded, sweetish as it slides over the tongue (oranges?), but with a bitter-sweet finish.

ABERLOUR

Category: Speyside (Upper Spey)
Distiller: Aberlour-Glenlivet Distillery Co., Ltd, Aberlour
Owner: Campbell Distillers Ltd, Brentford, Middlesex
(a subsidiary of Pernod Ricard)
Expressions: 10 Years Old, 1964, 1969, 1970; C 1963

Aberlour lies in the heart of Speyside, and its distillery was first noted in 1826, although whisky was almost certainly made on the site before this time, drawing water from St Drostan's Well.

St Drostan (or Dunstan) was made Archbishop of Canterbury in AD960. Previously, as Abbot of Glastonbury, he had led a mission into the Highlands and established a cell at Aberlour. The well was used for baptisms, and later, more prosaically, to power a meal mill and a saw mill.

Following a fire in 1879, the distillery was rebuilt. Much of the existing building dates from this time, with extensions in 1945 and more recent modernization by Pernod Ricard, which acquired it in 1974. Aberlour's distillery manager, Ian Mitchell, who died in 1992, was one of the longest-serving and best-regarded members of the industry. He was born within the distillery grounds, and both his father and his grandfather worked there before him.

Aberlour uses only Scottish barley and has uniquely broad-based stills; the product is matured partly in sherry casks, partly in bourbon. Cork bungs are used, not the usual wooden ones, which, it is believed, allow the harsher vapours to evaporate more easily.

Aberlour is available in all the major malt whisky markets, and is particularly strong in France. It claims to be the sixth best-selling malt worldwide (having risen from 22nd place in six years). It is the only malt whisky to have won both the Pot Still Trophy and the Gold Medal at the International Wine and Spirit Competition twice (1986, 1990), and, strangely, the week the first award was announced, St Drostan's Well, which had dried up, gushed forth once more!

Tasting Notes: Aberlour has a rich nose – a strong caramel aroma when nosed straight (this is a delicious whisky drunk neat) – with traces of mint, pine (fresh sawdust) and smoke, and a hint of peat as in a mountain burn. It has a voluptuous medium to full body. The flavour is attractively complex and well balanced, nothing is exaggerated: there are fruity elements and still a trace of peppermint. The finish is clean and smooth, neither dry nor sweet.

ALLT-A-BHAINNE

Category: Speyside (Dufftown)
Distiller: The Chivas & Glenlivet Group
Owner: The Seagram Co. Ltd, Montreal, Canada
Expressions: independent bottlings only – no stocks listed at time of writing

Allt-a-Bhainne (pronounced Alt-a-Bane) Distillery was built in 1975 by Seagram on the northern slopes of Ben Rinnes. It was built and equipped to a modern design and has the capacity of one million gallons (4.5 million litres).
Tasting Notes: (not available for tasting)

ARDBEG

Category: Island (Islay)
Distiller: Ardbeg Distillery Ltd, Port Ellen
Owner: Allied Distillers, 2 Glasgow Rd, Dumbarton
Expressions: 10 Years Old; C 1974; G&M 1974

It is said that the location of Ardbeg Distillery, on the south coast of Islay, was once the hideout of a gang of smugglers who dispersed after their cache was discovered by the Excise. What is certain is that there was a family of MacDougalls here from 1798, one of whom started a legal distillery in 1815 which was producing around 500 gallons (2,270 litres) per annum by 1835. This family retained their interest in the distillery until 1977.

Until the early 1980s Ardbeg Distillery had its own floor maltings and, unusually, there were no fans in the pagoda-roofed malting houses: the trapped peat smoke thoroughly permeated the malt, producing an extremely pungent whisky.

The strong character of Ardbeg tended to be too dominant for the blenders – yet almost all its output went for blending – and the distillery's history has been punctuated by closures. Since 1989 it has been working at only a third of its capacity, and no longer uses its own maltings (although the bought-in malt is heavily peated). Only about 200 cases are bottled as single malt every year: locals consider the dram to be variable, and very good indeed at its best.
Tasting Notes: Peat-smoke, iodine, seaweed and sawdust on the nose. Smoky, salty flavour, with a medicinal bite in the finish. The older expressions gain in depth; the younger has a somewhat shallow flavour-range, with all the powerful aromas associated with Islay malts.

ARDMORE

Category: East Highland
Distiller: Wm Teacher & Sons, Glasgow
Owner: Allied Distillers Ltd, 2 Glasgow Rd, Dumbarton
Expressions: 15 Years Old; C 1978; G&M 1977

The Ardmore Distillery was established by William Teacher's successors in 1898 (see **Teacher's**). Until this time the company had been concerned exclusively with blending, but during the 1890s whisky boom they quickly realized the importance of securing their own fillings.

The distillery stands deep in rural Aberdeenshire, near the ancient villages of Spynie and Kennethmont, close to the river Bogie. Despite some extensive modernization in the 1950s and 70s the buildings still retain several of their original features.

Ardmore is rarely bottled as a single malt by its owners (sometimes at 15 years old), but is available from independent bottlers. **Tasting Notes:** A dryish nose, with cereal notes; slightly oily; some smoke; 'meaty'. The flavour is agricultural – trace of silage, some salt, some vegetable mash – a sweet/dry balance.

AUCHENTOSHAN

Category: Lowland
Distiller: Morrison Bowmore (Distillers) Ltd, Carlisle St, Glasgow
Owner: as above
Expressions: 10 Years Old

Lowland malts were the first whiskies to be drunk in any quantity in England – their lightness had more appeal than the heavily flavoured Highland malts. However, following the arrival of consistent and well-made blended whiskies, after about 1870, the entire output of the Lowland distilleries went for blending.

The growing appreciation of malt whisky has led to several Lowland malts being made available as single malts. Auchentoshan is one, and it is unique in being created by 'triple distillation', formerly a traditional Lowland practice, introduced because it helped the spirit to mature more quickly.

Auchentoshan Distillery is on the northern edge of Glasgow, where the city gives way to the Kilpatrick Hills, from which the distillery draws its water. It was founded as early as 1800, largely rebuilt after the Second World War and re-equipped in 1974. A decade later it was bought by Stanley P. Morrison & Co. to complement its Highland and Islay distilleries (see **Bowmore** and **Glen Garioch**).
Tasting Notes: Nosed straight, the aroma is of sweet hay or straw. With the addition of water, this persists with cereal notes (dry barns); very slightly oily. The hay notes are also apparent in the flavour, now with a slightly lemony tinge. The overall impression is well balanced, clean and dry, and the finish is dry.

AUCHROISK
(see **The Singleton of Auchroisk**)

AULTMORE

Category: Speyside (Strathisla)
Distiller: John & Robert Harvey & Co., Glasgow
Owner: United Distillers
Expressions: 12 Years Old

The Aultmore Distillery has been in production since 1897, having been built two years earlier by Alexander Edward, the owner of **Benrinnes** Distillery. Its name is Gaelic for 'the big burn', and derives from a neighbouring stream. The distillery is situated two and a half miles north of Keith, in the hills between that town and the Moray Firth. The district was popular with smugglers in the old days on account of its relative remoteness and the peat-rich springs of the Foggie Moss, from which the distillery draws its water.

In 1898 Alexander Edward bought **Oban** Distillery, and the following year the new company was nearly brought down by the collapse of a principal customer, Pattison's of Leith. Production was cut, and times remained difficult until in 1923 the two distilleries were offered for sale: Aultmore was bought by John Dewar

& Sons for £20,000, and thus, two years later, became part of DCL, which licensed it to John & Robert Harvey & Co. Ltd.

In 1952 DCL embarked on a programme of modernization at the distillery, including a pioneering scheme for treating and making use of distillery effluent – the protein-rich draff and pot ale left after distillation has taken place. The experiments here and at Imperial Distillery were successful, and now 'dark grains', an animal feed, is made by all distilleries. A new effluent recovery plant was built at Aultmore in 1972.

Aultmore has long been well respected by blenders and, since 1992, a small amount has been bottled by United Distillers as a single malt.

Tasting Notes: The initial aroma is slightly sweet, with solvent notes (nail-varnish remover). Then the classic Speyside pear-drop aroma develops, with a subtle trace of walnuts. The flavour is dry and malty, with a nutty tang and a scented finish, which Michael Jackson describes as 'gentian or quinine'. Who am I to disagree?

BALBLAIR

Category: North Highland
Distiller: George Ballantine & Son, Dumbarton
Owner: Allied Distillers, 2 Glasgow Rd, Dumbarton
Expressions: 5 Years Old; C 1965; G&M 10 Years Old, 1959, 1964

On the southern shore of the Dornoch Firth, close to the village of Edderton, sits Balblair. Founded in 1749, it claims to be the second oldest distillery in Scotland. Some of the buildings – reminiscent of a farmsteading – date from its foundation, but they were considerably enlarged in the late 19th century. Balblair was bought by Hiram Walker in 1969, and has long been a major component of Ballantine's brands.

As with many areas where water and peat are in generous supply, this was a favourite site for smuggling activities. Edderton is known as the 'parish of peat' and the peat here is curiously dry and crumbly – presumably because of the plants from which it is composed, or perhaps because it is relatively young, which some distilleries deem to be an advantage (see **Highland Park**). The water used by the distillery trickles through this peat, which is said to account for the whisky's distinctive spicy character.

Tasting Notes: This is an uncommon whisky, since it is only bottled by the distillery from time to time.

(10 Years Old) The nose has a distinct salty tang, with some spice and an elusive freshness (pine-sap?). The taste is also fresh, clean, sweet-sour, with pinewood traces, perhaps a dash of lemon.

BALMENACH

Category: Speyside (Upper Spey)
Distiller: distillery closed 1993
Owner: United Distillers
Expressions: 12 Years Old; C 1981

Early in the 19th century, three Macgregor brothers left Tomintoul for Cromdale, a small village about five miles away across the hills. James Macgregor settled in Balmenach and established a farm there, on which he kept an illicit still. Sir Robert Bruce Lockhart KCMG, one of Macgregor's direct descendants, and the author of *Scotch* (1951) describes how, in 1823, his great-grandfather received a visit from the local exciseman, whose suspicions had been aroused by seeing a building with a mill-wheel and lade. Asked what it was, the farmer told him that it was a peat shed. Later, after receiving generous hospitality, and as he was about to leave, the exciseman gently advised Macgregor to take out a licence for his peat shed.

James Macgregor died in 1878, and was succeeded by his brother, who had made his fortune in New Zealand, but was summoned home to take control of what was by then a well-established distillery. In 1897 a limited company was formed as the Balmenach-Glenlivet Distillery Co. Ltd, and in the same year a private railway line with sidings was laid down, linking the distillery to the station at Cromdale.

The distillery was closed during the 1914–18 War and for a time thereafter. Having been acquired by Scottish Malt Distillers in 1930 it closed again and was used as a billet for the Royal Corps of Signals during the Second World War. During the great storm which blew down the Tay Bridge on 29 December 1979 – immortalized by William McGonagall – the distillery's chimney collapsed and there could have been a catastrophic fire but for the quick reaction of the stillman who opened the discharge cocks and allowed the spirit to run away to prevent the fire from spreading. Subsequently production resumed and continued until 1993, when Balmenach was mothballed.

Tasting Notes: A sweet, slightly sherried, very slightly smoky, rich and perfumed nose. The perfume comes through in the taste, with some maltiness, and the flavour embraces every area of the tongue: sweet to start, then an appetizing tinge at either side (like acid drops), even a slight dry note as it slides over the back of the tongue. A beautifully balanced, complex and satisfying whisky.

BALVENIE

Category: Speyside (Dufftown)
Distiller: William Grant & Sons
Owner: William Grant & Sons Ltd, The Glenfiddich Distillery, Dufftown
Expressions: Founder's Reserve (10 Years Old); Classic (18 Years Old); C 1979

In 1892, five years after building the **Glenfiddich** Distillery, William Grant bought the ground adjacent to it and built a second distillery. Its nucleus was 'new' Balvenie Castle, which had been designed by James Gibb and built in 1724 for the 1st Earl of Fife in the Adam style.

The ruins of 'old' Balvenie Castle stand on the hill behind. It was founded at the turn of the 13th century by the 3rd Earl of Buchan, who entertained King Edward I of England there and forfeited it to the Earls of Douglas in 1326. The 'Black' Douglases themselves forfeited the castle to the Crown in 1355, but James II returned it to Lady Douglas, on condition that she marry his supporter Sir John Stewart and pay an annual rent of a single red rose. Stewart was created 1st Earl of Atholl and Lord Balvenie, and his descendants lived there until 1610. The rose is repeated in the coat of arms which decorates Balvenie's label.

In 1673 the castle was bought by Alexander Duff of Braco, who gave his name to nearby Dufftown and whose descendants became earls of Fife.

Balvenie is unusual in having its own maltings and growing (some of) its own barley. It also has its own coppersmith's shop and cooperage (which it shares with Glenfiddich), and eight stills, which have much longer necks than those at its sister distillery. It matures its product in situ – partly in new wood, partly in fino sherry casks and partly in oloroso casks (the latter are used for the final year's maturation only) – and both expressions are bottled in most elegant flasks. The unique label-shape of The Balvenie Classic is supposed to echo the doors of the distillery's peat kiln.

Tasting Notes: (10 Years Old) Deep amber colour; medium body; sherried, honeyed, orangy nose; sweet flavoured, profound and rich, with a dryish finish. A first-rate after-dinner malt.

BANFF

Category: East Highland
Distiller: distillery closed 1983
Owner: United Distillers
Expressions: independent bottlings only – C 1976: G&M 1974

The distillery was founded in 1824 by James McKilligan & Co., at the Mill of Banff, close to the ancient town of the same name. Some years later it was taken over by James Simpson & Co., but closed in 1863.

Simpson's son then built a new distillery at Inverboyndie, a mile west of Banff and strategically placed to take advantage of the recently established railway line. In 1877 a fire destroyed the new distillery apart from its maltings and warehouses, and when it was rebuilt a fire engine was installed to prevent further disasters.

During the Second World War the distillery was closed and the buildings used to billet soldiers from the King's Own Scottish Borderers. On the afternoon of Saturday 16 August 1941 a single enemy aircraft bombed the site. By fluke no-one was injured, but the warehouse was burned to the ground. Exploding whisky casks were seen to fly into the air and those remaining were smashed to prevent the fire spreading. *The Banffshire Journal* reported that "thousands of gallons of whisky were lost, either by burning or running to waste over the land ... and so overpowering were the results that even farm animals grazing in the neighbourhood became visibly intoxicated". It is said that ducks and geese dabbling in the Boyndie burn were recovered at the sea-shore, some dead, some drunk, and that cows could not stand to be be milked.

At one time Banff (it was more commonly known as Inverboyndie) was purveyed to the House of Commons, but for many years before its final closure in 1983, the entire production of the distillery was sold for blending.

Tasting Notes: Malty, sweet but slightly astringent nose, with a whiff of smoke. The flavour is bland and light, with a quick, slightly soapy finish. Pleasantly unassertive.

BEN NEVIS

Category: West Highland – also Standard Blend
Distiller: Ben Nevis Distillery (Fort William) Ltd, Lochy Bridge, Fort William
Owner: Nikka Whisky Distilling Co. Ltd
Expressions: 19 and 25 Years Old

Ben Nevis is the highest mountain in the British Isles. Its summit is a 100-acre (40 ha) plateau with a sheer 1500-foot (450 m) fall on its north-eastern edge. From here you can see every peak in the Western Highlands.

The distillery which takes the mountain's name was built in 1825, by 'Long John' Macdonald (see **Long John**) who produced the famous blend Dew of Ben Nevis. He stood 6'4" (1.93 m) and was a renowned figure in the whisky industry. His distillery was the first licensed operation in the area.

In 1955 the distillery was bought by Joseph Hobbs, a colourful character who had made and lost a fortune in Canada during the 1920s by breaking the US Prohibition laws. When he came to Scotland he began buying up distilleries – at one time he owned **Bruichladdich**, **Glenkinchie**, and a share of **Glenury**, and traded as Associated Scottish Distillers. He also started an American-style cattle ranch along the Great Glen, allowing his beasts to roam semi-wild on the mountain slopes (this is still in existence). Some of his ranch hands took the idea a stage further and dressed as cowboys, complete with stetsons, chaps and spurs!

After he sold his interest in Associated Scottish Distillers, he bought Inverlochy Castle (now a luxurious hotel), Ben Nevis and Lochside distilleries, and introduced grain stills into their operations in order to produce both a malt and grain whiskies under the same roof, but the move was not a great success. The brand name had been sold to Seager Evans in the 1920s before Hobbs bought the distillery.

In 1981 the name and the distillery were reunited when the latter was bought by Long John International, a subsidiary of Whitbread & Co., the major brewer. Ben Nevis Distillery had been silent for many years after Hobbs' death and, alas, its new owners took it out of production in 1983.

Tasting Notes: The nose is very rich – rum toffee, fruit cake, caramel and sherry, but with intriguing herbal/floral notes – sherbet and violets. The taste is full-flavoured – sweet, smooth and rich – and the finish is slightly dry. An impressive whisky.

BEN RIACH

Category: Speyside (Lossie)
Distiller: The Chivas & Glenlivet Group
Owner: The Seagram Co. Ltd, Montreal, Canada
Expressions: independent bottlings only – G&M 1976, 1982, 1982 cask strength

This distillery was built by John Duff & Co. Ltd in 1897 but remained closed between 1903 and 1965. In 1985 two new stills were added to the complex to boost its annual output to over 780,000 proof gallons (3.5 million litres) of pure alcohol. The product is highly regarded by blenders although it is presently only available as a single malt in Gordon & MacPhail bottlings.

Tasting Notes: A big toffee nose when sniffed neat, modified with water. A noticeable sherry aroma, some floral fruitiness, with a hint of liquorice. Taste is positive, malty with a trace of toffee. Sweetish with a dry finish. Sound but uninspired.

BENRINNES

Category: Speyside (Upper Spey)
Distiller: A & A Crawford Ltd, Constitution St, Leith
Owner: United Distillers
Expressions: 15 Years Old; C 1971; G&M 1969

Benrinnes Distillery was built 700 feet (213 m) above sea level on the northern slopes of the mountain of the same name which dominates eastern Speyside.

The earliest reference to the distillery was in 1826, when one Peter Mackenzie was recorded as the licensed distiller. In 1864 it was bought by David Edward and his son Alexander, who owned and promoted many distilleries in Speyside, including Aultmore and Craigellachie. Alfred Barnard described the Scurran and Rowantree burns, from which the distillery draws its water, as rising *"from springs on the summit of the mountain and [which] can be seen on a clear day, some miles distant, sparkling over the prominent rocks on its downwards course, passing over mossy banks and gravel, which perfectly filters it"*.

The Benrinnes-Glenlivet Distillery Company was formed in 1897, but suffered badly when Edward's brokers collapsed two years later. However, production continued and it attracted the attention of one of the big four, John Dewar & Sons, which acquired control in 1922, taking Benrinnes into DCL with it in 1925. Ownership was transferred to Scottish Malt Distillers, the DCL subsidiary, in 1930.

In 1955 major reconstruction was undertaken in the interests of more efficient production; unfortunately the new buildings do nothing for their picturesque setting. Today the licensed distillers are A. & A. Crawford, which uses much of Benrinnes' output for their 3 and 5 Star blends (see **Crawford's**).

Tasting Notes: Pleasant fruity aroma – rich, with some sherry, traces of beeswax and a hint of liquorice. Medium body. Smooth and rich-tasting, with traces of fresh brambles and some smoke (cigar boxes). Clean, and surprisingly dry finish.

BENROMACH

Category: North Highland
Distiller: distillery closed 1983
Owner: United Distillers
Expressions: independent bottlings only – G&M 1970/1

Benromach Distillery was founded in 1898 by Duncan MacCallum of Glen Nevis Distillery (Campbeltown) and F.W. Brickmann, a broker from Leith. They were encouraged by Alexander Edward, the well-known promoter of Scotch whisky in Speyside, who granted them the land on which to build the distillery.

Unfortunately in October 1899, before the distillery had commenced production, Pattison's of Leith collapsed and Brickmann, who was closely associated with the company, was forced to withdraw from the partnership. MacCallum was only able to maintain production for a short time and then had to fight a lengthy battle against the Inland Revenue.

The distillery remained silent until 1909, operated until the war, underwent several changes of ownership, and then in 1938, was acquired by Joseph Hobbs, the eccentric Englishman who had made and lost a fortune in Canada (see **Ben Nevis**) and Hattim Attari, a London financier. Having bought up several distilleries they then sold them to National Distillers of America, which in turn returned them to the Scottish ownership of DCL in 1953. Its subsidiary Scottish Malt Distillers Ltd managed the Benromach Distillery, which was licensed until its closure in 1983, to J. & W. Hardie Ltd of South Queensferry.

Tasting Notes: Benromach has a curiously scorched aroma when nosed neat. With water this becomes a distant spent-firework note with, below a fresh, lightly perfumed, sweet aroma. The flavour is sweetish, clean and light; smooth and pleasant, with a hint of liquorice in the finish.

BEN WYVIS

Category: North Highland
Distiller: The Invergordon Distillers Ltd, Salamander Place, Leith
Owner: as above
Expressions: occasional independent bottlings only

The Ben Wyvis Distillery was established in 1965 as part of the Invergordon grain distillery complex on the northern shore of the Cromarty Firth. Its product is almost entirely used for blending and seldom found bottled as a single malt.

BLADNOCH

Category: Lowland
Distiller: Arthur Bell & Sons, Perth
Owner: United Distillers
Expressions: 10 Years Old; G&M 1984

Bladnoch Distillery lies deep in the pastoral south-west corner of Scotland, on the Machars peninsula in Wigtownshire, by the river Bladnoch whence it draws its water. 'Machars' signifies flat or low country in Gaelic, and well describes the landscape in which Scotland's most southerly distillery is located. It is a landscape rich in early Celtic remains, and inspired Sir Walter Scott's *Bride of Lammermoor*.

The distillery itself has been producing whisky since 1818, when it was established by two brothers, John and Thomas McClelland. It flourished as a typical winter-operating distillery until the 1930s, when it was closed for 18 years and its equipment sold to Sweden. Since re-opening it has been expanded twice and been sold twice, the second time to Bell's (1983) which brought Bladnoch with it when it joined United Distillers. Alas, the distillery was again closed in 1993: United Distillers will continue to use the site for warehousing, and it has opened discussions with the local authorities and enterprise agencies to consider how the distillery might be retained to function as a whisky museum and tourist centre.

Tasting Notes: An uncommon whisky, Bladnoch is an example of the Lowland style – the colour of pale straw, and smelling of damp hay and cereal mash. Concentration extracts light floral notes (violets?), a trace of orange and a smell of ground bones. To taste this whisky is thin, dry and 'boney'.

BLAIR ATHOL

Category: Highland (Perthshire)
Distiller: Arthur Bell & Sons, Perth
Owner: United Distillers
Expressions: 12 Years Old; C 1966

Blair Athol Distillery was founded in the late 1790s by John Stewart and Robert Robertson – not at Blair Atholl (double l) village itself, but 11 miles south at Pitlochrie. The whole district around Pitlochrie was once busy making whisky: there were over thirty distilleries in the area, although only three have survived.

Alfred Barnard wrote in 1887 that the water of the Allt Dour Burn ('the burn of the otter') which flowed from Ben Vrackie, rising above the snow-line close to Blair Athol Distillery was *"of the purest description, sparkling as clear as crystal"*.

In the 1850s Blair Athol was bought by P. Mackenzie & Co., which considerably enlarged the buildings and added two new granaries and malting floors. By the turn of the century there was a capacity for 100,000 gallons (over 454,000 litres). However the distillery was closed in 1932 and was out of production until 1949.

In 1933, P. Mackenzie & Co. was bought by Arthur Bell & Sons – an event which one writer describes as Bell's 'coming of age' – and in 1949 Bell's substantially rebuilt the distillery, happily without spoiling its attractive character. It was described as "almost a model distillery" by Professor McDowall, who goes on to describe its product as "one of the best malts".

Tasting Notes: The owners always insisted on using Orkney peat, preferred for its young character. It has a dry, sharp nose, becoming sweeter and creamier as the alcohol settles – with some cereal notes (fresh baking), light caramel and heathery overtones (perhaps heather flowers). Its flavour is deliciously smooth and sweet, with a gingery finish and mossy overtones.

BOWMORE

Category: Island (Islay)
Distiller: Morrison's Bowmore Distillery, Bowmore, Islay
Owner: Morrison Bowmore (Distillers) Ltd, Carlisle St, Glasgow
Expressions: 12 Years Old (also some rare special bottlings: 1966, 1979)

Nestling in the hills above the shores of Loch Indaal is the village of Bowmore, considered to be the 'capital' of Islay. It is a fine example of a late 18th-century planned village, with its quirky round church sitting at the head of the main street, which runs down to the shore through a huddle of houses. The distillery buildings are on the quayside.

Bowmore Distillery was established in 1779 by a local merchant, one John Simpson. One of the earliest legal distilleries on the island, it was also owner-operated which, at that time, was unusual, since most proprietors on Islay leased out their distilleries. It was later taken over by one James Mutter and his family: Mutter, as well as being a farmer and distiller had the unlikely role of Ottoman, Portuguese and Brazilian Vice-Consul in Glasgow.

Mutter considerably expanded the distillery, using his own steamship to bring barley and coal to Bowmore and deliver the whisky to Glasgow. Thus the Bowmore name began to travel and demand grew. The family kept the distillery until the 1890s when it was sold and became the Bowmore Distillery Co. During the Second World War the buildings were used as a coastal command base by the Air Ministry and after a brief spell of ownership by William Grigor & Son of Inverness in the 1950s the distillery was acquired by Stanley P. Morrison Ltd in 1963.

Morrison's rebuilt and renovated many of the buildings, retaining the malting floors which are still used today. Bowmore is a gentle whisky, only a little peat is used in malting and some claim that its geographical situation on the island gives it a balance between the intense malts of the southern shores and the subtler ones of the north.

Tasting Notes: A much more complex nose than the southern Islays, and fuller than their northern cousins. The nose is peaty, but not medicinal; there is a rich toffee undercurrent, some sherry, and a faint floral top note (Jackson identifies it as lavender). The flavour is big, sweet and resonant: there are traces of linseed oil and pure turpentine, reminiscent of a painter's studio; a salty tang, some sherry and a peppery finish.

BRAES OF GLENLIVET

Category: Speyside (Upper Spey)
Distiller: The Chivas & Glenlivet Group
Owner: The Seagram Co. Ltd, Montreal, Canada
Expressions: independent bottlings only – no stocks listed at time of writing

This distillery, not far from Dufftown, in the heart of Speyside was built in 1973 during Seagram's expansion in Scotland. The entire output is used for blending. The architecture of the complex was kept close to traditional distillery designs whilst employing the most advanced modern production technology.
Tasting Notes: (not available for tasting)

BRORA

Category: North Highland
Distiller: Ainslie & Heilbron (Distillers) Ltd, Edinburgh
Owner: United Distillers
Expressions: independent bottlings only – G&M 1972

Brora, the original part of Clynelish Distillery, stands close to the village of the same name on the east coast of Sutherland (see **Clynelish**). In 1967/68 a new distillery was built at Clynelish. The old distillery was closed for seven years, refurbished and renamed Brora to distinguish it from the new Clynelish Distillery. Brora closed in May 1983. (See **Clynelish** for G&M 1972)).

BRUICHLADDICH

Category: Island (Islay)
Distiller: Bruichladdich Distillery Co. Ltd, Bruichladdich, Islay
Owner: The Invergordon Distillers Ltd, Leith, Edinburgh
Expressions: 10, 15, and 21 Years Old; Stillman's Dram (extra long matured) will be produced from time to time; G&M 1965 (cask strength); C 1969

Bruichladdich (pronounced Brewickladdie), meaning 'the brae on the shore', is the most westerly of Scotland's working distilleries – situated in that western peninsula of the Island of Islay, known as the Rhinns.

The distillery was built in 1881 by William, Robert and John Harvey, with money from a trust established by their father, a well-known distiller in Glasgow (see **Harvey's**). The building used a newly patented material in its construction – namely concrete – and has changed little in appearance since its construction, with smart, whitewashed buildings overlooking the pebbled shore of Loch Indaal. Much of its equipment, including cast iron brewing tanks and mash-tun, and one of its stills (which is riveted rather than being welded), date from the distillery's foundation. The warehouses have traditional earthen floors. (Visitors are welcome, but should make an appointment.)

In 1929 the Harveys were obliged to close the doors on this, their last remaining distillery. Eight years later it was bought by the redoubtable Joseph Hobbs (see **Ben Nevis**). It closed again during the war, and was acquired by Invergordon in 1969.

Bruichladdich's product is highly regarded by other distillers on Islay – no mean accolade. It is lighter than most Islays, and less heavily peated (mainly owing to its water source, although the tall necks of its four stills may also contribute to this).

Bruichladdich became part of the Invergordon Group in 1968, and since then the whisky has become increasingly popular in discerning malt markets, like Italy, France and Holland.

Tasting Notes: A delicate nose, biscuity, slightly oily, a hint of seaweed – no trace of peat until water is added, and then only slight – little to betray its Islay origin; fresh flavour at first, with almonds, moss (rather than peat) and sea breeze, developing into a sweetish finish (marzipan). A complex and subtle malt.

BUNNAHABHAIN

Category: Island (Islay)
Distiller: Bunnahabhain Distillery, Port Askaig, Isle of Islay
Owner: The Highland Distilleries Company, plc
Expressions: 12 Years Old

Bunnahabhain Distillery was built between 1881 and 1883 by the Greenlees brothers – local farmers who wanted to make good use of their barley crop – at the mouth of the river Margadale (the name, pronounced Bunahavan, is Gaelic for 'the mouth of the river'). Their company was named The Islay Distillery Co. Ltd, and amalgamated with Glenrothes-Glenlivet Distillery in 1887 to become The Highland Distilleries Company.

The attraction of the site was the abundant supply of fresh peaty water, tumbling down a burn from Loch Staoinsha, combined with ready access to the Sound of Islay for shipment. Otherwise it was remote and desolate, without a tree in sight, let alone a human habitation. A mile-long road had to be constructed up a steep slope behind the distillery to join the track from Port Askaig; a strong pier had to be built and stone quarried for the distillery buildings, warehouses and accommodation. In due course an entire village grew up in the shadow of the distillery, complete with a school and a village hall.

Bunnahabhain's product was used almost exclusively for blending until the late 1970s when the 12 Years Old was launched, labelled with an illustration inspired by the old song Westering Home. It now sells well in France, Italy, Germany, the USA and Canada.

Bunnahabhain is the lightest of the Islay malts, and the distillery ensures this by drawing spring water from underground (before it has run through peat), and by taking a very narrow cut from the second distillation. Maturation is done on site, in a mix of sherry and bourbon casks.

Tasting Notes: Light in colour, Bunnahabhain has a very fresh, salty nose and a light to medium body. In flavour it is smooth and only subtly phenolic – a faint, flowery hint of peat, with a malty sweetness. Flavour develops well, and the finish is refreshing.

CAMERON BRIG

Category: Single Grain
Distiller: John Haig & Co., Markinch, Fife
Owner: United Distillers
Expressions: 9 Years Old (no age statement)

The Haigs have a good claim to be the oldest Scotch whisky distillers in Scotland. Their first recorded association with distilling was in 1655, when Robert Haig was summoned before the Kirk Session, charged with working his still on the Sabbath!

The distilling interests of the family continued over many years and it was 21-year-old John Haig who built the Cameronbridge Distillery in 1824, near the house in which he was born and brought up.

The distillery's original product was a Lowland malt, but Haig was a keen experimenter. In 1827, the year that his cousin, Robert Stein, invented the continuous still, he installed one at Cameronbridge, and after the repeal of the Corn Laws in the 1840s (which made grain cheaper) he installed a pair of Coffey stills and concentrated on the production of grain whisky. By the 1870s the distillery was producing 1.25 million gallons (over 5.6 million litres) of spirit a year, a stupendous amount for that era.

In 1877, only a year before he died, John Haig was instrumental in the merging of Cameronbridge and five other grain whisky producers to become The Distillers Company Ltd, of Edinburgh. He and his son Hugh became directors of the new company and another son, Henry, was appointed company secretary. In 1878, John Haig died leaving Hugh to manage the distillery and the whisky blending company, John Haig & Co. Ltd, which was excluded from the merger (see **Haig's**). Two other brothers set up Haig & Haig Ltd in order to concentrate on exporting to the expanding American market. Another brother, who was a young soldier at the time, was later to become Field Marshall Earl Haig, Commander-in-Chief of the British Forces in France during the Great War.

In 1919 John Haig & Co. Ltd was taken over by the Distillers Company and a great many technological improvements were made to Cameronbridge distillery, which continued to operate without interruption until 1941 when wartime grain shortages halted production for six years.

Further modernization took place during the 1960s and again between 1989–92 (when £20 million was invested and output was trebled), making Cameronbridge one of the most efficient distilleries in Europe.

Although most of the product goes for blending, a small amount is bottled as a single grain and sold as Old Cameron Brig – the main markets being local and in Edinburgh. Grain whiskies are lighter than malts owing to the extended rectification process used in distillation. As there is no peat used in the production of grain whisky it also lacks the smoky, phenolic flavour of malt.

Tasting Notes: Grain whiskies do not offer the range of aromas and flavours offered by malts – they are somewhat monochrome – but they have a robust, industrial attractiveness of their own, and, tasting them provides a fascinating insight into blending. Cameron Brig is rich coloured (caramel?). The nose is oily – reminiscent of machinery – with hay-like traces, and to me a trace of haggis(!). The taste is sweet and viscous, with an indefinable spiciness. The finish is disappointingly short.

CAOL ILA

Category: Island (Islay)
Distiller: Bulloch, Lade & Co. Ltd, Glasgow
Owner: United Distillers
Expressions: 15 Years Old; C 1978; G&M 1978, 1978 cask strength

Coal Ila (pronounced 'Cull-eela') is Gaelic for 'the Sound of Islay' (the strait separating that island from the Isle of Jura), and the distillery was built in a cove overlooking the Sound in 1846 by Hector Henderson who had been in partnership at **Littlemill** Distillery. The site was chosen for its abundant supply of good water from Loch Nam Bam – of which Alfred Barnard wrote, "*over which ever and anon the fragrant breeze from the heather and myrtle is wafted*" and which, more prosaically, was used to power the distillery's generator as well as to make its whisky.

Henderson soon went out of business and the distillery was bought by Bulloch Lade & Co. (1857), which, among other things, established a mission hall at Caol Ila, where each Sunday a seminary student from Edinburgh or Glasgow preached to the distillery workers and their families.

In 1927, its management passed to the Distillers Company Limited. The distillery remained in production until 1972 when it was decided to demolish the entire structure (apart from the warehouses) and build a larger distillery in the same architectural style as the original, but with new and better equipment and another pair of stills. Production was resumed in 1974. Today Caol Ila obtains its malt from Port Ellen and the whisky once dispatched by DCL's own vessel from the distillery's private pier now reaches its destination by road and ferry from Port Askaig and Port Ellen.

For many years Caol Ila was only available in independent bottlings, but it has been bottled by its owners since 1988/89.
Tasting Notes: Very pale in colour, with a greenish tinge. The first impression on the nose is of peat, but there are distinct floral notes (rhododendrons?), and less seaweed/iodine than one would expect from an Islay malt. The taste has been described by SMWS as 'pastel-coloured': it is lightly medicinal, smoky, salty; sweet, with a dry, peppery finish. Surprisingly complex.

CAPERDONICH

Category: Speyside (Lower Spey)
Distiller: The Chivas & Glenlivet Group
Owner: The Seagram Co. Ltd, Montreal, Canada
Expressions: independent bottlings only – C 1977; G&M 1968/80/82

Caperdonich was originally built as Glen Grant No. 2 Distillery (see **Glen Grant**) in 1897, across the road from its parent: although it used the same source of water, the same malt and the same distilling practice, its product turned out to be quite different, and, owing the market slump at the turn of the century, it was only in production for three years.

It is now active again as part of the Chivas & Glenlivet Group, its product being used almost exclusively for blending. Although the complex has been extensively modernized it still retains the original copper pot stills. Caperdonich is bottled by both Cadenhead's and Gordon & MacPhail.
Tasting Notes: Cadenhead's describe Caperdonich tersely as: "An abrasive whisky." The nose is spiritous, slightly sherried, malty; the

flavour is slightly smoky, but somewhat nondescript. The finish is accurately described by Michael Jackson: "Seems at first abrupt, but turns out to be lingering."

CARDHU

Category: Speyside (Upper Spey)
Distiller: John Walker & Sons, Kilmarnock and London
Owner: United Distillers
Expressions: 12 Years Old

Cardhu – the name derives from the Gaelic for 'black rock' – looks down upon Strathspey from Upper Knockando, on the slopes of the Mannoch Hill. For over 150 years the Cumming family farmed and made whisky here: John Cumming leased the property in 1811, and like so many in the district he had been involved in illicit distilling for many years. His wife, Helen, was famous for her skill in avoiding the excisemen: when the officials were on their rounds of the area they would lodge for the night at the farm, and when she had them safely seated at table she would steal into the farmyard and raise a flag above the barn which was a sign for the neighbourhood smugglers to hide their gear. Despite the efforts of his wife, John Cumming was convicted of unlicensed distilling three times before 1824, when he acquired a licence and went on to build up a thriving business.

In 1846 he died and left the farm to his son Lewis, who in turn died in 1872 leaving the running of both the farm and distillery (not to mention three young children) to his wife Elizabeth.

Elizabeth Cumming was a remarkable woman, overseeing the distillery and business at Cardhu (pronounced Car-doo) for nearly twenty years, and becoming known as 'The queen of the whisky trade'.

During this period the 'Glenlivets', as all Speyside malts were termed, became in great demand for blending. Realizing that if the firm was to take advantage of this, the distillery had to be expanded and updated, Elizabeth acquired a lease of 4 acres (1.6 ha) of land adjacent to the farm and built a new distillery capable of producing 60,000 gallons (over 270,000 litres) annually (1886). With her son John, Elizabeth Cumming transacted and determined the business of the distillery, dealing directly with agents and brokers herself, and by 1888 Cardhu was in demand by blenders, and was being sold in London as a single malt (as Cardow).

Such success attracted interest from larger companies, and over the years Elizabeth turned down several takeover bids, on the grounds that the distillery should be retained by the family. However, in 1893 she negotiated a deal with John Walker & Sons of Kilmarnock (see **Johnnie Walker**), (Cardhu's major customer), whereby her son would become a salaried director of the larger company, while remaining at Cardhu to manage the distillery. John Walker & Sons then bottled Cardhu (as Old Vatted Cardhu, then, post-1908, as Cardow).

John Cumming retired from the board in 1923, when John Walker & Sons was floated as a public company, and spent the rest of his days farming. He was succeeded on the board by his son Ronald – later Sir Ronald – who eventually became chairman of Walker & Sons and then of its parent company, DCL. During the war and the post-war period of barley shortage all the distillery's production went into the Johnnie Walker brands, but in the 1960s Ronald Cumming reintroduced Cardhu as a single malt, and it is now a leading brand.

Tasting Notes: Cardhu has been described as a ladies' whisky. Strongly perfumed with violets and sweet almonds, there are notes of peach-stones and honeycomb, a whiff of smoke and a hint of sherry. The flavour is fresh and sweet, with traces of pencil shavings (cedarwood) and aromatic spices (cinnamon?). The spiciness is reminiscent of a Highland, but the sweetness is pure Speyside.

CLYNELISH

Category: North Highland
Distiller: Ainslie & Heilbron (Distillers) Ltd, Glasgow
Owner: United Distillers
Expressions: 12 Years Old; G&M Brora 1972, Clynelish 12 Years Old

Originally named Brora, Clynelish Distillery was established in 1819 at the fishing port and golfing resort of Brora, on the northeast coast, by the Duke of Sutherland, to provide a use for the barley grown by the tenants on his farms. He was the son of the Marquis of Stafford and acquired the vast Sutherland estates by marriage to the Countess of Sutherland. He is remembered by history for ordering the removal by force of some 15,000 men, women and children from his estates in order to make room for the more economical Cheviot sheep.

Many of the crofters were forced to emigrate; others moved to the coast at Brora where the land was better for growing barley, and where there was a coal field, which it was hoped would power the distillery's machinery. The Duke sank a pit but the coal turned out to be of inferior quality and ran out quickly.

James Ainslie & Co. bought the distillery in 1896 (see **Ainslie's**). Soon after the years of the whisky boom at the turn of the century there followed a collapse of the market for fillings and Ainslie's barely survived bankruptcy until 1912 when the distillery and company were bought jointly by one John Risk and the DCL. In 1925 Risk was bought out and the Clynelish Distillery became part of the DCL empire. In 1967 a new distillery was built, also named Clynelish. The original, renamed Brora, was closed down in the 1980s.

Clynelish is very highly regarded. No less a connoisseur than the great Victorian Professor George Saintsbury declared it a favourite (he believed a blend of it with The Glenlivet to be a sublime dram). Many writers comment that it has the character of an island malt, perhaps because of the distillery's proximity to the sea.

Tasting Notes: (12 Years Old) Fresh, fragrant, complex nose, with a dash of seaweed and a whiff of smoke. Medium bodied. Sweet tasting, with a slightly smoky, dry finish. Unmistakably Highland. (Brora 1972) Could easily be mistaken for an Islay. The aroma is much more phenolic – smoky and iodiney, but fuller than most Islays. Latakia tobacco dominates the taste, which is still as sweet as the younger expression.

COLEBURN

Category: Speyside (Lossie)
Distiller: distillery closed 1985
Owner: United Distillers
Expressions: independent bottlings only – G&M 1972

John Robertson & Son Ltd (est. Dundee, 1827) built the Coleburn Distillery in 1896/97, six miles south of Elgin. The site was near the Glen Burn, which provided the water for production and the Great Northern Railway, which provided a goods station for the distillery traffic, and the distillery was designed by Charles Doig, an experienced distillery engineer. The owners described the appearance of the complex as: "*Faced on one side by a ... plantation of Scotch firs and birches, and swept by the cool mountain breezes of Brown Muir ... in a snug corner shut off from the surrounding country... complete itself, compact and clean with a cleanliness that can only be attained in Highland air.*"

In the early years of the century the distillery was the site of a number of successful experiments at purifying effluents and the process perfected at Coleburn was used in a number of other distilleries in the area.

In 1916 Coleburn was bought by the Clynelish Distillery Co. (see **Clynelish**), and went into DCL with that company in 1930.

Although the buildings retain their original appearance some conversion was done in the late 1950s and 60s – the mash house was rebuilt , condensers replaced the worm tubs and the stills were provided with internal steam coils. The licensed distillers at Coleburn were J. & G. Stewart Ltd, the well-known Edinburgh blenders (see **Usher's Green Stripe**). Coleburn closed in 1985.

Tasting Notes: Coleburn has an unusual aroma – reminiscent of dried seaweed, with some salt and a trace of rubber, and a faint floral mustiness. It is smooth and sweet-tasting , with an interesting 'fishiness', and a smooth, short finish.

CONVALMORE

Category: Speyside (Dufftown)
Distiller: distillery closed 1985
Owner: United Distillers
Expressions: independent bottlings only – G&M 1969

The distillery takes its name from the Conval Hills, north of Dufftown, from whence it draws its water. It was built in 1894 by the Convalmore-Glenlivet Distillery Co. Ltd. *The Elgin Courant* announced that: "*Its situation (close to the railway and within a mile of the town of Dufftown) is most convenient and central and will save considerable time and money in cartage ... the natural contour of the ground has been largely taken advantage of....*"

The company was bought by W.P. Lowrie & Co. Ltd, of Glasgow in 1904 following a recession in the whisky trade. Lowrie was a very successful stockholder, blender and bottler for wholesale whisky merchants who had no premises of their own (see **Lowrie's**). James Buchanan was one of his customers, and some years later he acquired most of the company from Lowrie, whose business was suffering from the lack of demand for mature whiskies.

In 1909 a fire broke out at Convalmore and much of the distillery was destroyed. The rebuilding which immediately followed included some innovations, one of which was a continuous still with the capacity to distil 500 gallons (2,270 litres) of wash every hour, using a similar process to that used in grain distilleries. This experiment was not a success, however, since the spirit would not mature evenly. It was abandoned in 1915.

The distillery was extended in 1965 and mothballed in 1985.

Tasting Notes: A full-bodied aroma including scents of beeswax, some sherry, malt and a curious sweet caramel note which can best be described as fresh meringues. The taste is sweetish, slightly salty and vaguely musty.

CRAGGANMORE

Category: Speyside (Upper Spey)
Distiller: D. & J. McCallum, Edinburgh
Owner: United Distillers
Expressions: 12 Years Old; G&M 1974, 1976; 1976 cask strength

John Smith, the founder of Cragganmore Distillery, is said to have been the most experienced distiller of his day. He had been manager of Macallan, Glenlivet and Wishaw distilleries, and was lessee of Glenfarclas distillery when he persuaded his landlord, Sir George Macpherson-Grant, to lease him the land to build a new distillery at Ballindalloch beside the Strathspey railway line, in 1869.

Cragganmore (the name is that of the hill behind the distillery, whose springs supply the water for production) was the first distillery to be deliberately sited to take advantage of railway transport, and a private siding was built on the Speyside railway to accommodate distillery traffic. John Smith himself was a great railway enthusiast, but since he weighed 308 pounds (140 kg) and was too wide to enter a railway carriage, he was obliged to travel in the guards van! He died in 1886, leaving the business to his son Gordon, who largely rebuilt the distillery in 1901.

In 1923, Gordon's widow sold the distillery to the Cragganmore Distillery Co. Ltd, a subsidiary of White Horse Distillers Ltd (see **White Horse**) and when White Horse merged with DCL in 1965, Cragganmore became a wholly owned subsidiary.

The licensed distillers are D. & J. McCallum Ltd, of Edinburgh (see **McCallum's Perfection**), which for many years exported Cragganmore mainly to Australia and New Zealand. In 1988/89, however, the brand was deservedly chosen by United Distillers to represent Speyside in their Classic Malts series. It was magnificently relabelled and widely promoted, and as a result it has become much better known.
Tasting Notes: Nosed straight, Cragganmore has a distinct oloroso sherry aroma; when water is added, other sweet scents emerge – pine essence, spices, cider apples, leathery notes. The overall impression is complex, clean and fresh. The taste begins dry and finishes sweet; there is plenty of sherry, but it doesn't mask a variety of other herbal notes. There is some restrained peat-smoke. Overall it fills the mouth with flavours and has a long finish.

CRAIGELLACHIE

Category: Speyside (Lower Spey)
Distiller: White Horse Distillers, Edinburgh
Owner: United Distillers
Expressions: 14 Years Old; C 1972; G&M 1974

The Craigellachie Distillery Co., founded in 1898 during the whisky boom, overlooks Thomas Telford's famous single span bridge across the Spey. It was established by Peter Mackie who, after inheriting Lagavulin Distillery on Islay, formed a partnership with Alexander Edward (see **Aultmore** Distillery), whose father, David, was a leading Speyside distiller (see **Benrinnes**).

Mackie eventually took over complete ownership of Craigellachie and thus it came under the mantle of White Horse Distillers Ltd. Mackie, or 'restless Peter' as he was known among his employees for his unrelenting energy, held his annual general meetings at Craigellachie, during which he was wont to air his views on the industry and the Empire in forceful terms. He was later knighted for his services as one of the leading figures in the whisky business (see **White Horse**).

Tasting Notes: Pale gold in colour, Craigellachie has a light, sweetish nose, with distinct traces of cereal and smoke. Light to medium bodied and delicately flavoured. Somewhat bitter finish.

DAILUAINE

Category: Speyside (Upper Spey)
Distiller: Dailuaine-Talisker Distilleries Ltd, Isle of Skye
Owner: United Distillers
Expressions: 16 Years Old; C 1962; G&M 1971, 1972

Dailuaine (pronounced Daal-yewann) is Gaelic for 'the green vale', and must refer to the site of the distillery, built in 1851 by William Mackenzie on the lush ground between Ben Rinnes and the river Spey, near Ballindalloch. Twelve years later the Strathspey railway reached the opposite bank of the river, and when a new road bridge was constructed close to the distillery Dailuaine could reach its distant markets directly.

In 1891, Mackenzie & Co. became a limited company and merged with the successful Talisker Distillery of Skye to form the Dailuaine-Talisker Distilleries Ltd. By this time the business was in the hands of Mackenzie's son who had built the Imperial Distillery at Carron and owned a further, grain, distillery in Aberdeen. During the pre-war recession, however, the company came under increasing pressure, and in 1916 it was bought jointly by Dewar's, DCL, W.P. Lowrie and John Walker & Son, thus becoming part of DCL.

Dailuaine has always been a filling malt, and until recently the distillery's entire production went for blending, apart from the occasional cask bottled independently. Since 1988/89 a small quantity has been bottled by its owners at 16 years.

Tasting Notes: Nosed straight, Dailuaine has a rich rum-toffee aroma. With the addition of water this becomes gentler and more sherried. The nose is quite hot and peppery, which adds to an already dry impression. However, there is plenty of rich malt present. The flavour is an interesting balance of sweet and dry, with more than a little sherry, some fruity notes and a bitter finish.

DALLAS DHU

Category: North Highland
Distiller: distillery closed 1983
Owner: United Distillers
Expressions: independent bottlings only – G&M 1971, 10 Years Old

Alexander Edward, the eminent Speyside distiller, laid the plans for Dallas Dhu Distillery in 1898 and sold the rights to build it (on his own land) to Wright & Greig Ltd, the Glasgow blenders.
The name of the distillery (pronounced Dallas Doo) is taken from the Gaelic *Dalais Dubh* which means 'black water valley'.

In 1919 ownership passed to J.P. O'Brien & Co. Ltd, then, in 1921, to an English consortium which had set up a company called Benmore Distilleries Ltd, based in Glasgow, *"with a view to creating an organisation of brewers, merchants and others interested in the whisky trade, for the purpose of assuring supplies of Scotch malt whisky, and also for securing the manufacturers profits."* This company was bought by

DCL in 1929, and ownership of Dallas Dhu transferred to Scottish Malt Distillers.

A fire in 1939 caused considerable damage, gutting the still-house and damaging most of the production equipment. Fortunately the warehouses, which contained hundreds of thousands of pounds worth of maturing stock, were saved. Apart from the war years production continued during most of this century until the distillery was closed in 1983, although it is preserved as an industrial museum by Historic Scotland.

Tasting Notes: Dallas Dhu has a rich nose, perfumed with a distinct 'barber's shop' aroma. It is medium-bodied. The flavour is smooth, complex and well balanced; neither sweet nor dry; with some maltiness, traces of wood and some pleasant mustiness.

DALMORE

Category: North Highland
Distiller: Dalmore Distillery, Dalmore, Alness, Ross-shire
Owner: Whyte & Mackay Group plc, 310 St Vincent St, Glasgow
Expressions: 12 Years Old

The Dalmore Highland Malt Distillery was founded in 1839 and acquired by the Mackenzie brothers, a local farming family, in 1867. The distillery has a fine position overlooking the Cromarty Firth and the Black Isle, and its appearance has been compared to an old-fashioned country railway station, its offices partly panelled with carved oak from a shooting lodge. The harbour here was once an important embarkation point for timber which was being shipped to Newcastle and South Shields. It has exclusive rights to the water of the river Alness, and one of its stills dates from 1874.

A diary dating from this time is still in the possession of the Mackenzie family. It holds detailed entries of tastings and day-to-day transactions, showing the importance of whisky as a part of the agriculture and commerce of the area. During the First World War, when the distillery was closed, it was used for the assembling of mines.

The Mackenzie brothers had been friendly with James Whyte and Charles Mackay, and Dalmore had always been a key component in their leading brand, **Whyte & Mackay**. In 1960 the two companies merged, although the Mackenzie connection was not lost: until recently there was still a representative of the family on the board of the larger company. Much of the distillery's output now goes to Whyte & Mackay blends although Dalmore has an established market as a single malt.

Tasting Notes: The immediate aroma is of cereal, with a whiff of smoke and a trace of rubber; after only a few moments these give way to sweetish notes – heather-honey, caramel and some sherry. The whisky is medium-bodied, smooth and sweetish to taste, with cereal (straw) notes.

DALWHINNIE

Category: North Highland
Distiller: James Buchanan & Co. Ltd, Glasgow and London
Owner: United Distillers
Expressions: 15 Years Old; G&M 1970

Dalwhinnie, the highest distillery in Scotland, stands in the Drumochter Pass at the head of Strathspey. The area is steeped in history. The placename itself means 'meeting place', where cattle drovers and smugglers met on their way to markets in the south. Prince Charles Edward Stuart passed down Drumochter after raising his standard at Glenfinnan in 1745. Part of General Wade's road – built after the '45 to help control the Highlands, still remains in the grounds of the distillery.

The distillery was originally named Strathspey when it was established during the whisky boom of the late 1890s by two men from Kingussie. They chose the site for its access to a supply of clear spring water from Lochan-Doire-Uaine, above the snow line, and abundant peat from the surrounding moors.

The business was not a great success, however, and in 1905 Dalwhinnie was sold to the largest distilling company in America, Cook & Bernheimer. This gave rise to great concern within the whisky industry in Scotland, which feared that the Americans might attempt to take over the market. Worries were dispelled by the introduction of Prohibition in 1922, and in 1926 the distillery passed into the ownership of the Distillers Company Ltd, which licensed it to James Buchanan & Co. Ltd (see **Black & White**).

Until 1988/89, the brand was only available locally, but it was chosen by United Distillers for their Classic Malts series, and is much better known today as a result.

Tasting Notes: The advertising slogan for Dalwhinnie is 'The Gentle Spirit', but this does not mean it lacks character. Pale gold in colour, the nose is very aromatic, with traces of solvent and peat-smoke, and malty-fruity undertones The taste is very sweet and smooth – honey and flowers, with a malty-heathery finish. 'Heather-honey' is promised on the label!

DEANSTON

Category: Highland (Perthshire)
Distiller: Burn Stewart Group Ltd, Barrhead, Glasgow
Owner: as above
Expressions: 12 Years Old; C 1977

Deanston Distillery is situated at Doune in Perthshire, just north of the Highland Line and about a mile up stream of the picturesque ruins of Doune Castle, seat of the 'Bonnie Earl o'Moray', who was brutally butchered in February 1592 near North Queensferry.

The distillery is housed in a cotton mill built in 1785 and designed by Richard Arkwright (1732–92), the inventor of the 'Spinning Jenny', and one of the fathers of the Industrial Revolution.

The mill was closed in the early 1960s and converted to a distillery in 1965/66. It was perfectly suited to such a purpose on account of, first, its good supply of clean water from the river Teith (the mill had been powered by this source) and, second, its airy weaving halls, designed to maintain a constant temperature and humidity in the days before air conditioning, and thus ideally suited to the maturing of whisky.

The conversion was inspired by Mr Brodie Hepburn, a well-known figure in the industry. The internal reconstruction involved removing three very solid floors in order to accommodate four stills.

Deanston prospered during the 1970s, then ceased production temporarily during the difficult mid-1980s. It was acquired by Invergordon Distillers in 1972, which sold it to Burn Stewart Distillers in 1991.

Tasting Notes: Deanston was originally known as Deanston Mill. It is pale in colour and light bodied. The malt used is very lightly peated, so sweet maltiness predominates, although there is some dryness at the back of the nose. In flavour it is well balanced, with malty notes and some fruitiness. Sweet with a dry finish.

DEERSTALKER

Category: Highland (district unknown)
Distiller: undisclosed
Owner: Hedges & Butler Ltd (parent Bass Export Ltd, Glasgow)
Expressions: 12 Years Old

This brand was launched in 1991, exclusively in export markets. It is attractively packaged – indeed the packaging won awards – and the colourful remarks on the label (penned by the present writer) tell one nothing at all about the whisky. The distillery that created Deerstalker is also a mystery.

Tasting Notes: Light in colour and body. The aroma is grassy with some estery notes and perhaps a trace of smoke, becoming more like damp hay. The flavour is thin and dryish, with some sweetness which is out of balance. The finish is dry, becoming bitter.

DUFFTOWN

Category: Speyside (Dufftown)
Distiller: Arthur Bell & Sons, Perth
Owner: United Distillers
Expressions: 15 Years Old; C 1979

In 1895, two Liverpudlian entrepreneurs, Peter Mackenzie and Richard Stackpole, visited Speyside with the aim of purchasing a property on which to build a distillery. Having toured the Kirkton of Mortlach, they settled on a meal mill near Dufftown on land owned by John Symon, one of whose farms, Pittyvaich, stood at the top of the hill overlooking the mill (see **Pittyvaich**). A deal was struck and the Dufftown-Glenlivet Distillery Company was founded (soon incorporated as P. Mackenzie & Co. Ltd).

Within a year the mill was converted and barley from Pittyvaich farm was being mashed for distillation. The first batch filled nine hogsheads. Water came from 'Jock's Well', famous in the district for its quality and quantity, and just a few miles from the distillery. On more than one occasion, men from the nearby Mortlach distillery attempted to divert the water.

As business prospered the company acquired **Blair Athol** Distillery and expanded its outlets for their whisky, even to the USA shortly before Prohibition. In 1933 P. Mackenzie & Co. was bought by Arthur Bell & Sons (see **Bell's**).

Apart from the war years, when grain shortages forced most distilleries to shut down, Dufftown has been in continuous production, its product well regarded by blenders.

In 1968, a major expansion programme doubled the capacity of the distillery, and in 1979 further expansion included the introduction of a stainless steel lauter mash tun and two more stills, allowing Dufftown the capacity to produce over 6 million gallons (over 27 million litres) of whisky per annum. In 1985, Arthur Bell & Sons amalgamated with Scottish Malt Distillers to become United Distillers.

Tasting Notes: Dufftown has a light body and traces of biscuits and diesel oil on its nose. It is sweet and estery, but this is balanced by a dryish smokiness. In flavour, the smoke and oiliness persists, and to my mind it has a somewhat cloying finish.

EDRADOUR

Category: Highland (Perthshire)
Distiller: Glenforres-Glenlivet Distillery Co. Ltd, Edradour Distillery, Pitlochry
Owner: Campbell Distillers Ltd, 924 Great West Rd, Brentford, Middlesex (a subsidiary of Pernod Ricard)
Expressions: 10 Years Old; occasional vintages

Edradour is Scotland's smallest distillery, and many would say her prettiest. It is a classic example of a farm-distillery, and was established as such in 1825, by a group of Perthshire farmers. The fact that it has been preserved is largely thanks to William Whiteley, known as the 'dean of distillers', one of the characters of the industry in the 1920s, who bought Edradour in 1922 with a view to keeping it as it was.

Apart from the conversion of the malt barn into a visitors' centre, and the reluctant installation of electricity (in 1947), little has changed: there is no automation, much of the equipment is still made of wood, the stills are the smallest permitted by the Customs & Excise, and the brewing and distilling methods are traditional. Today the distillery has a staff of three, and its annual production is equivalent to the weekly output of an average Speyside distillery.

William Whiteley's principal reason for purchasing Edradour was his belief that its product was perfect for blending, indeed, with it he produced King's Ransome, the blend which in the 1920s was considered 'the world's most excellent and expensive whisky'. Until the late 1980s Edradour was not available as a single malt, except in rare bottlings by, for example, Gordon & MacPhail.

Tasting Notes: An extraordinarily floral nose (dog-roses, almond blossom) and a light but substantial body. At 10 years old, this is a beautifully developed whisky, with layers of flavour which unravel across one's tongue – sweetish to start with, spicy to finish – just a trace of sherry, more of mint. Clean and fresh. A dram for any time of the day or night.

FETTERCAIRN

Category: East Highland
Distiller: Whyte & Mackay Distillers Ltd, Dalmore House, 296 St Vincent St, Glasgow
Owner: as above
Expressions: 10 Years Old; C 1980

Fettercairn is situated at Laurencekirk, in the heart of the Mearns, one of Scotland's most fertile areas. It commenced business in 1824. The Fettercairn Distillery Co. was formed in 1887 with Sir John Gladstone, father of the great Victorian Prime Minister, as chairman.

In 1939 Fettercairn was acquired by Associated Scottish Distillers, through its Glasgow subsidiary Train & MacIntyre which controlled it until 1971 when it came under the private ownership of an Aberdeen businessman. The distillery was later bought by Whyte & Mackay which markets the brand in the UK, Europe and the Far East.

Tasting Notes: A light nose – sweet and estery, with traces of fudge. The light toffee persists in the flavour, and there is a very slight rubbery taste on the back of the tongue. In spite of these sweet-associated notes, the overall impression, and the finish, is dry. An unusual and well-balanced flavour.

GLEN ALBYN

Category: North Highland
Distiller: distillery closed 1983
Owner: United Distillers
Expressions: independent bottlings only: C 1964: G&M 1972

Glen Albyn was started in 1846 by the then Provost of Inverness, James Sutherland, using the site of an abandoned brewery. It is thought that its owner was attracted by the prospect of sales to the great urban markets in the south, which could be reached via the Caledonian canal, on whose bank stood Glen Albyn. However, the main buildings were destroyed by fire three years later, and although rebuilding commenced immediately, Sutherland went bankrupt in 1855.

The complex was briefly used as a flour mill, then for twenty years Glen Albyn lay silent. One A.M. Gregory, a grain merchant, acquired the site in 1884 and built an entirely new distillery with the same name and its own railway siding, connecting to the main line.

During the First World War Glen Albyn became a US naval base for the manufacture of mines, then in 1920 Mackinlays & Birnie Ltd – which had built a neighbouring distillery called Glen Mhor – bought Glen Albyn and worked the two as a single operation.

In 1972 DCL took over both distilleries: both remained in production until the early 1980s, when they were closed and subsequently demolished.
Tasting Notes: More of a Speyside nose than a Highland – estery, with some maltiness and fruit, and a trace of nail-varnish remover (Cadenhead's notes make mention of lavender). The flavour is well-rounded, sweet but with a dryish finish, and some light smokiness.

GLENALLACHIE

Category: Speyside (Upper Spey)
Distiller: Glenallachie Distillery Co. Ltd, Leith
Owner: Campbell Distillers Ltd, Brentford, Middlesex
(a subsidiary of Pernod Ricard)
Expressions: old independent bottlings occasionally available
Glenallachie Distillery was built in 1967 near Aberlour in the heart of Speyside, by Charles Mackinlay & Co. (see **Mackinlay**), a company which at that time was owned by Scottish Newcastle Breweries. It was a constituent of the Mackinlay brands.

The distillery was designed by Delmé Evans, as were Tullibardine and Isle of Jura distilleries (both part of the Invergordon stable). After being closed for a time during the late 1980s, the distillery was sold to Campbell Distillers, which now use its product exclusively for its own blends.
Tasting Notes: A rather closed and nondescript nose – some heather notes; some malt. The flavour is smooth and medium bodied; sweet and syrupy with hints of digestive biscuits.

GLEN AVON

Category: Speyside (district unknown)
Distiller: undisclosed
Owner: Avonside Whisky Ltd, George House, Boroughbriggs Rd, Elgin

Expressions: 8, 15, 25 Years Old; 1953, 1955, 1958, 1962

(see **MacPhail's, Avonside**) Avonside Whisky is a subsidiary of Gordon & MacPhail of Elgin which, for longer than any other company, has been buying new spirit at the distillery and holding it in its own warehouses for an exceptionally long time. It is not disclosed which distillery Glen Avon comes from: it is on Speyside and still in operation.

GLENBURGIE

Category: North Highland
Distiller: James & George Stodart Ltd, Edinburgh
Owner: Allied Distillers
Expressions: independent bottlings only – C 1963, 1978; G&M 8 Years Old, 1960, 1968; 1966 cask strength

Glenburgie Distillery was established as early as 1810 by William Paul, and was originally known as Kilnflat.

In 1884 it was acquired by Alexander Fraser & Co. of Elgin and as the demand for Speyside malt increased so did the distillery's output – by 1890 the wash still capacity had grown to 1,500 gallons (6,800 litres) from its original 90 gallons (400 litres).

In 1925, Fraser & Co. went into liquidation and control passed into the hands of an Elgin lawyer, Donald Mustard. Ballantine's acquired Glenburgie in 1936, since when there has been a steady programme of rebuilding and upgrading, with great pains to preserve the original character of the buildings. Floor malting ceased at Glenburgie during the 1950s; malt is now in from Ballantine's central maltings in Kirkaldy.

Between 1958 and 1981, Glenburgie was actually producing two different whiskies. This came about because during that period the distillery housed a pair of Lomond (Lowland) stills (see **Inchmurrin**) in addition to its conventional stills. The spirit produced was quite different and was known as Glencraig, after the director of Ballantine's Highland Malt Distilleries. Some of this whisky remains in bond but it is unlikely to be distilled again as the two Lomond stills have been replaced by traditional Highland malt stills. Glenburgie is not presently bottled as a single malt by its owners.

Tasting Notes: The aroma is slightly astringent, oily, with traces of rum toffee and sherry and some maltiness. The flavour is strangely nondescript, sweetish with a touch of saltiness in the finish. Michael Jackson detects "bourbon, vanilla and perhaps even cinnamon".

GLENCADAM

Category: East Highland
Distiller: The Glencadam Distillery Co. Ltd
Owner: Allied Distillers Ltd, 2 Glasgow Rd, Dumbarton
Expressions: independent bottlings only: C 1980; G&M 1974

Glencadam is situated about half a mile outside the ancient Royal Burgh of Brechin (see **North Port-Brechin**). The distillery was built in 1825, and from 1827 until 1837 it was owned by David Scott. A succession of owners followed, before it was acquired by Gilmour, Thomson & Co. Ltd in 1891. The latter, an established firm of blenders, retained ownership until 1954 when they sold Glencadam to Hiram Walker.

The distillery later became the responsibility of Stewart & Son of Dundee Ltd which use it in the popular Cream of the Barley blend.

Tasting Notes: Glencadam has a relatively closed nose: the aroma is of damp wool, with some sherry and distinct tangerine notes. The flavour is light and smooth, sweetish, also with some traces of tangerine.

GLENCRAIG

Category: Speyside (Lossie)
Distiller: James & George Stoddart Ltd
Owner: Allied Distillers
Expressions: not currently available, except rare old stocks

Glencraig was a brand of malt whisky produced on Lomond stills between 1958 and 1981 at **Glenburgie** Distillery, Forres, when the distillery was owned by Hiram Walker & Sons, which later became Allied Distillers. The Lomond stills were dismantled in 1981 (see **Inverleven** for a description of Lomond stills).

GLEN DEVERON

Category: East Highland
Distiller: William Lawson Distillers Ltd
Owner: William Lawson Distillers Ltd, Coatbridge, Lanarkshire
Expressions: 12 Years Old; named Macduff in independent bottlings – G&M 1975; C 14 Years Old

Macduff Distillery, near Banff, was built in 1962 and bought by William Lawson & Co. ten years later, in order for the company to secure its malt whisky stocks. The premises were extended and a dark grains plant was built close by. (Dark grains are a by-product of the distillation process. Traditionally the draff and pot-ale were fed as a mash to cattle; by drying and compressing the by-product into small cubes, the foodstuff (known as 'dark grains') is more easily stored and transported.)

The distillery's water comes from the Deveron, a well-known salmon river, after which its product is named. Most of the output goes into **William Lawson's** Finest Blended although some is available as a single malt.

Tasting Notes: (1975) A sweet nose (boiled sweets, some rum toffee), overlain with traces of diesel oil, and an attractive spiciness; some light smoke. Medium body. The flavour is salty and peppery; still traces of oil and boiled sweets. A fairly short and dry finish. Macduff has been described as a "traditional east coast whisky, sea-breeze salty, with a hint of fisherman's cottage smoke"!

GLEN DOCHART

Category: region unknown
Distiller: undisclosed
Owner: Winerite Ltd, Gelderd Rd, Leeds
Expressions: 10 Years Old

This is Winerite's own-label single malt, launched in 1991 and available from the company's retail outlets throughout the UK. Where it comes from is kept secret, and it may be that the company will change the malt marketed under this label from time to time (see **Royal Game**), so no tasting notes are provided.

GLENDRONACH

Category: Eastern Highland
Distiller: The Glendronach Distillery Co. Ltd
Owner: Allied Distillers Ltd, 2 Glasgow Rd, Dumbarton
Expressions: 12 Years Old (two versions – matured in sherry and in plain wood); 18 Years Old

The distillery straddles the Dronac burn in Glen Forgue, near Huntly (West Aberdeenshire). Built in 1826 by James Allardes, the son of a local landowner, its product was favoured by the 5th Duke of Gordon – the peer responsible for the 1823 Act which provided for the licensing of distilleries and reduction of taxation. The duke was so impressed by this whisky that he introduced Allardes into London society, which resulted in him neglecting the management of his distillery to such an extent that it burned down in 1837 and was sold to one Walter Scott (no relation).

Glendronach means 'the valley of the brambles'. There is an old nonsense rhyme which runs:

> Red-currant jelly is good for the belly.
> Ginger and nuts are good for the guts.
> But the wine of Glendronach is good for the stomach!

In 1960 the distillery was bought by William Teacher & Sons, which has doubled its production capacity while preserving the traditional production methods. These include old-fashioned floor maltings (much of the barley used is grown locally, to order), Oregon pine washbacks, a peat-fired drying kiln and coal-fired stills. The whisky is matured at the distillery, some in sherry casks, some in plain oak – giving rise to the two versions of the malt available, and making possible a valuable study of the effects of maturation in sherry-wood.

Tasting Notes: The Glendronach Original (i.e. plain wood matured) – gold colour; dry nose, malty with a hint of sherry; dry flavour, slightly smoky, trace of peat; clean, full, scented finish.

The Glendronach Matured in Sherry Casks – deep amber colour, with red tinge; intense sherry nose with some vanilla; luscious body; a good balance of sherry and malt, some caramel notes and peat smokiness; surprisingly dry.

It is most interesting to taste the two alongside one another.

GLEN DULLAN

Category: Speyside (Dufftown)
Distiller: Macdonald Greenlees Ltd, Edinburgh
Owner: United Distillers
Expressions: 12 Years Old; C 1965

Founded in 1897 by William Williams & Sons Ltd of Aberdeen, this was the last of the seven distilleries to be built in Dufftown – which prompted the saying: "Rome was built on seven hills and Dufftown stands on seven stills." The location was chosen for its proximity to the river Fiddich, which not only provided water for production, but drove a water wheel for power.

At the outset Williams & Sons used most of the output for its own blends (Strathdon and Three Stars), although a small amount of the single malt was known to have been supplied to Edward VII in 1902. Following the hardships of the First World War the company merged with Macdonald Greenlees to become Macdonald Greenlees and Williams (Distillers) Ltd in 1919 (see Old Parr) and was acquired by DCL in 1925.

Tasting Notes: Pale coloured, spirity/biscuity nose, turning to damp grass. Markedly dry aroma. Very sweet, smooth and clean as it slides over the tongue; fresh tasting but with few noticeable characteristics. Short finish. Warming.

GLEN ELGIN

Category: Speyside (Lossie)
Distiller: White Horse Distillers Ltd, Edinburgh
Owner: United Distillers
Expressions: 12 Years Old

The distillery was established in 1898 – during the years of the whisky boom – by a former manager of Glenfarclas, William Simpson. During construction, however, Pattison's Ltd, the Leith blends who were one of the country's principal buyers of malt fillings, went into liquidation, taking with them the market for malt whisky.

So Glen Elgin ended up much smaller than originally planned, and it was the last distillery to be built on Speyside until Tormore in 1958. Within six months of commencing production, the distillery was taken over by a consortium of local businessmen, who registered themselves as the Glen Elgin-Glenlivet Distillery Co. Ltd. In turn they sold on to J.J. Blanche, a Glasgow distiller and blender, and in 1936 the company was sold to DCL, which placed it under the management of its subsidiary, Scottish Malt Distillers, and licensed it to White Horse Distillers (Glen Elgin had long been a key ingredient of White Horse). Glen Elgin is a pleasant dram and deserves to be better known.

Tasting Notes: A positive, aromatic nose, presenting a combination of heather flowers, sherry and a trace of mint with a whiff of smoke. Medium bodied and oily in appearance. Honey sweet, with an attractive floral (or fruity) finish. Remains sweet and clean throughout.

GLEN ESK

Category: East Highlands
Distiller: distillery closed 1985
Owner: United Distillers
Expressions: independent bottlings only

Originally a flax mill at the mouth of the river South Esk at Montrose, 'Highland Esk' Distillery (its original name) was converted in 1898 by James Isles, a wine merchant from Dundee.

The site enjoyed both a ready supply of water and access to the Mearns, one of Scotland's great barley-growing regions. Before the First World War the distillery was bought by a J.F. Caille Heddle who changed the name to North Esk Distillery. During the war operations ceased and the buildings were used to billet soldiers. Part of the distillery was burnt down at this time and remained in disrepair, and for some years only the distillery's maltings were in use.

In 1938 it was acquired by Associated Scottish Distilleries, Joseph Hobbs' company (see **Ben Nevis**): the distillery's name was changed again – to Montrose – and it was also converted to grain whisky production. Following the 1939–45 War ASD ran into difficulties and Montrose was bought by DCL, which used only the warehouses and maltings until the 1960s when it was reconverted to malt whisky production. A large mechanical drum maltings was also installed which enabled the distillery to supply a number of SMD's other operations.

The complex was finally renamed Glenesk Distillery and Maltings in 1980 and the licence is held by William Sanderson & Sons Ltd, which used most of the output for its **VAT 69** blend.

Tasting Notes: (1981 at 64.7%) "Pale straw colour (American oak cask?).... With water it shows sweet, fruity flavours; the lack of colour belies a voluptuous and passionate nature. Very agreeable. Would be good with fish." (SMWS)

GLENFARCLAS

Category: Speyside (Upper Spey)
Distiller: J. & G. Grant International Ltd, Rechlerich, Ballindalloch, Banffshire
Owner: J. & G. Grant
Expressions: 8 (@ 60%), 10, 12, 15, 21, 25 Years Old; '105' (cask strength); occasional limited bottlings; C 1979

Glenfarclas is one of only two malt whiskies of world status which remains in the ownership of the family that originally created it. The company's directors, George and John Grant, are the great-grandson and great-great grandson of the founder.

The first licence was granted to Rechlerich Farm in 1836, but distilling remained low-key until the property was bought by a neighbouring farmer, John Grant, in 1865. Less than fifty years later, John's son, George, was shooting with the king at Balmoral, such was the fame of his whisky.

Glenfarclas means 'the valley of the green grass', and the Grants still breed pedigree Aberdeen Angus cattle, as did their forebears. The distillery stands in meadows at the foot of Benrinnes and draws its water from a spring fed by snow-melt high in the mountain – soft water filtered through heather and over granite. The still-house itself is modern and its stills are the largest on Speyside. The distillery was one of the first to build a visitors' centre (1973), and this was refurbished recently to include an exhibition, a film theatre and a tasting room constructed from a stateroom in the RMS *Empress of Australia* (built 1913).

Glenfarclas is matured in sherry casks – some first-use, some re-fill and some new wood. This lends a sherried quality to the finished product; an assertive, vigorous character, typical of the robust school of Speysides, yet with all the finesse one associates with these superb whiskies. It is popular in Scotland, has a well-developed market throughout Europe and North America, and is found in Australasia, the Far East and South Africa.

Tasting Notes: Glenfarclas is a whisky of classic status; usually it is numbered among the top handful of Speysides by professional tasters. The fact that it is available at so many ages (and at cask strength) makes for fascinating comparative tastings, the older expressions become more sherried, as one would expect, and fill out the subtle wood notes and sweetness of the more youthful members of the tribe.

GLENFIDDICH

Category: Speyside (Dufftown)
Distiller: William Grant & Sons, The Glenfiddich Distillery, Dufftown, Banffshire
Owner: William Grant & Sons

Expressions: Special Reserve; 18 Years Old; 21 Years Old; 30 Years Old; Classic (Japan and Far East duty-free only); Excellence 18 Years Old (Japan and selected duty-free only); 50 Years Old (a limited edition of 500 bottles)

Glenfiddich is not only the world's best-selling malt whisky, it is the whisky which introduced the world to the pleasures of single malt.

The statistics relating to the brand's sales performance are impressive: 35% share of the total world export market for malt whisky, with a high market share in Germany (47%), Scandinavia (70%), Spain (48%), Australasia (51%) South America (46%), Canada (47%), France (40%) and USA (25%). It accounts for 54% of world duty-free sales (number one wine and spirit brand for the past four years) and is the UK brand-leader, outselling its nearest competitor by three to one.

William Grant (1839–1923) was the son of a tailor in Dufftown. He served an apprenticeship as a cobbler, then learned the art of distilling at Mortlach Distillery, where he worked for 20 years. Although he earned only £200 a year, he patiently saved part of his wage until he had enough to establish his own business. He chose a site close to Dufftown, in the field of Glenfiddich ('the valley of the deer'), drawing his water from the Robbie Dubh spring and buying his stills and plant second-hand from **Cardhu** Distillery for £120. The first whisky ran from the stills of Glenfiddich on Christmas Day 1887.

William Grant brought his eight children into the business, and the company is still directed and managed by his descendants (see **Grant's**). This sense of family tradition and continuity runs through all the company's operations: Glenfiddich still has its own cooperage and coppersmiths, grows some of its own barley and has its own maltings; it retains open mash tuns and traditional Douglas fir washbacks, and it fires its stills directly, with coal. The distillery is unique in bottling in situ, reducing the spirit with the same water from the Robbie Dubh as is used in its making.

Throughout its history, all but a minute amount of Glenfiddich went for blending. Then, in the early 1960s, the directors of William Grant & Sons determined on a bold plan: to sell it in southern Scotland and England as a single malt, marketing it in the same way as blended whisky. Single malt whisky had never been widely promoted: the popular palate found it too strong in flavour and body. Glenfiddich is a light-bodied whisky with a delicate flavour, however, and within only a few years it had won markets abroad as well as in England. In 1964, 4,000 cases were sold in export markets; ten years on the figure was 119,500 cases, and in 1974 William Grant & Sons became the first whisky company to be honoured with the Queen's Award for Export Achievement.

William Grant & Sons has always been adept at packaging its products. In 1957 the firm introduced a triangular bottle – wildly eccentric at the time – and was the first to put its products in tubes and gift tins. It was also the first to realize the significance of the duty-free trade and to take advantage of these worldwide outlets. Many of their foreign distributors have been handling the company's products for decades, and it supports them with advertising and promotions which are tailored to their individual markets. Above all, Glenfiddich's success is attributable to the fact that it is a most 'accessible' malt and easy to drink at any time of the day.

The result is that, today, one in every three bottles of malt whisky sold in the world is a bottle of Glenfiddich.

Tasting Notes: Very pale in the standard version (which makes no age statement, but is usually bottled at 8 years), becoming deeper in older expressions; light, fresh, slightly sweet, slightly oily nose; dry flavour, with a hint of smokiness and some malt and citric notes. Often described as the 'perfect beginner's malt'.

GLEN GARIOCH
Category: East Highland
Distiller: Morrison Bowmore (Distillers) Ltd, Carlisle St, Glasgow
Owner: Morrison Bowmore
Expressions: 10 Years Old; C 1974

The distillery – pronounced 'Glen Geerie' – is sited in a small glen near the village of Old Meldrum in Aberdeenshire. It was founded in 1797 but had a patchy history, owing to the unreliability of its water source. In 1884 William Sanderson bought Glen Garioch (see **VAT 69**), and in 1937 it passed into the DCL empire.

After sporadic periods of closure, the distillery was bought by Stanley P. Morrison (1968), as part of his bid to build a portfolio of distilleries which represented all the geographical areas of whisky production. After digging a deep well in a nearby field, a reliable source of water was secured and the distillery has been in production ever since. An innovative, ecologically sound development is that the waste heat from the distillery is piped into hothouses nearby for the purpose of growing tomatoes and other greenhouse fruits.

Tasting Notes: The initial aromas are of lavender and sawdust, with sandalwood traces. This quickly develops into a remarkable ginger aroma – the nose is complex with spices. Ginger persists in the flavour, and the finish is hot and spicy, almost oriental, with traces of cinnamon and spiced rum.

Glen Garioch is, however, more variable than any other malt I have come across; I have tasted supermarket bottlings which were a shadow of the proprietory bottlings, and I once tasted a single cask bottling from a 'rogue' cask which was heavenly – like a divine ginger cordial.

GLENGLASSAUGH

Category: East Highland
Distiller: The Highland Distilleries Co., 106 West Nile St, Glasgow
Owner: as above
Expressions: G&M 1983

Glenglassaugh Distillery was built between 1873 and 1875 on lands known as 'Craig's Mills', after the three mills situated there. Two were water mills, and powered the distillery until well into this century, the third was one of the few windmills in Scotland and formed the entrance to the distillery, even though it is some way off, since the road passed through it.

Highland Distilleries bought Glenglassaugh (pronounced Glenglassoch) in 1892 and completely refurbished it in 1959. It has always been in demand by blenders, but its owners have never felt it stands up as a single malt. From time to time great efforts have been made to 'improve' it – its owners going so far as to transport water in from their distillery at Glenrothes. This was not a success and the distillery was mothballed in 1986.

Tasting Notes: Grainy, with some floral notes (gorse?), unusual but unintegrated. Sweetish and floral to taste, again a trace of gorse (very slight coconut), a fresh, almost minty finish. A pleasant dram. "Sackcloth ... hessian ... Flax perhaps? Fresh linen? Newly-made beds", quotes Michael Jackson of his tasting panel!

GLEN GORDON

Category: Speyside (district unknown)
Distiller: undisclosed
Owner: The Glen Gordon Whisky Co. Ltd, George House, Boroughbriggs Rd, Elgin
Expressions: 15 Years Old; 1947, 1958

Glen Gordon Whisky Co. is a subsidiary of Gordon & MacPhail of Elgin (see **MacPhail's**, **James Gordon's**, **Glen Avon**).

GLENGOYNE

Category: South Highland
Distiller: Lang Brothers Ltd, 106 West Nile St, Glasgow
Owner: Robertson & Baxter Ltd, 106 West Nile St, Glasgow
Expressions: 10, 12 (export only) and 17 Years Old

The distillery lies in a wooded glen on the western edge of the Campsie Fells, not far from Loch Lomond. It is one of the most attractively sited in Scotland, with a pretty waterfall plunging into the natural hollow which forms the distillery's dam, where ducks swim and preen. The distillery retains many of its 19th-century features, and its layout is well adapted to viewing the distilling process in a compact space. Being so close to Glasgow, it attracts a large number of visitors (30,000 in 1991) and has a good new visitor centre to entertain them.

Glengoyne was established in 1833 (when it was known as Glenguin, later as Burnfoot of Dumgoyne). It was bought by Lang Brothers in 1876, and its product is used in the Lang blends. The Highland Line, which notionally divided Highland from Lowland Scotland, runs through the distillery grounds, and although technically a Highland, Glengoyne has many of the characteristics one would associate with Lowland malts: pale in colour, fresh and light to taste.

What distinguishes Glengoyne, however, is that it is the only malt distillery to use completely unpeated malt. It is suggested that by avoiding peat smoke in the drying process, the more subtle flavours in the barley (only Golden Promise is used) are allowed to emerge. About one-third of the output is matured in sherry casks.
Tasting Notes: Ian Taylor, Glengoyne's distillery manager, goes to great lengths to ensure that no single flavour dominates his creation. The result is a delicately balanced whisky, with a fresh, slightly fruity nose, a light to medium body and a clean, slightly sweet taste.

GLEN GRANT

Category: Speyside (Lower Spey)
Distiller: The Chivas & Glenlivet Group
Owner: The Seagram Company Ltd, Montreal, Canada
Expressions: 5 Years Old (Italy); 10 Years Old ; 12 Years Old; G&M 15 (40% and 57%), 21 and 25 Years Old, 1936, 1948, 1949, 1950, 1951, 1952, 1954, 1959, 1960

In 1840 an Elgin lawyer, James Grant, went into partnership with his older brother, John, to establish Glen Grant Distillery in the village of Rothes on the river Spey. Their father farmed six miles away – John had worked on the farm and had established a grain merchant's business – and both brothers had been engaged in illicit distilling before going into partnership (in about 1833) with the owners of Aberlour Distillery.

In 1839 the brothers leased some land from the Earl of Seafield and proceeded to build the first Glen Grant distillery. James Grant was a railway enthusiast and was instrumental in the completion of the Morayshire Railway, (indeed he is most remembered in Elgin, where he became Lord Provost, for his work on the railway enterprise) and this was vital for the efficient transport of their new product, which was one of the first malt whiskies to be sold outside its locale.

The distillery used water from the Black Burn close by and coal-fired stills were installed. The technical innovation of electric light was introduced to the buildings and workers' houses making Glen Grant one of the first industrial premises in Scotland to be so equipped.

When the brothers died, in 1864 and 1872, the distillery passed to James Grant's son, also named James. Soon after he took over, the demand for whisky grew and in 1897 he began to build another distillery across the road: Glen Grant No. 2. It lasted only four years: Pattison's – the large Edinburgh firm of brokers and blenders – were major clients, and when this company collapsed in 1898 Glen Grant No. 2 ceased operation. (It reopened in 1965 as Caperdonich Distillery.)

The original distillery continued to prosper, and Glen Grant was one of the earliest single malt whiskies to be generally available throughout Scotland (from about 1900).

When James Grant died in 1931 he left the business to his grandson, Major Douglas Mackessack, who immediately set about increasing production and expanding the market for Glen Grant. During the Second World War the distillery had to close ('The Major', as he was always known, was captured at St Valéry and spent four years as a POW).

In 1952 Glen Grant merged with George and J.G. Smith Ltd, to form The Glenlivet and Glen Grant Distilleries Ltd This was followed, in 1972, by a merger with Hill, Thomson & Co. Ltd and Longmorn Distilleries, then, six years later, the company was acquired by the largest producer of alcoholic drinks in the world, The Seagram Company, Canada (see **Chivas Regal**).

Glen Grant is a world brand – one of only two malt whiskies to feature in the top 20 export best-sellers. It has long done especially well in Italy, owing to the efforts of Armando Giovanni, a Milanese hotelier, who travelled to Scotland in the late 1950s to investigate malt whisky, returning with 50 cases of Glen Grant, with which he literally introduced his country to malt whisky. By 1970, 60,000 cases were being sold in Italy each year; today the number is in excess of half a million.

Tasting Notes: There is a marvellous range of Glen Grant expressions, and it is fascinating to compare one with another and see the mellowing effects of ageing. The younger versions are spirity and dry, then an attractive nuttiness develops and the whisky becomes sweeter and gains delectable honeycomb notes. Sherry notes also develop with age, but these will depend on the wood in which the spirit has been matured. In terms of flavour, Glen Grant's hallmark is probably its nuttiness – hazel in the younger expressions, almonds in the older (even marzipan). A very well-made whisky, Glen Grant strikes a delicate balance between sweet and dry.

GLEN KEITH

Category: Speyside (Strathisla)
Distiller: The Chivas & Glenlivet Group
Owner: The Seagram Co. Ltd, Montreal, Canada
Expressions: independent bottlings only – G&M 1965

In 1957 Seagram acquired the site of an old meal mill on the opposite bank of the river Isla from their beautiful distillery of **Strathisla**, and built this complex.

It was apparently the first distillery to employ gas-fired stills, and pioneered the use of computers in the monitoring and control of production. Vast bonded warehouses were also built at Keith, which are now used to house the products from most of the Chivas & Glenlivet Group's distilleries. Apart from merchant bottlings the entire output of Glen Keith goes for blending.
Tasting Notes: Slightly oily texture and nose; rum toffees, rich and sherried nose. Sweet and slightly salty; very smooth, viscous. Fairly rapid finish. A pleasant, full-bodied dram.

GLENKINCHIE

Category: Lowland
Distiller: John Haig & Co. Ltd, Markinch, Fife
Owner: United Distillers
Expressions: 10 Years Old; G&M 1974

Glenkinchie is a Lalland corruption of the name 'de Quincy', a family which owned tracts of East Lothian – the 'garden of Scotland' – in the 14th century.

The distillery was founded in 1837 by the Rate brothers near the village of Pencaitland. They were originally farmers and grew and malted their own barley on the premises to produce a high quality Lowland whisky which has only recently been made available as a single malt (1988/89), as part of United Distillers' Classic Malts range.

In 1853 the Rate brothers were bankrupted and the buildings of the distillery lay empty, being used primarily as a cowshed, with part being converted into a saw mill. In the 1880s Glenkinchie was bought by a consortium of whisky merchants and blenders from Edinburgh and Leith, which re-established production after rebuilding the distillery and maltings.

In 1914 Scottish Malt Distillers was formed with a view to consolidating the interests and resources of Lowland distilleries in troubled times. Glenkinchie was bought and has remained in operation under the license of John Haig & Co. The distillery has always maintained its close associations with local agriculture, and its farm was for many years managed by the distillery manager W.J. MacPherson, who was nationally acclaimed for his championship herd of Aberdeen Angus cattle.
Tasting Notes: The colour of Sauternes. A fragrant nose, sweet, slightly estery with hay or grass notes. The flavour is very clean and fresh, sweet for a Lowland. Light, but by no means insipid – a good, positive flavour. An interesting gingery note appears in the finish.

THE GLENLIVET

Category: Speyside (Upper Spey)
Distiller: George & J.G. Smith Ltd

Owner: The Seagram Company Ltd, Montreal, Canada
Expressions: 12 Years Old; C 1974 & 1972 (55.6% & 54.9%);
G&M 1943/46/48/49/50/51, 1977 cask strength

In 1823 an Act was passed which gave positive encouragement to
licensed whisky distilling by cutting duty dramatically and permit-
ting weaker washes (which made for more palatable distillate). The
Act had been steered through Parliament by the Duke of Gordon,
whose estates in the north-east of Scotland included Glenlivet. He
encouraged one of his tenants, George Smith, to build a legal distillery on his farm.

The fame of Glenlivet was already well established. In 1815
there were reputed to be 200 illicit stills in the area. Elizabeth
Grant of Rothiemurcus recorded in her Diary of a Highland Lady
that, on her father's instructions, she sent some Glenlivet whisky -
"*long in wood, mild as milk, and with the real contraband* goût *in it*"-
to George IV, when he visited Edinburgh in 1822. While the king
was in Scotland he would drink nothing else.

Like his neighbours, George Smith had been involved in illicit
production and smuggling, but unlike them he saw the opportunity presented by legal distilling, and seized it. He did this in some
trepidation, however, since his neighbours were still committed
smugglers and considered him a turncoat. He wrote in his journal:
"*The outlook was an ugly one. I was warned that they meant to burn the
distillery to the ground, and me in the heart of it. The laird of Aberlour
presented me with a pair of hair trigger pistols worth ten guineas, and they
were never out of my belt for years...*" Captain William Grant, the
officer in command of guarding the distillery, courted and
married George Smith's daughter and established a distillery at
Auchorachan on the other side of the glen.

George Smith took his son James Gordon Smith into partnership in about 1850. In 1858 they built a larger distillery close by,
at Minmore, to meet the growing demand for their product –
notably from Andrew Usher & Co. (see **Usher's of Green
Stripe**). This location benefited mightily from the construction of
the Speyside railway line in 1863, and the following year the first
bottle of Glenlivet was sold south of the Border.

J.G. Smith succeeded his father, who died in 1871. By this time
the name Glenlivet had become the benchmark for fine malt
whisky, and had been adopted by some 18 other distilleries, none
of them situated in the glen itself. In 1880 J.G. Smith took legal
action against the pretenders and the court ruled that there was
only one Glenlivet (hence the definite article 'The Glenlivet'). The
others could only use the appellation as a suffix to their brand
name.

The distillery passed to J.G.'s nephew, Colonel George Smith
Grant of Auchorachan, and in 1921 his son, Captain Bill Smith
Grant MC, assumed control. Even before the end of Prohibition,
Captain Grant had visited the United States and laid the foundations of what was to become the brand's principal market. In 1952
he guided the company into a merger with Glen Grant Distillery
and subsequently (1970) the company merged with Hill,
Thomson & Co. to form The Glenlivet Distilleries Ltd. This company was acquired by Seagram in 1978, whose marketing power
has helped establish The Glenlivet as the largest selling single malt
in the American market.

Tasting Notes: (12 Years Old) An 'uncluttered nose' – sherry
immediately apparent, but not so strong as to mask the delicate
spice and floral notes; some vanilla, all aromas very well integrated.
The taste is smooth and clean, again, marvellously balanced: the

first impression is sweet and lightly sherried, becoming drier and spicier, perhaps a hint of almonds. Long sherry and nuts finish.

GLENLOCHY

Category: West Highland
Distiller: distillery closed 1983
Owner: United Distillers
Expressions: independent bottlings only – G&M 1974

Glenlochy Distillery was established in 1898 by David McAndie of Nairn. It was built a mile outside Fort William, on the bank of the river Nevis and in the shadow of Ben Nevis which afforded a good supply of water – described as "coming off the mountain at great speed" – with which to power the distillery. The West Highland Railway was close by.

Unfortunately, the distillery's owners could not have chosen a worse time to commence business. The whisky boom of the 1890s turned to recession the year Glenlochy opened, and it ran at only a fraction of its capacity, even going out of production for several seasons.

In 1920 the shareholders sold out to a group of English breweries, but production remained patchy and in 1935 Joseph Hobbs, a colourful character who had made and lost his fortune in Canadian distilling, bought the distillery through his new company Associated Scottish Distillers Ltd. Production resumed in 1938 (see **Ben Nevis**).

In 1940 Hobbs sold his interest in ASD and retired to Inverlochy Castle (now a luxurious hotel) to develop plans for his Great Glen Cattle Ranch, where beef cattle roamed semi-wild and largely fended for themselves, as they did on the North American prairies. ASD was sold to DCL in 1953 and its distilleries were managed by Scottish Malt Distillers, which re-equipped Glenlochy in the 1960s, and undertook renovations in the 1970s.

Due to world recession Glenlochy was closed in 1983. Its closure was part of the measures taken by SMD to reduce output in order to bring the level of maturing stock into line with the anticipated level of future sales.
Tasting Notes: Glenlochy has a rich nose – sherried and perfumed, with some spicy notes and a trace of orange. Its flavour is sweet, with some sherry and scent, with a good balance, but somewhat nondescript. It fades rapidly.

GLENLOSSIE

Category: North Highland
Distiller: John Haig & Co. Ltd, Markinch, Fife
Owner: United Distillers
Expressions: 10 Years Old; G&M 1972

Glenlossie Distillery was built in 1876 by John Duff, a publican who had been the manager of **Glendronach** for several years. He had two partners in the business, Alexander Grigor Allan, Procurator Fiscal for Morayshire and H. Mackay, a land agent and burgh surveyor of Elgin. By 1887 John Hopkins & Co. Ltd was entirely responsible for the sale of the fillings. John Duff & Co. was liquidated in 1897 and the Glenlossie-Glenlivet Co. was formed. A private railway siding constructed on the line that ran between Elgin and Perth significantly cut the costs of transporting incoming supplies and consignments of whisky to the markets in the south. Many improvements and extensive additions to the buildings were made over the years (including the installation of a horse-drawn fire engine, which the distillery preserves to this day), and in 1930 Glenlossie became fully owned by Scottish Malt Distillers, the subsidiary of DCL. During the 1950s and 60s new warehouses were built and the distillery was fully powered by electricity. In 1971 Mannochmore distillery was built within the same complex and John Haig & Co. Ltd became the licensed distillers. Glenlossie is prized by blenders.

Tasting Notes: Slightly green tint. Full fresh nose, with some sherry. Heather honey predominates. Taste is sweet and sherried, with more honey, but the finish is smooth and dry.

GLEN MHOR

Category: Highland (Inverness)
Distiller: distillery closed 1983
Owner: United Distillers
Expressions: independent bottlings only – C 1976; G&M 8 Years Old (40% & 57%), 1963/5, 1978 cask strength

Glen Mhor Distillery faces **Glen Albyn** across the Great North Road on the western outskirts of Inverness. The manager of the Glen Albyn, John Birnie, tried in vain to gain a significant shareholding in his distillery, and so formed a partnership with Charles Mackinlay & Co. of Leith (see **Mackinlay**), he bought a site opposite Glen Albyn and built a new distillery, designed by the architect Charles Doig of Elgin. Named Glen Mhor, the distillery was completed and in production by 1894. The partnership became a private company in 1906 with the participation of John Walker & Sons Ltd, which held 40% of the shareholding.

In 1920 Mackinlay & Birnie Ltd bought Glen Albyn and set about an extensive modernization plan for both distilleries. DCL made a successful offer for Mackinlay & Birnie's shares in the distilleries in 1972, and in 1983 both distilleries were closed.

Tasting Notes: The aroma is malty, with cereal, grassy and nutty notes. The taste is sweet, fresh and smooth but unremarkable. It has a nutty finish.

GLENMORANGIE

Category: North Highland
Distiller: The Glenmorangie Distillery, Tain, Ross-shire
Owner: Macdonald Martin Distilleries plc, Leith
Expressions: 10 and 18 Years Old; 10 Years Old (cask strength); 1963, 1971, 1972

Glenmorangie has been for many years the best-selling malt in Scotland and the third-ranking malt whisky worldwide in volume terms. So it comes as a surprise to discover that the distillery itself is relatively small.

It is situated on the southern shore of the Dornoch Firth, near the Royal Burgh of Tain in Ross-shire – one of the oldest towns in Scotland, with a bishopric dating from the 9th century – on the site of a brewery which was established in 1738. The site is attractive because of the nearby Tarlogie Spring, which provides a copious supply of extremely hard and mineral-rich water – unusual, this, since traditional wisdom maintains that soft water is best for whisky-making. Illicit distilling took place on Morangie Farm from at least the 1660s.

The foundation of the distillery dates from 1843, when the farm was bought by William Matheson, a partner in Balblair Distillery. Matheson lacked capital, so was unable to realize his plans to develop the distillery. His first pair of stills were second-hand, and of an unusual pattern (they are immensely tall – the highest in Scotland) but were so successful that they have been carefully copied ever since. When Alfred Barnard visited in the mid-1880s he described Glenmorangie Distillery as *"certainly the most ancient and most primitive we have seen, and now almost in ruins"*. He was amazed that, in spite of its condition it produced 20,000 gallons (over 90,000 litres) of whisky a year.

Indeed, by this time Glenmorangie was selling widely throughout Britain, and even abroad, wherever Ross-shire expatriots travelled: the *Inverness Advertiser* reported that a consignment had been seen en route to San Francisco, and another to Rome.

The distillery was incorporated in 1887, and the directors immediately undertook its complete renovation. The new stills, modelled on the old, were heated by internal steam coils rather than by direct firing – a pioneering move, and one which was to be followed by the industry generally. By the outbreak of the First World War, Glenmorangie was being exported all over the world, although principally trade remained in the home market, including such prestigious outlets as the Savoy Hotel in London.

During the war barley rationing and shortage of manpower (75% of the local men aged between 15 and 35 signed up) caused the distillery to close for two years. In 1918 the need for capital persuaded the directors to sell the distillery to their largest single customer, the Leith-based distillers and blenders Macdonald & Muir Ltd (see **Highland Queen**).

By 1920 production exceeded pre-war levels, but that year Prohibition was introduced, and this, combined with high taxation and the General Strike of 1926 kept profits down. In 1929 the collapse of the American Stock Market heralded the first great world recession: this proved nearly fatal for Glenmorangie, and the distillery was closed from 1931 to 1936.

By the outbreak of the Second World War production had again reached unprecedented levels, but again barley was rationed, and whisky production ceased between 1941 and 1944. Not until 1948 were pre-war levels reached, but these were soon exceeded: during the 1960s and 70s the demand for Glenmorangie was such that stock rationing had to be introduced. In 1980 the number of stills was doubled (to four), but even this was not enough and ten years later a further four were added.

By maintaining traditions and adhering to the strictest production standards, Macdonald & Muir have done much to promote the enjoyment of malt whisky throughout the world. The company has pioneered the study of the effects of wood upon maturation, and it exercises the most stringent 'wood regime', buying its oak as standing timber in the Ozark Mountains of Missouri, airdrying the staves and filling the casks with Kentucky bourbon. The company eschews the use of sherry wood (except, in occasional bottlings, to round off a long period of maturation – a procedure pioneered at Glenmorangie in the early 1960s). It argues convincingly that sherry masks the flavour of such a delicate whisky. The entire production of the distillery is bottled as single malt. None goes for blending.

Tasting Notes: (10 Years Old) Clean fragrance, with floral and citric notes (mandarin, vanilla) and a trace of smoke. (A leading Parisian perfumier has identified no fewer than 26 individual aromas, including apricot, bergamot, cinnamon and quince). Medium bodied; smooth tasting, well balanced. Almonds, some spice and wood smoke. The overall effect is fresh and aromatic; the finish is clean and dryish. Glenmorangie is the quintessence of a 'well-mannered' Highland malt.

The older expressions fill out and enrich the flavours noted above: caramel and butterscotch appear, marzipan and increased nuttiness, but the finish is still fresh and dry, even minty.

GLEN MORAY

Category: Speyside (Lossie)
Distiller: Glen Moray-Glenlivet Distillery Co., Elgin
Owner: Macdonald Martin Distilleries plc
Expressions: 12, 15, 17 Years Old; also 1962, 1964, 1966, 1967, 1973

Glen Moray Distillery was established in 1897, on a site which was famous for the quality of its water (which drains off the Dallas Moor into the river Lossie), and which had been occupied by a brewery since the 18th century – the buildings on two sides of the distillery's central courtyard date from this time.

The distillery's site was also on the main road west out of Elgin, and until 1680 the town's gallows had stood here – a grim warning to visitors. Excavations in 1962 at Gallowcrook Hill, within the distillery's grounds (to make room for a new warehouse), revealed seven skulls, including one with a musket ball embedded in its jaw.

The Royal Burgh of Elgin is the gateway to Speyside, and the 'capital' of the whisky industry. It was once the centre for the extensive whisky trade with the Baltic states. The surrounding area, known as the Laich o'Moray, is famous for its barley crop: according to an old saying (repeated on Glen Moray's label) "The Laich o'Moray has forty days more summer than any other part of Scotland."

The distillery was acquired by Macdonald & Muir in 1920 (see **Highland Queen** and **Glenmorangie**) after a lengthy period of closure, and was considerably expanded in 1958. Its product has a good name amongst blenders – and the huge majority of its 1.6 million litre (over 350,000 gallons) annual output goes for blending. Since 1976 some has been bottled as a single malt, and more recently in very limited vintages.
Tasting Notes: (12 Years Old) A typical estery, Speyside nose – cereals, hay, fresh-mown grass, a trace of smoke and violets (the malt is hardly peated at all: the peat flavour comes from the water). Light but smooth bodied; fresh-tasting, clean, with barley coming through. Well balanced with a clean, dry finish.

GLEN ORD

Category: North Highland
Distiller: John Dewar & Sons Ltd, Perth
Owner: United Distillers
Expressions: 12 Years Old

Built on the site of an illicit still at Muir of Ord in Ross-shire, the distillery was licensed in 1838 by a Mr Maclennan. Its product has been known variously as Ord, Glenordie and Glen Ord.

In 1924 Muir of Ord Distillery was acquired by Dewar's, and accordingly passed to DCL the following year. Ord has long been a contributor to Dewar's blends. An unusual feature of production is that heather is thrown into the kilns during malting – this is believed to impart a dry, rooty, flavour.

Tasting Notes: Described as having a profound nose, with sweet and dry malt notes and a hint of peat. Medium to full body, very smooth. A clean, malty taste, slightly sweet; well balanced, very smooth. The finish is dry and spicy.

GLENROTHES

Category: Speyside (Lower Spey)
Distiller: Glenrothes-Glenlivet Ltd, Rothes, Morayshire
Owner: The Highland Distilleries Co. plc
Expressions: 12 Years Old (limited stocks in numbered bottles from Berry Bros & Rudd); G&M 8 Years Old, 1956, 1957; C 1971

Glenrothes Distillery was started in 1878, the year in which the City of Glasgow Bank collapsed. The collapse had dire consequences for the firm building the distillery – it had borrowed heavily to finance the venture, and two of the directors were employed by another bank, which might well have gone the same way.

All was well, as it happened, and work continued on the distillery, the partners appointing one James Booth Henderson as brewer. Henderson, a renowned judge of livestock, used to stable his stock of horses and cattle in the distillery, to the displeasure of his employers when they found out.

Glenrothes is ranked among the top six malt whiskies by blenders, who pay a premium for it and take all they can get. It is also a constituent of the popular Famous Grouse brand. All this results in it being difficult to find as a single malt , and apart from the independent bottlers, Berry Bros & Rudd has the exclusive license to bottle it as such.

Tasting Notes: Michael Jackson says of Glenrothes that it "quietly embodies all the nobility and complexity of a fine Speyside malt, and is beautifully balanced". It has a deep, fruity nose, slightly sherried, with a medium to full body and a well rounded, raisiny palate. There is a trace of malt, and the sweetness this implies, but this is balanced by a smooth dryness in the finish.

GLEN SCOTIA

Category: Campbeltown
Distiller: Glen Scotia Distillery Co. Ltd, Campbeltown, Argyll
Owner: Gibson International Ltd and James McAlistair Ltd
Expressions: 8 Years Old; 12 Years Old; C 1977

Glen Scotia is one of only two distilleries in Campbeltown (the other being **Springbank**): once there were over 30 distilleries. First registered in 1835, it was thoroughly overhauled in the early 1980s to increase efficiency and capacity. In spite of this, the distillery was closed in 1984 and only reopened after it had been sold to its present owners in 1989. Glen Scotia has long been popular with blenders and now sells well as a single malt in North America and Germany.

The distillery is small, has the appearance of a good townhouse, and is reputed to be haunted by a previous owner who drowned himself in Campbeltown Loch after being swindled. Its entire production is now matured in Campbeltown (previously, part was matured in Dumbartonshire). Glen Scotia is especially popular in North America and Germany.

Tasting Notes: Campbeltown malts are famous for their briny, 'sea-mist' character. Glen Scotia has this in full measure. The nose is aromatic, fresh and slightly peaty; the body medium and very smooth; the taste full, rounded, salty, with some peat. Long finish.

GLEN SPEY

Category: Speyside (Lower Spey)
Distiller: Glen Spey Distillery, Rothes, Speyside
Owner: International Distillers & Vintners Ltd, 151 Marylebone Rd, London NW1 (parent: Grand Metropolitan)
Expressions: independent bottlings only

The distillery was built in 1884 with the name Mill of Rothes, by James Stuart. In 1887 it was sold to Gilbey Vintners Ltd which was expanding its interests into whisky distilling (see **The Singleton of Auchroisk, Knockando, Strathmill**). The distillery was substantially reconstructed in 1970.

Glen Spey has seldom been available as a single malt, although for a short time it was sold through Unwin's as a house brand, and it is now used entirely for blending except for merchant bottlings. It is a key ingredient in **J&B Rare** and Spey Royal blends.
Tasting Notes: (1978 at 56.8%) "Sharp, attacking nose which develops astonishingly with time; sherry with overtones of new-mown grass. Very sweet – toffee and sugar tablet – take it with your pudding, or instead of it." (SMWS)

GLENTAUCHERS

Category: Speyside (Lower Spey)
Distiller: William Teacher Ltd
Owner: Allied Distillers Ltd, 2 Glasgow Rd, Dumbarton
Expressions: independent bottlings only – G&M 1979

The Glentauchers-Glenlivet Distillery was built by James Buchanan (see **Buchanan's**) in 1898 when he realized that in order to complete the range of his operations he should secure a supply of malt whisky. By this time Buchanan's was one of the 'big three' whisky houses, along with Dewar's and Walker's, and in 1925 they merged their interests with DCL. The ownership of Glentauchers (pronounced Glen-tockers)eventually passed to Scottish Malt Distillers Ltd, the DCL subsidiary. Between 1923 and 1925 extensive alterations and improvements had been made and a large new spirit store was built to the design of the distillery architect, Charles Doig of Elgin. Glentauchers was closed in 1985, then sold to Allied Distillers which reopened it in 1989. Currently its entire output goes for blending.
Tasting Notes: The nose is sweet and estery, a trace of solvent and an interesting 'waxy' development (like scented candles). The taste is smooth and sweet, with rich biscuity traces; the waxy flavour is still discernable. The finish is surprisingly dry, and quite lengthy.

GLENTURRET

Category: Highland (Perthshire)
Distiller: Glenturret Distillery Co. Ltd, Crieff, Perthshire
Owner: The Highland Distilleries Co. plc, 100 West Nile St, Glasgow
Expressions: 8,12,15, 21, 25 Years Old, and vintage bottlings; C 1965

Glenturret makes a strong claim to being the oldest distillery in Scotland. It was established by 1775 (some of the original buildings still exist) on a site which had been used by illicit distillers since 1717. Whisky-makers, then and now, use the water of the fast-flowing river Turret – said to be "as fine as any in the kingdom for distilling purposes" – and the site also appealed to smugglers on account of the vantage points provided by the surrounding hills.

The distillery itself was dismantled in the 1920s, then revived in 1957 by the noted whisky enthusiast, James Fairlie, with a view to preserving the craft traditions of malt distilling and developing its appreciation. To the latter end he was well ahead of his time in developing visitor facilities and making arrangements for tours and tastings. In 1964, he showed the British Prime Minister, Sir Alec Douglas-Home, round the distillery. Fairlie retired in 1990.

Today the distillery is a major tourist attraction (150,000 visitors per annum) and is provided with a heritage centre, exhibition museum (complete with life-size figures), an audio-visual display, a shop (selling souvenirs and the complete range of Glenturret products, including a limited edition 10 Years Old, which is available nowhere else) and a substantial restaurant.

Tasting Notes: (12 Years Old) Pale, with a slightly green tinge. A dryish, malty nose, some flowery aromas (elderflower?) and a hint of wood; fairly closed and unyielding. Malty flavour, with a hint of nuts and vanilla. The finish is dryish. Older expressions differ wildly, becoming more sherried, richer, creamier, more scented.

GLENUGIE

Category: East Highland
Distiller: distillery closed 1982
Expressions: independent bottlings only – C 1978, 1980; G&M 1966

Built on the site of an old brewery in 1875, the distillery was acquired by Long John International Ltd in 1937 (see **Long John**). Long John later became a subsidiary of Whitbread & Co. which sold on its whisky interests to Allied Distillers. which in turn sold Glenugie to a consortium of oilmen in 1975: it was closed in 1982 and later demolished.

Tasting Notes: (1965) There is an intriguing trace of incense on the nose – spicy and lightly sherried. The flavour is disappointingly flat: sweet turning to bitter.

GLENURY-ROYAL

Category: East Highland
Distiller: distillery closed 1985
Owner: United Distillers
Expressions: independent bottlings only; C 1966

Glenury is close to the coastal town of Stonehaven, south of Aberdeen. Founded in 1825, it was built in 1836 by Captain Robert Barclay of Ury, MP for Kincardine – a prominent farmer and landowner, and a renowned long-distance athlete. In 1799 he walked from London to Birmingham in two days and in 1808 became the first man in history to walk 1,000 miles in 1,000 successive hours. He also had a friend at court (whom he referred to as 'Mrs Windsor'), through whose influence he was permitted to suffix 'Royal' to his product.

Barclay died in 1847 and the distillery was put up for auction.

In 1857 it was bought by William Ritchie of Glasgow, and it remained in his family until 1938, when it was sold by its landlord, Lord Stonehaven, to Associated Scottish Distilleries (see **Ben Nevis**). In 1953 it became part of DCL and was licensed to the small Glasgow blenders, John Gillon & Co. Ltd (see **Gillon's**). Glenury was closed in 1985.

Tasting Notes: (1978 at 56.8%) "Highly aromatic on the nose. The taste is much stronger than the nose would suggest and to sweetness is added an overtone of spice. It would go well with Greek olives." (SMWS)

HIGHLAND PARK

Category: Island (Orkney)
Distiller: James Grant & Company, (Highland Park) Ltd, Kirkwall, Orkney
Owner: The Highland Distilleries Company plc
Expressions: 12 Years Old; Vintage 1967; G&M 8 Years Old (at 40% and 57%), 1983, 1974; C 1979

The world's most northerly whisky distillery was founded in 1798 by Magnus Eunson of Gallowhill, near the Parks of Rosebank, Kirkwall. Until it was licensed in 1825, its production was illicit, and Eunson was assisted in evading the excisemen by a kinsman, who was a kirk elder and hid the contraband under the pulpit.

By the 1880s Highland Park had an established reputation. In 1883 Sir Donald Currie, the founder of the Union Castle shipping line, took a party of distinguished guests to Kirkwall on the maiden voyage of the Pembroke Castle. They were entertained by one Baillie Peace, "*who produced his well-known big bottle of Old Highland Park whisky. No sooner had this famous brand been tasted than they one and all agreed that they had never met with any whisky like it before; that what was called Scotch in England was as different from this as chalk from cheese… A supply of Old Highland Park was at once sent on board… At Copenhagen, where the vessel called after leaving Kirkwall, the King of Denmark, the Emperor of Russia and a very distinguished party were entertained on board. The Highland Park was procured and pronounced by all to be the finest they had ever tasted.*"

In 1888, James Grant, whose father was manager of The Glenlivet Distillery, became managing partner, and later owner, of Highland Park. The Grants relinquished control to Highland Distilleries in 1937. Its product retains much that is traditional, even original. It has its own floor maltings and peat beds (the peat is cut shallow to impart a light, 'rooty' character) and two traditional peat-fired kilns. During malting a little heather is burned.

Highland Park has been promoted as a single malt since the early 1970s, and is currently the sixth largest selling malt in the UK. Its main export markets are France, Italy, Germany, Holland, Hong Kong and the USA.

Tasting Notes: Michael Jackson describes Highland Park as "the greatest all-rounder in the world of malt whiskies". Its aroma is heathery, slightly sweet, with clean smoky echoes; its flavour is succulent and smoky, with leafy, spicy and heather-honey notes. A subtle balance of sweet and dry, and a clean, dryish finish.

IMPERIAL

Category: Speyside (Upper Spey)
Distiller: Allied Distillers Ltd

Owner: as above
Expressions: independent bottlings only – G&M 1979

The Imperial Distillery was built in 1897, the year of Queen Victoria's Diamond Jubilee, by Thomas Mackenzie, who already had substantial interests in the Dailuaine and Talisker distilleries. The buildings were designed by the renowned distillery architect from Elgin, Charles Doig, and were constructed entirely from red Aberdeen bricks within a frame of iron beams. This specification was made in order to restrict the possibility of damage by fire, a common problem in so volatile an environment.

The progress of the distillery was reported by a local journalist, who noted that the malt kilns were being surmounted with a large imperial coronet which, *"once gilded, would flash and glitter in the sunlight like the crescent on a Turkish minaret ... among the dark pine woods of Carron and the brown hills which encircle it"*.

During the 1890s the demand for whisky outstripped supply, so Mackenzie merged his interests to form Dailuaine-Talisker Distilleries Ltd, to which Imperial was transferred. Following the crash in 1898 of Pattison's, the blenders in Leith, demand for malt fillings slumped and Imperial closed in 1900. It remained closed for twenty years. In 1925 production was resumed for one season only, then beset with problems of effluent disposal. During the next 30 years Imperial operated purely as a maltings. In the 1950s it was discovered that effluents could be recovered by drying, and used as a high protein animal foodstuff, so the earlier disposal problems were overcome. Production recommenced in 1954.

The business of Dailuaine-Talisker Distilleries Ltd was wound up in 1982 and Imperial was subsequently taken over by Scottish Malt Distillers, the DCL subsidiary responsible for malt whisky production. It was closed in 1985 then sold to Allied Distillers, which reopened it in 1989. The new owners use Imperial entirely for blending.
Tasting Notes: The nose is spiritous, slightly sherried with some smoky notes; generally lightweight. The flavour is also lightweight; sweet, with smoky traces and cereal undertones and lacks integration. The finish is sweet.

INCHGOWER

Category: Speyside (Strathisla)
Distiller: Arthur Bell & Sons, Perth
Owner: United Distillers
Expressions: 14 Years Old

The distillery was built in 1871 in an area renowned for illicit distilling. Although it is described as a Speyside, it is a long way from the region, on the Moray Firth, near the fishing port of Buckie.

Bell's acquired Inchgower in 1933 and undertook an extensive modernization programme, converting the power from coal to steam, and renovating the warehouses which were so vast that they provided bonding space for other distilleries in the region.
Tasting Notes: Dense floral notes, with some caramel and an aroma of mint toffee. the flavour is rich and very smooth, with toffee notes persisting, a trace of salt, an overall dryness and a curious impression of steam engines. A pleasant rich whisky.

INCHMURRIN

Category: South Highland
Distiller: Loch Lomond Distillery, Alexandria, Dumbartonshire

Owner: Glen Catrine Bonded Warehouse Ltd
Expressions: 12 Years Old

This malt is named after an islet in nearby Loch Lomond upon which stand the ruins of an ancient castle built by the Dukes of Lennox. More recently the island was used as a naturists' resort.

Loch Lomond Distillery, where Inchmurrin is made, is situated on a Victorian industrial estate at Alexandria, in a converted calico-dyeing factory. Calico-dyeing requires a copious supply of (preferably soft) water and this was provided by the river Leven, which runs from Loch Lomond to Dumbarton (at its mouth is Ballantine's massive blending and bottling factory). The Leven's water is very soft, which made it especially suitable for the bleaching and dyeing of calico: in 1768 there were as many as four bleach fields and three print fields devoted to this important industry.

Soft water is also favoured for the production of whisky and the old calico factory was converted to this purpose in 1965/6 by the owners of Littlemill Distillery. It was bought by Glen Catrine Bonded Warehouse Ltd in 1985.

Inchmurrin was first sold as a vatted malt, but now that it has had time to mature it is marketed as a single malt. It is made in Lomond stills (see **Inverleven**) which have rectifying columns within the still head, and can produce different styles of whisky, at different strengths: **Old Rosdhu** is made in the same stills.

Tasting Notes: Nosed straight the impression is of a weighty whisky with rum-toffee notes. This becomes lighter when water is added: there is still a slight toffee aroma but malty, grainy notes appear, becoming grassy and hay-like. Michael Jackson notes wintergreen and eucalyptus. The flavour is smooth and well integrated; some initial sweetness but the overall impression is dry. The finish is fairly quick.

THE INVERGORDON

Category: Single Grain
Distiller: The Invergordon Distillers Ltd, Invergordon
Owner: The Invergordon Distillers Ltd, Leith, Edinburgh
Expressions: 10 Years Old; Stillman's Dram (extra long matured) will be produced from time to time as stocks permit

The Invergordon Distillery occupies an 80-acre site on the northern shore of the Cromarty Firth in the north-east Highlands, surrounded by some of the best arable land in Scotland. The place takes its name from an 18th-century laird, Sir William Gordon. It is one of the best deep-water harbours in Europe and was formerly an important commercial port and naval base. The distillery was built in 1960 to create employment in the area, following the departure of the Royal Navy. The original owning company was part of the Hawker Siddeley Group, but a management buy-out in 1988 secured the distillery for nearly £100 million.

Production commenced in 1961 and now runs to between 8.4 and 8.8 million gallons (38–40 million litres) of grain whisky – which after being matured in oak for at least three years is used for blending, mainly in Invergordon's own products – and neutral grain spirit. The spirit is made without the addition of malted barley and is the basis of gin and vodka. This part of the operation will shortly be transferred to a new distillery in London. At any one time there are over 18 million gallons (around 85 million litres) of whisky maturing on site at Invergordon.

The Invergordon, one of only two single grain whiskies bottled as such (the other is **Cameron Brig**), was introduced in 1990 and targeted at first-time and occasional whisky drinkers. It is light and refreshing, and recommended over ice. Its creators describe it as 'distilled sunlight'.

Tasting Notes: Light cereal nose, with fresh grass and vanilla notes; very pale colour (the casks in which it is matured are selected for their lightness); clean, slightly sweet with a dash of iodine; a pleasant, lingering finish. Withal, it has a positive and distinctive flavour which will confound anyone who maintains that grain whisky is tasteless.

INVERLEVEN

Category: Lowland
Distiller: George Ballantine & Son Ltd, Dumbarton
Owner: Allied Distillers Ltd
Expressions: independent bottlings only – G&M 1979

This distillery originates from the early days of the Hiram Walker/Ballantine's relationship which was marked by the building of the Dumbarton Grain Distillery on the site of the McMillan shipyard, where the river Leven meets the Clyde beneath Dumbarton Rock – the former capital of the ancient British kingdom of Strathclyde. The distillery is currently mothballed.

From the outset, Inverleven supplied fillings for **Ballantine's** blends and it has never been available as a single malt, except from the specialist merchants. In about 1959 a new kind of still was installed alongside the distillery's two conventional stills: this, the first of its kind, was named a Lomond still and its product was occasionally bottled as a curiosity (named Lomond single malt) by independent bottlers.

Lomond stills were later installed by Hiram Walker at Glenburgie (producing **Glen Craig**), Miltonduff (producing **Mosstowie**) and Scapa (a wash still only). The first two have since been removed. Loch Lomond Distillery, which produces **Inchmurrin**, also has a pair of Lomond-style stills.

The idea behind the Lomond experiment was to produce a lighter whisky (in terms of its specific gravity) which would appeal to the American market. The stills themselves incorporated a cold-water coil within the still-head, which increased the reflux and acted as a kind of rectifier. Indeed, in some case, including the Inchmurrin stills, the coil was replaced by a small rectifying column (see Introduction, Grain Whisky Production).

Tasting Notes: An untypical Lowland. Highly perfumed nose, with complex, fresh-fruit aromas – peaches, nectarines, citric notes. The flavour is lightweight and sweetish – traces of soft fudge, and a catch of ginger in the finish.

ISLE OF JURA

Category: Island (Jura)
Distiller: Isle of Jura Distillery Co. Ltd, Craighouse, Jura, Argyll
Owner: The Invergordon Distillers Ltd, Leith, Edinburgh
Expressions: 10 Years Old; Stillman's Dram (extra long matured) will be produced from time to time.

'Jura' derives from the Norse for 'deer', of which some 6,000 share the island with 225 people. The first distillery here was set up in the 17th century in the grounds of its successor, which itself dates from 1810, although little remains since its roof was removed in 1901 to avoid paying rates (an odd feature of Scots Law).

In 1958 the present distillery was conceived by two Jura landowners as a way of creating work on the island. They obtained the assistance of Scottish Brewers, and employed the noted distillery designer, W. Delmé Evans. It was opened in 1963, and its first single malt came to market in 1974.

The distillery draws its water from Loch a' Bhaile-Mhargaidh (the market loch), a thousand feet (300 m) above Craighouse, the island's only village. The water is dark with peat, but Jura whisky is surprisingly light, and not at all like its cousins and closest neighbours in Islay.

Tasting Notes: Pale colour; delicate nose – slightly oily, with a hint of peat; light body; sweetish taste at first, with vanilla notes; becoming drier in the finish; a trace of saltiness, and very slight peatiness.

KINCLAITH

Category: Lowland
Distiller: distillery demolished 1982
Expressions: independent bottlings only – G&M 1967

The distillery was built in 1958 to complement the construction of the Strathclyde grain distillery complex constructed by Long John International, when this company was a subsidiary of Seager Evans. It was the last malt distillery in the City of Glasgow. Strathclyde incorporated vast storage, cooperage and blending facilities, and it was natural to have a malt distillery close by – making use of the water available from Loch Katrine. The output was used for blending and in 1982 Kinclaith was demolished to make way for the new distillery at Strathclyde.

Tasting Notes: Highly perfumed for a Lowland, with light grassy notes, a whiff of caramel. To taste – I cannot improve on Michael Jackson: "melon dusted with ginger".

KNOCKANDO

Category: Speyside (Upper Spey)
Distiller: Justerini & Brooks Ltd, St James's St, London SW1
Owner: International Distillers & Vintners (parent: Grand Metropolitan)
Expressions: various 'vintages' (bottles display the year of distillation and of bottling, usually 12 to 15 Years Old; older years are labelled as 'Extra Old Reserve'); also C 1980

Knockando Distillery is situated on a knoll overlooking the River Spey (hence the Gaelic name 'Cnoc-an-Dhu' – the dark hillock), and draws its water from the Cardnach Spring, described as an especially good source of water and used only for Knockando. The distillery was built in 1889, and was acquired by Gilbey's in 1904 for £3,500 (see **J&B Rare**).

The distillery has long made a practice of bottling casks only when they are deemed to be 'at their peak', and making an age declaration on the bottle, rather than automatically bottling at, say, 12 years old. Knockando was first exported in 1977/78 and is now sold in 40 markets worldwide.

Tasting Notes: Pale, even for a Speyside; nose dry and fragrant; mouth-feel smooth; complex flavour with layers of flowery, nutty, slightly smoky notes; a soft, clean, sweetish finish.

KNOCKDHU

Category: East Highland
Distiller: The Knockdhu Distillery Co., Knock, Banffshire
Owner: Inver House Distillers Ltd, Airdrie, Lanarkshire
Expressions: 12 Years Old

Knockdhu Distillery (pronounced Nock-doo) was opened in 1894, a showpiece of its day, and the first distillery to be established by the Distillers Company Ltd. Its two original stills are still in production.

The site is on the River Isla, beneath Knock Hill (from which the distillery draws its water), close to the fertile Laich o'Moray which provided abundant barley. For nearly 100 years Knockdhu's production went mainly into Haig's blends, then in 1983, it was closed. Five years later it was acquired by **Inver House**, with a view to making Knockdhu available as a single malt. As such it is now marketed successfully in Europe as well as the UK.

Tasting Notes: The nose is malty and sweet, with some fruit and a whiff of wood smoke; mouth-feel is soft and smooth; taste is sweet with orange notes and a surprisingly dry, smoky, lingering finish.

LADYBURN

Category: Lowland
Distiller: distillery closed
Owner: William Grant & Sons International Ltd, 84 Lower Mortlake Rd, Richmond, Surrey
Expressions: independent bottlings only – no stocks listed at time of writing

In the years following the Second World War William Grant & Sons (see **Grant's**) underwent considerable expansion and quickly realized that it would need to secure its supplies of fillings for blending.

In 1963 the company built the grain distillery at Girvan beside the Penwhapple Loch, followed, three years later, by the construction of a Lowland malt distillery called Ladyburn.

Ladyburn was bottled as a single malt for export to America, otherwise the entire production is used in blending. Like many other Lowland distilleries, Ladyburn was shut down in 1975, when the whisky industry was suffering from oversupply. Samples of Ladyburn still exist in merchant bottlings.

Tasting Notes: (not tasted) Michael Jackson describes it as: "a well-made Lowland malt, but it is a whisky meant to be blended. It has a certain fresh-faced charm, but no pretensions to depth of character."

LAGAVULIN

Category: Island (Islay)
Distiller: White Horse Distillers Ltd, Edinburgh
Owner: United Distillers
Expressions: 16 Years Old

Lagavulin Distillery stands near the ruins of Dunyveg Castle, once the stronghold of the Lord of the Isles, in a little bay on the south coast of Islay. In Gaelic the name means 'the hollow where the mill is', and in the late 1700s there were known to have been up to ten illicit stills operating in the district. A century on, when he visited the island in 1887, Alfred Barnard remarked: "*there are only a few of the Scotch distillers that can turn out spirit for use as single whiskies, and that made at Lagavulin can claim to be one of the most prominent.*"

By the 1830s there were two remaining distilleries in the bay; these amalgamated in 1837 to form Lagavulin Distillery, under the ownership of the Graham brothers and their partner James Logan Mackie, uncle of Sir Peter Mackie who later became one of the 'big five' in the whisky industry (see **White Horse**).

Indeed it was at Lagavulin that the young Peter learned his trade as a distiller. Soon after succeeding his uncle he earned the nickname 'Restless Peter' at the distillery – a comment on the fact that he was always planning new enterprises and seeking new methods to improving efficiency. These initiatives included a 'power flour' called Bran, Bone & Muscle, the development of dark grains cattlefeed, tweed manufacturing and the harvesting and distribution of Carragheen moss.

Mackie also instigated the restoration of two of the old buildings at Lagavulin which had at one time been a small distillery called Malt Mill, built in 1816. He intended to distil a whisky according to the original techniques – only peat was burned in the kilns – and the final product was quite different to Lagavulin. Sadly this was closed down in 1962 when it became necessary to build a larger still-house for the main distillery.

Sir Peter Mackie died in 1924 and Mackie & Co. Ltd changed its name to White Horse Distillers Ltd. Three years later it joined DCL, and in 1930, when the malt whisky distilling activities of DCL were reorganized, Lagavulin was taken over by Scottish Malt Distillers.

Tasting Notes: Very dry nose; Lapsang Suchong tea – smoky, some toasted peat, but all in balance – nothing over-dominant. Big body. The flavour begins sweetish and malty, with some sherry, then becomes very dry and smoky. It finishes almost bitter, with lingering peat smoke and some salt. Lagavulin has been described as the aristocrat of Islays.

LAPHROAIG

Category: Island (Islay)
Distiller: D. Johnston & Co. (Laphroaig)
Owner: Allied Distillers, 2 Glasgow Rd, Dumbarton
Expressions: 10 Years Old; 15 Years Old

The name is Gaelic for 'the beautiful hollow by the broad bay', and it was in this place on the south coast of the island of Islay that two brothers, Donald and Alex Johnston, established a distillery in 1815 which they built up during the 1820s. Many of the original buildings remain, including the floor maltings. Alas, one of the founding brothers died in 1847 by drowning in a vat of fermenting wash. Ownership passed through the family, until, between 1954 and 1972 the company was chaired by Mrs Bessie Campbell.

Laphroaig has the justified reputation of being the most pungent of all Scotch whiskies. It is very heavily peated at every stage – the distillery owns its own peat banks, and malts its own barley; the water in which the malt is mashed is dark with peat (they say that Islay water tastes of whisky!). Maturation takes place close to the sea, which may account for the slightly salty flavour that can be detected in Laphroaig.

Laphroaig's principal markets are the UK, the USA, France and Italy, and it is among the top five best-selling malts. It has come to be regarded as the epitome of Islays, which is unfortunate, since it is far and away the most strongly flavoured.

Tasting Notes: Nose is powerfully phenolic – smoky, medicinal, seaweedy (fishing nets), peaty. The body is medium and oily. The taste translates the smell element for element: peat smoke, tar, diesel oil, seaweed, iodine, salt. The finish is dry and lingering. The overall impression is clean and straightforward.

Laphroaig is an old tar, a salty dog, amongst whiskies – not a drink for the faint-hearted, but its mighty flavour is unique.

LEDAIG

Category: Island (Mull)
Distiller: Tobermory Distillers Ltd, Ledaig Distillery, Tobermory, Isle of Mull
Owner: Tobermory Distillers Ltd, St John's Place, Cleckheaton, West Yorkshire
Expressions: 1974, 1975 Vintage and 20 Years Old planned

Tobermory Distillery, or Ledaig Distillery, as it is also known, occupies the ground beside the Ledaig burn on the foreshore of the picturesque 18th-century harbour of Tobermory. In 1798, John Sinclair took a lease of this land from the British Fisheries Society, an offshoot of the Highland Society of London, which was responsible for developing the port.

Sinclair was a well-established merchant with a fleet of ships already sailing from the island to Glasgow and Liverpool with cargoes of kelp. This made the transportation of barley from the mainland easy, and in its first year the distillery produced 292 proof gallons (1,327 litres) of whisky.

On Sinclair's death in 1863 the distillery went out of production and remained silent until 1890, when it was bought by John Hopkins & Co. which resumed distilling. In 1916, Hopkins & Co. was bought by DCL, which kept open the distillery until June 1930, when it closed. It remained silent for forty years.

In 1972 it was reopened as Ledaig Distillery by a consortium representing some Liverpool shippers and the Domecq sherry group from Spain. The distillery was extensively reconstructed and the annual output raised to 800,000 proof gallons (over 3.6 million litres). However, this was a difficult time for the whisky trade, and it proved to be too much for Ledaig's owners. In 1979, the distillery was bought by a Yorkshire family with wide business interests, especially in Scotland. The new owners reopened the distillery but, owing to depressed market conditions, closed operations between 1981 and 1990, until the industry stabilized.

During this period, Tobermory was vatted with other island malts and sold in limited quantities in a dark green 'dump' bottle.

Since it resumed production, the company is concentrating on selling new fillings to established customers and expanding its market for Tobermory (vatted malt). In 1992 the distillery began bottling some 1974 Ledaig as a single malt, and it plans to bottle limited quantities of 1972, 1973 and 1975 stocks.

Tasting Notes: (not sampled)"Fine fruity nose with a soft finish. Gentle flavour with a soft finish. A good subtle malt" (Milroy).

"Lightly peated for an Island malt ... smell of violets. A good introduction to Island whiskies, it has peat and sweetness too: old-fashioned humbugs or bog boilings, if your imagination will stretch that far. Cinnamon and spice, peaty but not medicinal. An Island whisky for dwellers in a semi rather than a blackhouse." (SMWS)!

LINKWOOD

Category: Speyside (Lossie)
Distiller: John McEwan & Co. Ltd
Owner: United Distillers
Expressions: 12 Years Old; C 1968; G&M 15(40% & 5%) and 21Years Old, 1939, 1946, 1954, 1961, 1967

Linkwood is the distillery closest to the sea on the river Lossie, just south of Elgin. It was founded in 1821 by Peter Brown, an estate factor (i.e. manager) and agricultural improver (whose brother, General Sir George Brown, commanded the ill-fated Light Brigade during the Crimean War).

Little is known of the distillery in its early days, except to say that it passed to Brown's son, who completely demolished then rebuilt it.

In 1898, at the height of the whisky boom, a public company was formed and with doubled capacity and access to railway transport the whisky began to fetch a good price in the markets in the south.

In 1936 Scottish Malt Distillers took over the company and brought in a new manager, who, according to Professor McDowall, was "a Gaelic speaking native of Wester Ross, who for many years supervised its making with unremitting vigilance. No equipment was replaced unless was essential. Even the spiders' webs were not removed for fear of changing its character." Extensive rebuilding programmes were undertaken in 1962 and 1971, and the distillery remains in production under the licensed distillers John McEwan & Co. Ltd.

Tasting Notes: An initial cereal impression, quickly taken over by a strong estery perfume – bananas and bubblegum (New World Chardonnay), with some nail-varnish remover and a trace of fino sherry. The flavour begins delicately sweet, and finishes dry – even bitter. The overall impression is that the flavours are not well integrated.

LITTLEMILL

Category: Lowland
Distiller: Glen Scotia Distillery Co Ltd, Bowling, Dumbartonshire
Owner: Gibson International Ltd
Expressions: 8 Years Old; 12 Years Old

Littlemill, standing at Bowling on the north bank of the Clyde close to Glasgow, makes a strong bid to being the oldest distillery in Scotland, claiming its foundation at least as early 1772 (when accommodation for excise officers was erected). There was a brewery on the site, attached to nearby Dunglass Castle and probably of even date with it (14th century), so it is likely that distilling took place here from very early times.

The site has a good source of water in the Kilpatrick Hills and readily available barley from the fertile fields along the Clyde. When the first government survey of the whisky industry was conducted in 1821, Littlemill was producing 20,000 proof gallons (over 90,000 litres) a year. During its long history the distillery has changed hands several times, and periodically been out of production. Its current owners, Gibson International (since 1988) have undertaken extensive refurbishment and improvement.

Tasting Notes: Littlemill is a typical Lowland malt: the colour of white wine with a light body; gentle, fresh, slightly sweet, malty (marshmallows?), with a dry, quick finish.

LOCHSIDE

Category: East Highland
Owner: Macnab Distilleries Ltd, Lochside Distillery, Montrose
Distiller: distillery closed 1992
Expressions: independent bottlings only – G&M 1966

Lochside Distillery was a brewery in the 18th century, and in the early 19th century it was owned by William Ross who sold it to James Deuchar & Sons Ltd – the Edinburgh brewers, who are now part of Scottish & Newcastle Breweries Ltd. In 1957 the site was bought by Joseph Hobbs, who converted it to a distillery, introducing a grain still alongside the traditional malt pot stills, as he had at **Ben Nevis**. The managing company was Macnab Distilleries Ltd, and produced a successful blend called Sandy Macnab's.

Lochside was sold in 1973 to Destilerias y Crienza del Whisky SA, a Spanish drinks company, which closed down the grain stills and successfully marketed the blend for many years. The manager of the distillery, Mr Sharpe (who worked with Hobbs on leaving the Royal Navy), tells me that the distillery was closed in 1992. He assures me, however, that there is enough bonded stock to keep the warehouses busy for at least two years if no buyer can be found, and no doubt there will be some independent bottlings available for some years to come.

Tasting Notes: A lightly sherried nose, with traces of toffee and rubber, then a deep fruity note (blackcurrants?). The flavour is innocuous – slightly sweet and sherried, becoming dry – then suddenly explodes into more sherry towards the end.

LOMOND

Category: Lowland
Distiller: George Ballantine & Son Ltd, Dumbarton
Owner: Allied Distillers Ltd
Expressions: rare independent bottlings only (e.g. SMWS)

Lomond was made at Inverleven Distillery, Dumbarton on Lomond stills: the plant is currently mothballed (see **Inverleven**).

Tasting Notes: The sample tasted had the sharp flavour associated with maturation in plain oak casks. The nose was initially reminiscent of fresh paint and oily bourbon-like notes, then became mossy/dusty/fusty. The flavour was reminiscent of fresh lint bandages, with a sweetish start and a dry even bitter finish. SMWS unaccountably noted peaches which is interesting in view of the tasting notes for Inverleven.

LONGMORN

Category: Speyside (Lossie)
Distiller: The Chivas & Glenlivet Group
Owner: The Seagram Co. Ltd, Montreal, Canada
Expressions: 10 Years Old; C 1974; G&M 12 Years Old, 1956/62/63, 1969 cask strength

The name 'Longmorn' comes from the Old British word, *Lhanmorgund*, meaning 'place of the holy man' (Morgund or Morgan being a holy man) and history suggests that there was an ancient chapel here. A warehouse now stands on what was reputedly the chapel site, and long after the chapel itself had disappeared a water-driven meal mill was established there (in about 1600).

John Duff (who built Glenlossie Distillery in 1876) bought the site – which is about half-way between Glenrothes and Elgin – in 1893 and built two distilleries on it – Benriach and Longmorn – to take advantage of the 1890s whisky boom.

Longmorn Distillery opened in 1897 and has remained in continuous production. It has an ample supply of local peat and abundant springwater from the Mannoch Hill. In 1899 responsibility for its management passed to James R. Grant and later to his two sons, who became known as 'The Longmorn Grants'. Until 1970 the distillery remained with this family, when they joined with the Grants of Glen Grant to form The Glenlivet Distillers Ltd, later a subsidiary of the Canadian giant Seagram (see **The Glenlivet**).

Longmorn retains its own floor maltings, and the water-wheel and steam-engine which used to power the distillery can still be seen on the premises. Longmorn is as highly prized by blenders as **Glen Grant** and **Glenlivet** and it is generally regarded as one of the best Speysides.

Tasting Notes: Professor McDowall talks of Longmorn's "outstanding bouquet".

(1963) A highly sherried nose, slightly oily, buttery; a rich malty/fruity aroma; traces of shortbread (aromas tight and well integrated). Full bodied. Sherry on the palate; extremely smooth; malty and sweetish, becoming slightly drier in the long finish, but no trace of bitterness. Younger expressions are not so sherried – fresher and more flowery. An exceptionally well-made malt.

LONGROW

Category: Campbeltown
Distiller: J. and A. Mitchell & Co. Ltd, Springbank Distillery, Campbeltown
Owner: as above
Expressions: 16 Years Old; 17 Years Old (export only); C 1974

Longrow is made at Springbank Distillery in Campbeltown and is distilled in the same stills as **Springbank**, yet the two whiskies are utterly different. The former is made from very heavily peated malt – the distillery has its own floor maltings, and uses local peat – and the resulting whisky is powerfully phenolic. In blind tastings it is usually mistaken for an Islay.

There was a distillery named Longrow, established in 1824, occupying part of the site on which Springbank now stands.

Tasting Notes: Longrow has a pungent, earthy, peaty nose (a colleague described it as "the aroma of wet sheep"); it is medium to full bodied and very oily, and has a creamy, malty palate, phenolic and extremely dry; its finish is tenacious, salty and intense.

THE MACALLAN

Category: Speyside (Lower Spey)
Distiller: Macallan-Glenlivet plc, Craigellachie, Banffshire
Owner: Macallan-Glenlivet plc
Expressions: 7, 10, 12, 18, 25 Years Old, and vintage bottlings; C 1980

The Macallan has become a benchmark against which other malts are measured. This is somewhat unfair, for as *the* exemplar of the heavier class of Speysides it is unique, and the flavour developed by its creators at Easter Elchies, near Aberlour in the heart of Speyside, is simply not that sought by other distilleries.

A farm-distillery was established in the early 18th century and its product had a wide reputation even beyond Speyside, assisted by the fact that Macallan Farm was situated above one of the few fords across the Spey and was on one of the cattle-drove routes from the Laich o'Moray to the south.

Macallan's popularity will have encouraged its owners to apply for a licence earlier than most (1824), but the distillery changed hands several times throughout the 19th century, and in 1892 was bought by an Elgin merchant, Roderick Kemp, who owned Talisker Distillery in Skye. The descendants of his two daughters – one of whom married a Shiach, the other a Harbinson – still form the largest shareholding group. Until 1968, when it went public, the company was family-owned: since then its shares have increased 2,000-fold. Allan Shiach, the current chairman, is a scion of the original owning family. He is a noted Hollywood script-writer (*Don't Look Now, Castaway*, etc.), and is largely responsible for the company's idiosyncratic and intelligent advertising.

A programme of modernization and expansion was begun in the 1950s (trebling the output by 1959), but such was the demand that, in 1968, the directors decided to expand the distillery further and to follow a policy which, in time, would rely more on sales of single malt. New stills were installed, all built to exactly the same pattern as the original stills (which are among the smallest in the industry), and bonded stores built to house the maturing spirit. This includes what is currently the largest single-roofed whisky warehouse in Europe, built in 1990.

It is easy to forget that, in the early 1970s, there were relatively few single malts available beyond Scotland. Macallan had long been considered a 'top dressing' by blenders, who invariably place it in the top three of such malts, and are prepared to pay a premium for it, so the decision to concentrate on selling the brand as a single malt was a bold one.

Macallan's directors also determined at this time that their entire output should be matured in sherry wood – it is the only distillery to use sherry wood exclusively. Within a few years, the availability of casks became a problem, so in 1976 the company began to buy its own new wood in Spain and have it seasoned in the *bodegas* of Jerez for three or four years before shipping it and filling it with whisky. This is an expensive policy (the cost of a sherry butt is about ten times that of a bourbon cask), but it makes a major contribution to Macallan's uniqueness.

The first batch of The Macallan was not deemed to be ready for the market until 1980: since then its popularity and success has been phenomenal. The brand currently stands at number three in the UK malt whisky market, number five in the world. It is also a favourite among the local people of Speyside.

Tasting Notes: (12 Years Old) Deep amber colour. The bouquet is as rich as fruitcake, with powerful sherry and butterscotch notes; round and deep. Full bodied. The flavour is full and well rounded, reminiscent of old armagnac: sherry, fruit (currants? cherries?), a hint of wood (this becomes more noticeable in the older expressions); withal clean, intense and well-rounded. The finish is surprisingly dry, with a lingering, sherry wood aftertaste. A classic *digestif*.

MACDUFF

Category: East Highland
Distiller: William Lawson Distillers Ltd

Owner: William Lawson Distillers Ltd, Coatbridge, Lanarkshire
Expressions: G&M 1975; C 14 Years Old; as Glen Deveron, 12
Years Old

Macduff Distillery is near Banff. Its owners name their product
Glen Deveron, while it is named Macduff by independent bottlers.
(see **Glen Deveron**).

MACPHAIL'S

Category: Speyside (district unknown)
Distiller: undisclosed
Licensee: Gordon & MacPhail, 58–60 South St, Elgin
Expressions: 10 (and @ 60.5%), 15, 21, 25, 30, 40 Years Old, and
vintages 1937, 1938, 1939, 1940, 1945, 1946, 1947, 1950, 1951,
1960, 1965, 1973

In 1895 Messrs Gordon & MacPhail set up as 'Italian
Warehousemen' in the Royal Burgh of Elgin, where many of the
Speyside distillers had their offices.

James Gordon was a whisky broker and with his partner, John
Alexander MacPhail, and a young assistant, John Urquhart, they
commenced trading as 'Family Grocers, Tea, Wine & Spirit
Merchants'.

Initially they were concerned with provisioning the local clien-
tele, but quickly the firm made a speciality of whisky – blending
and bottling under its own labels, as well as broking and dealing in
mature whiskies. The latter was a pioneering move – indeed
Gordon & MacPhail can boast of being the first company to stress
the virtues of aged single malt whisky.

As early as 1896, the firm was advertising their Moray Brand
Old Highland Liqueur Scotch Whisky in a London magazine, and
by 1914 its whiskies were being exported abroad. In the 1930s
ownership of the company passed to the Urquhart family: today
the entire board is made up of children and grandchildren of the
original John Urquhart, and the firm remains in their hands.

The firm's policy has always been to buy new whisky direct
from the distillery, to warehouse it itself, and bottle it when it is
considered to be at its best. The 'laying down' of malts has been
going on for so long that some of its stock is now extremely rare,
either because of its age, because stocks are in very short supply or
because the distillery has gone out of production. Several of the
whiskies offered by Gordon & MacPhail would never have seen a
bottle had it not been for the firm's commitment to invest in otherwise unknown malts. Apart from blending its own brands, the
company has become best known for specializing in fine Highland
malts. Unfortunately, legal injunctions have prevented it from
continuing to bottle certain prominent brands where the distillery
proprietors wish to retain their exclusive right to do so.

The single malt which bears the founder's name is a case in
point: its creator is kept a close secret, although apparently the distillery is very well known.

Tasting Notes: (10 Years Old @ 60.5%) Maturation in sherry
wood is immediately apparent, but the nose also has a lot of fresh
hay and barley, and a peppery top-note. Upon tasting, the sherry
and malt lend a sweet smoothness, but the finish is dry.

(1973) The aroma has developed into a profound fruitiness –
plums, stewed apples, rumtoft (although there is a freshness to the
fruit that suggests fruit salad to some noses); the sherry notes almost
vanish in the fruitiness. The flavour is not as sweet as the nose

would suggest; there is a faint sandalwood mustiness, and the finish is on the dry side, with cigar-box afterthoughts. The two expressions are utterly different.

MANNOCHMORE

Category: Speyside (Lossie)
Distiller: John Haig & Co. Ltd, Markinch, Fife
Owner: United Distillers
Expressions: 12 Years Old

Mannochmore was built in 1971 by John Haig & Co. Ltd, a few miles south of Elgin, beside their distillery at Glenlossie. It has a capacity to produce a million proof gallons annually. All but a tiny amount of this goes for blending, and this small amount has only been available as a single malt since 1992.
Tasting Notes: Pale straw colour (matured in bourbon casks?); a fresh, perfumed nose – unmistakably Speyside, with a strong estery aroma (sweet acetone/nail-varnish remover) – and a restrained scent of cereals. Light bodied, but with a delightful, firm flavour – well balanced; slightly salty, with a trace of smoke and a satisfying sweet-sour finish.

MILLBURN

Category: North Highland
Distiller: distillery closed 1985
Owner: United Distillers
Expressions: independent bottlings only – C 1969; G&M 1971, 1972

Millburn was founded in 1807 which makes it one of the earliest distilleries. At that time distilling was a difficult business in which to make a profit, owing to excessive competition from illicit distillers, who paid no fees or taxes, and were more or less endemic throughout the Highlands. But Millburn survived and in 1853 it became the property of David Rose, an Inverness corn merchant, who largely rebuilt it in 1876.

In 1892 Millburn was acquired by two members of the Haig family (see **Haig**), under whose ownership it was considerably expanded. In 1921 it was sold again, to Booth's Distillery Ltd, the famous London gin-makers. However a fire in 1922 destroyed most of the essential buildings and it had to be completely rebuilt. It was taken over by DCL in 1937 and was in continuous production from after the war until 1985, when it was dismantled.
Tasting Notes: A robust nose, full of promise – estery, malty, well-scented, clean. The flavour does not disappoint: some sherry, smooth mouth-feel, pleasant malty notes, well balanced – with a good, slightly dry finish.

MILTONDUFF

Category: Speyside (Lossie)
Distiller: Miltonduff Distillery, Elgin, Morayshire
Owner: Allied Distillers Ltd, 2 Glasgow Rd, Dumbarton
Expressions: 12 Years Old (40% vol.); C 1978

Miltonduff Distillery is three miles outside Elgin – the whisky capital – close to Pluscarden Priory, which at one time was said to produce the finest ale in Scotland, so good that it *"filled the abbey with unutterable bliss*". The Benedictine monks of Pluscarden drew their water from the Black Burn and accounted its excellence to the fact that it had been ceremonially blessed by a saintly abbot in the 15th century. Miltonduff uses the same source of water today.

The distillery was licensed in 1824 as Miltonduff-Glenlivet. It was renovated in the 1890s, at which time it was producing 300,000 proof gallons (over 1.3 million litres) a year, but it suffered badly in the whisky crash of 1898. It was sold to Hiram Walker in 1936, which licensed it to George Ballantine & Sons. Considerable modernization has taken place in recent years, including the installation of a pair of Lomond stills for a short period (see **Inverleven**) with which a whisky named **Mosstowie** was produced. Apart from this experiment, every replaced still is identical to its predecessor, of which Alfred Barnard, visiting Miltonduff in 1877 wrote: "*some of the oldest fads and methods are in use [here], and the ancient style of stills and utensils, as carried on by the smugglers, have also been continued.*"

Miltonduff's main markets outside the UK are Japan, France, Germany and the USA.

Tasting Notes: Miltonduff is an elegant malt, fragrant and complex. Its nose is flowery with vanilla and almond notes; its taste lightly smoky, with faint almonds and a hint of honey; its finish is long and aromatic, with some malty dryness.

MORTLACH

Category: Speyside (Dufftown)
Distiller: John Walker & Sons Ltd, Kilmarnock, Ayrshire
Owner: United Distillers
Expressions: 16 Years Old; G&M 15 and 21 Years Old; 1936, 1960, 1965, 1966

Until 1887, Mortlach was the only distillery in Dufftown; today there are seven. The site had been used by smugglers for many years, on account of an excellent spring, known as 'Highlander John's Well'. The distillery was licensed in 1823, following the changes introduced by the Excise Act of the same year.

Mortlach Distillery was established by three local men on a feu of land leased from the Earl of MacDuff. By 1854 only one of the founders was still active, and he took one George Cowie into partnership. The latter, who became sole owner ten years later, sought markets beyond the immediate vicinity and Mortlach-Glenlivet became known as far afield as London.

By 1903 Cowie was able to refurbish the distillery, and brought in his son, Dr A.M. Cowie, who had studied medicine at Aberdeen University and was a senior medical officer in Hong Kong. He returned to Scotland to run the family business and became a much respected local figure, eventually being appointed Deputy Lord Lieutenant for Banffshire.

For many years Mortlach was only available through independent bottlers, but it has long been regarded locally as one of the best Speyside malts and is now bottled by its owners at 16 years.

Tasting Notes: Mortlach is a rich red colour in the United Distillers bottling (paler and more tawny in the independent bottlings). It has a deeply perfumed nose, like an oriental garden – full of mysterious scents, tropical fruits and spices. It is very smooth tasting, somewhat bland until the finish, when it explodes into a wonderful range of fresh, perfumed (even soapy) flavours, with a smoky-dry aftertaste.

MOSSTOWIE

Category: Speyside (Lossie)
Distiller: George Ballantine & Son Ltd
Owner: Allied Distillers Ltd, 2 Glasgow Rd, Dumbarton
Expressions: independent bottlings only – G&M 1975

This malt was produced at the Miltonduff-Glenlivet Distillery (see **Miltonduff**) in Lomond stills fitted with rectifying columns within the still head (see **Inverleven** for a description). These have now been dismantled and although old stocks of their product can still be found, Mosstowie is not common.

Tasting Notes: A pleasant, malty nose with fruity aromas quickly developing – figs, nectarines – then with some sherry coming through. The flavour is sweet, smooth and well balanced – almost fruit-syrupy – but with a refreshing dryness and even a trace of wood in the finish.

NORTH PORT-BRECHIN

Category: East Highland
Distiller: distillery closed 1983
Owner: United Distillers
Expressions: independent bottlings only – G&M 1970

The Royal Burgh of Brechin in Angus is of great antiquity. From early times it was an important religious centre – it was sacked by the Danes in 1012, and its splendid little cathedral incorporates a Pictish 'round tower'. Its bishopric dates from 1150. The town was once walled, and traces of its gates – or 'ports' – are still evident: hence the name of North Port-Brechin.

The distillery was founded in 1820 by David Guthrie, who had established the first bank in the town and had served as Provost (i.e. mayor). The Guthries were farmers in Angus, where some of the country's best barley is grown. Alfred Barnard wrote in 1887: *"the district around Brechin being highly cultivated, barley of the finest quality is grown and carted by the farmers into the lofts of the distillery where nothing but the best barley is malted."*

In 1892 the company changed its name to Guthrie, Martin & Co. and became a limited company the following year. DCL acquired the entire shareholding in 1922, in conjunction with W.H. Holt & Co. Ltd, an independent wine and spirit merchants in Manchester. In 1922 it was licensed to Mitchell Brothers, Glasgow. It was closed down in 1983 and dismantled.

Tasting Notes: The nose is dry and astringent, spiritous, with some light smokiness, and sweet scents beneath the spirit – marzipan and a trace of aniseed? The flavour is likewise dry and astringent, with a brief blooming of sweet malt followed by a rapid finish.

OBAN

Category: West Highland
Distiller: John Hopkins & Co. Ltd
Owner: United Distillers
Expressions: 14 Years Old; G&M 1972

Situated on the west coast, midway between the Caledonian and Crinan canals, Oban is known as the Gateway to the Isles.

Two brothers of the name of Stevenson settled in Oban in 1778 and were responsible for greatly enriching the prosperity of what had previously been no more than a hamlet. The brothers had been involved in slate quarrying, housebuilding and shipbuilding and in 1794 Hugh Stevenson built the Oban Distillery, hiring an experienced Lowland distiller to manage the whole operation.

The distillery remained in the hands of the family until 1866 and was eventually acquired by one Walter Higgin (1883). By this time Oban was a busy port with wool, whisky, slate and kelp being shipped to Liverpool and Glasgow by steamship. The railway also brought a new era of prosperity to the area: tourism, with the first scheduled passenger trains arriving from Glasgow in 1880.

According to Alfred Barnard (1887) Higgin had made *"vast improvements in the machinery and appliances, and built two new warehouses"*. While engaged in this renovation, rock was blasted from the cliff behind the distillery to accommodate the enlargements and during this process a cave was discovered which contained human bones and implements from the Mesolithic era (c. 4500–3000 BC).

In 1898, Alexander Edward, owner of Aultmore Distillery, bought Higgin out. In its first year the Oban & Aultmore Distilleries Ltd suffered near fatal losses, when the major blending company, Pattison's of Leith, collapsed.

In 1923 Aultmore was acquired by John Dewar & Sons Ltd and Oban by a new company, Oban Distillery Co. This in turn came under the wing of DCL when Scottish Malt Distillers bought the entire share capital in 1930.

Tasting Notes: A sweet nose, with a distinct seaside note, and also a flowery/herbal hint of bog myrtle. The flavour begins sweet and finishes dry with a whiff of smoke. It is smooth, slightly viscous and fruity.

OLD ROSDHU

Category: South Highland
Distiller: Loch Lomond Distillery, Alexandria, Dumbartonshire
Owner: Glen Catrine Bonded Warehouse Ltd
Expressions: 8 Years Old

Old Rosdhu is produced at the Loch Lomond distillery, which Glen Catrine has owned since 1985, and which also produces **Inchmurrin** on the same Lomond stills (see **Inverleven**).

One of the feature of Lomond stills is that it is possible to produce whiskies of differing strengths from the same still: Rosdhu has a slightly lower specific gravity than its sister whisky and a slightly different style of malt is used in its production, so the flavour is also different. It is available in the UK and export markets, but is not common.

Tasting Notes: The nose is rich, heavy and malty, with some heathery notes. The taste is succulently smooth – sweet, even on the roof of the mouth, but not in the slightest cloying. The heather traces remain, with some almonds.

PITTYVAICH

Category: Speyside (Dufftown)
Distiller: Arthur Bell & Sons, Perth
Owner: United Distillers
Expressions: 12 Years Old; C 1977

Pittyvaich Distillery was built in 1974 as part of Bell's huge extension programme, close to the older, more traditional Dufftown Distillery, and part of the Dufftown complex. It is situated in the Dullan Glen, close to Mortlach Church (see **Mortlach**), and draws its water from the Convalleys and Balliemore Springs.

Bell's has taken great pains to ensure that the new distillery is similar to the old in every respect: its four stills are exact replicas of Dufftown's, and the storage and vatting facilities are matched, one with the other. Yet its product is quite different, and in my view better. Most goes for blending, but since 1992 some has been bottled by United Distillers as a single malt. The distillery was closed in 1993.

Tasting Notes: Sweet, fruity-estery nose, lightweight, with the faintest trace of aniseed. Medium bodied. Sweet tasting, delicious caramel flavours; smooth and well balanced. A fresh, spicy finish.

PORT ELLEN

Category: Island (Islay)
Distiller: distillery closed 1983
Owner: United Distillers
Expressions: independent bottlings only – C 1981: G&M 1977, 1978 cask strength

The distilleries of Islay are all built on the shore, where piers could be erected for convenient transportation. Port Ellen is no exception: the village which grew up around the distillery is now one of the largest on the island and its harbour has superseded Bowmore as the principal port.

The distillery was first established by A.K. Mackay in the 1820s, but he soon was involved in bankruptcy proceedings and Port Ellen passed into the hands of John Ramsay.

Ramsay was a remarkable man. Liberal MP for Stirling and chairman of the Glasgow Chamber of Commerce, he was a leading figure in the whisky industry of his day. It was he who first saw the benefits of exporting whisky to America – which he did, direct from Port Ellen. He pioneered the spirit safe, which is now a standard item in every distillery. He assisted Aeneas Coffey and Robert Stein with their experiments which led to the invention of the Patent Still for the manufacture of grain whisky – much of their research was done at Port Ellen. He persuaded the government to allow Islay whisky to be bonded free of duty for many years. And he introduced the first regular cargo and passenger service from Islay to Glasgow by steamer.

Following his death, ownership passed to his wife and son who sold their interest to the Port Ellen Distillery Ltd. In 1925 the distillery was acquired by DCL and closed down. It reopened in 1967 following an extensive modernization programme when it became licensed to Low Robertson & Co. Ltd of Edinburgh. The distillery has been closed since 1983.

Tasting Notes: Port Ellen is unmistakably an Islay malt – phenolic, with peat-smoke and iodine, but also having gentler, spicy, mossy notes which lend interest and complexity. It is full-flavoured, sweet then dry, salty with a hint of bonfires, and a good lingering finish.

PULTENEY

Category: North Highland
Distiller: George Ballantine & Son Ltd

Owner: Allied Distillers Ltd
Expressions: independent bottlings only – G&M 8 (40% & 57%) and 15 Years Old, 1961

Located at Wick in Caithness, Pulteney is the most northerly distillery on mainland Scotland. It was founded in 1826 by James Henderson and remained in possession of his family until 1920, when it was sold to James Watson & Co. Ltd. In 1923 it was bought by John Dewar & Sons Ltd. Later the distillery came under the ownership of Hiram Walker and thus under the wing of Allied Distillers Ltd. It is currently available from Gordon & MacPhail as an 8-year-old bottling.
Tasting Notes: Pulteney is known as the 'manzanilla of the north', but its flavour is a complex balance of dry and sweet. The first impression is of almonds, almost marzipan, with pear-drop notes, and some traces of lemon sherbet. The almond/marzipan comes through when the whisky is tasted and there is even a sherbet 'fizz' apparent. The texture is smooth, viscous, the finish long and dry.

ROSEBANK

Category: Lowland
Distiller: The Distillers Agency Ltd, Edinburgh
Owner: United Distillers
Expressions: 12 Years Old: C 1980; G&M 1979

Until recently, Rosebank was the only single Lowland malt generally available, and it is still regarded by many as the classic representative of the species.

The distillery is at Camelon, just north of Falkirk, on the bank of the Forth-Clyde Canal, which was built by James Smeaton in 1773. The first record of distilling activity here was in 1798 by Messrs Stark.

During the 1840s the maltings of the Camelon distillery were acquired by James Rankine, a local grocer and wine and spirit merchant. He rebuilt the distillery and began to produce a whisky of great quality and such was the demand from the blenders that he sold it on allocation, and was able to charge warehouse rent to his customers (at the time he was the only distiller at that time to be able to do so, although this has since become universal practice). These were the beginnings of this, the most well-known of the Lowland malts.

In 1894 Rosebank Distillery Ltd was formed, with Rankine holding half the capital. A second issue of shares in 1897 was fully subscribed. Unfortunately, Rosebank was hit by the collapse of the market in 1900, and the ensuing slump, so much so that in 1914 it was among the companies which amalgamated to form the Scottish Malt Distillers Ltd. Subsequently this group became part of DCL.

Rosebank continued the Lowland tradition of 'triple distillation', and maintained that the lightness of its fine product is attributable to this. Unusually, the mash tun is cast iron with a copper lid, and the traditional worm tubs used in the first distillation have been retained in place of more modern condensers.

In spite of being widely regarded as the most distinguished Lowland malt, Rosebank Distillery was closed in 1993.
Tasting Notes: (1979) Amber colour, with a reddish hue. Sweet, and very scented (Parma violets, Russian toffees, boiled apples), very lightly sherried, traces of honey. Much drier flavour than one would expect, still perfumed; perfectly balanced. Very elegant.

ROYAL BRACKLA

Category: North Highland
Distiller: John Bisset & Co. Ltd, Leith
Owner: United Distillers
Expressions: 10 Years Old; C 1966; G&M 1972

The small Brackla Distillery was established in 1812 on the Cawdor Estate, near Nairn, a district made famous by Shakespeare's 'Thanes of Cawdor'. The distillery's founder, Captain William Fraser, found it difficult to compete with the many illicit producers in the neighbourhood, and set about establishing a market in the Lowland and south of the Border.

In 1835 William IV granted Fraser a Royal Warrant as a sign of his appreciation of the whisky; this was renewed by Queen Victoria in the 1850s. After several changes of ownership, the lease of the Brackla Distillery Co. passed to two Aberdeen wholesale wine and spirit merchants, who rebuilt the distillery (1898). In 1926 it was sold to John Bisset & Co., a firm of blenders. Royal Brackla became a key ingredient of its two well-known blends, Bisset's Finest Old and Gold Label. The firm joined DCL in 1943 and in 1965 the new owner renovated Brackla Distillery and built new maltings. Royal Brackla has long been rare as a single malt, but United Distillers now bottles a small quantity.

Tasting Notes: Pale gold in colour, aromatic, estery nose; some faint smoke, some fruit (bananas?) and a trace of cereal. Sweet and malty, with a touch of salt. Bitter/dry finish, and a lingering fruity taste (bananas again).

ROYAL LOCHNAGAR

Category: East Highland
Distiller: John Begg Ltd, Glasgow
Owner: United Distillers
Expressions: 12 Years Old

> *…Oh for the crags that are wild and majestic*
> *the steep frowning glories of dark -Loch-na-gar.*

These are the words of Lord Byron, himself a Scot who spent much of his boyhood in this area of Deeside.

Lochnagar is a small distillery, founded in 1825, close to the Royal Family's summer residence at Balmoral Castle, in the shadow of the mountain of the same name. The founder was a local man, John Crathie, who took advantage of the 1822 Act which encouraged licensed distilling, but the present buildings date from 1845, by which time the distillery was owned by John Begg.

In the same year, the Balmoral estate was bought by Queen Victoria and in 1848, only three days after she and the Prince Consort arrived at Balmoral, Begg invited them to visit his establishment (he had heard how fascinated Prince Albert was with anything mechanical)The very next day he was honoured with a royal visit. In his diary he recorded that after the tour, "*I asked whether he [Prince Albert] would like to taste the spirit in its matured state, as we had cleared some that day from bond, which I thought was very fine.*" Some days later a letter arrived granting a royal warrant to supply the Royal Household.

John Begg was an innovative businessman. He was a close friend of William Sanderson, to whom most of the distillery's product went, chiefly for the blending of **VAT 69**. He also created his own brands, realizing that the future of whisky was in blending (see **John Begg Blue Cap**).

As late as 1967, Professor McDowall wrote: "It is a privilege to have tasted such a rich whisky. It is not generally available. Perhaps it is kept at the distillery in case the present Queen and her Consort pay a call, but there is enough of it made to justify a single bottling. At one time it was the most expensive whisky in Scotland." John Begg & Co. became part of DCL in 1916, and United Distillers now bottle a small quantity of Royal Lochnagar as a single malt, lavishly packaged and distinctively labelled. It sells especially well in the Far East.

Tasting Notes: Royal Lochnagar has a rich toffee-gold colour, and toffee/caramel/ butterscotch notes predominate on the nose, with a clear wisp of smoke. It is full-bodied and luscious; mouth coating and very smooth. So the very clean, dry finish comes as something of a surprise when the whisky is tasted: it is balanced by an initial malty sweetness, and rounded off by a heathery fruitiness (raspberries?).

ST MAGDALENE

Category: Lowland
Distiller: distillery closed 1983
Owner: United Distillers
Expressions: independent bottlings only – G&M 1965

The name derives from the lands near Linlithgow upon which the distillery was built in the late 18th century, known as St Magdalene's Cross – once the site of a hospital of the same name, and of an annual fair. The distillery was also known as 'Linlithgow': the town itself was once an important brewing and distilling centre, with five distilleries.

The first recorded licensed distiller was Adam Dawson in 1797, who was one of the loudest voices for the Lowland distillers against the exemptions granted to Highland distillers by the Board of Excise.

St Magdalene was well placed for communications, especially after the opening of the Forth-Clyde (Union) Canal in 1822, upon which the distillery had its own wharf. Many of the buildings are now listed as being of historic interest, but have been turned into bijou flats. The malt store pre-dates the repeal of the malt duty as it still has iron bars on its windows.

In 1894 A. & J. Dawson were incorporated, and extended and modernized the distillery. But competition between the Lowland distillers was fierce, and in 1912 Dawsons went into liquidation, all its assets being acquired by DCL. Here began the origins of Scottish Malt Distillers, the DCL subsidiary which was created by an amalgamation of five Lowland distillers. SMD made radical improvements at St Magdalene and by 1927 most of the complex was electrified. The floor maltings were retained, and although the Depression of the 1930s caused most distilleries to close, the maltings at St Magdalene remained active throughout. The output from the distillery resumed after the war and production was maintained until1983, when it was closed.

Tasting Notes: (1965) The colour of amontillado sherry, shot through with red-gold. The aroma is dry and spicy and strongly perfumed – attar of roses, fresh black pepper, dry hemp rope, dusky – oriental and delightful. The flavour is very smooth and perfectly balanced, with a distinct smoky artichoke flavour. Clean and dryish, with a perfect tapering finish. An experience!

SCAPA

Category: Island (Orkney)
Distiller: Taylor & Ferguson Ltd
Owner: Allied Distillers, 2 Glasgow Rd, Dumbarton
Expressions: independent bottlings only – G&M 1983

Scapa Distillery stands on the north shore of Scapa Flow in Orkney, where the German High Seas Fleet scuttled itself at the end of the First World War. For many years the shadowy shapes of the giant battle cruisers, *Hindenburg* and *Seidlitz*, were visible beneath the waves, their masts above water at low tide.

An earlier fragment of Scapa history is recorded by the Reverend John Brand in 1701, concerning a drinking custom of the hamlet: "*In Scapa, about a mile from Kirkwall to the south-west, it was said there was kept a large and ancient Cup, which they said belonged to St. Magnus, King of Norway, who first instructed them in the principles of the Christian religion, and founded the church of Kirkwall, with which full of some strong drink their Bishops, at their first landing were presented. If the Bishop drank it out, they highly praised him, and made themselves believe that they should have many good and fruitful years in his time.*"

'Orkney's other distillery' (the best-known being **Highland Park**) was designed and built by J.T. Townsend, a well-known figure in the Speyside distilling business in 1885, and it was acclaimed as one of the most up-to-date distilleries of its day. It is situated on the Lingro Burn, from which the distillery takes its process water and the cooling waters for the pot stills. The barley for malting and the coal for firing the stills is brought in by sea to Kirkwall.

There have been continuous and extensive additions to the distillery over the years as demand for the product increased; the original buildings covered only an acre and a-half but today the site covers some seven acres as more warehouses have been required.

During the Second World War a fire threatened to destroy the entire distillery, but Naval ratings who were billeted in the area came to the rescue by the boatload and managed to save the buildings. After the war the distillery underwent two changes of ownership and was eventually acquired by Hiram Walker & Sons, now a subsidiary of Allied Distillers which licenses it to Taylor & Ferguson Ltd. At present the entire product of the Scapa distillery goes for blending, although independent bottlings of the single malt can be found.

Tasting Notes: Scapa has an unusual nose: the first impression is of old-fashioned oilskins (a little like plastic), next comes a hint of heather-flowers and a trace of bourbon. The flavour begins dryish, with a slight tang, but finishes with caramel notes (even chocolate). The texture is silky-smooth (even at 8 years old), the body medium to full. A good, dry finish. A most interesting whisky, difficult to locate in blind tasting if you had not sampled it before.

THE SINGLETON OF AUCHROISK

Category: Speyside (Strathisla)
Distiller: Auchroisk Distillery, Mulben, Banffshire
Owner: International Distillers & Vintners Ltd, 151 Marylebone Rd, London NW1 (parent: Grand Metropolitan)
Expressions: minimum 10 Years Old

Auchroisk Distillery was opened in 1974 and is something of a :howpiece. Its total production is bottled as a single malt, launched in 1986. Pronunciation of the name 'Auchroisk' was considered to be too hard for non-Scots, so the cunning marketing people added 'The Singleton'.

As well as indicating that it is a single malt, the word 'Singleton' is an expression which was used by the industry earlier this century to describe single casks of malt whisky at auction. The fact they came as single items, rather than in 'parcels', often implied exceptional quality or age.

The water used at Auchroisk comes from Dorie's Well, a local spring which rises from granite through sandstone, and produces the soft water which is traditionally sought by distillers: the head distiller at Auchroisk claims it accounts for the whisky's character. This is enhanced and enriched by part of each bottling being matured for two years in sherry butts, then vatted with bourbon-matured spirit of the same year.

The resulting whisky has done exceptionally well in tastings, winning gold medals at the International Wine & Spirit Competition and at the Monde Selection in 1992. The brand is already well established in North America, Japan, Spain and Portugal, as well as the UK.

Tasting Notes: Gives little away on the nose: traces of cereal, spirity, with straw or hay notes. the taste is inoffensive and somewhat bland – some beeswax notes, some nuts, very slight wood smoke; a very clean flavour, with a sudden fade.

SPEYBURN

Category: Speyside (Lossie)
Distiller: Speyburn-Glenlivet Distillery Co., Rothes, Morayshire
Owner: Inver House Distillers, Airdrie, Lanarkshire
Expressions: C 1975; G&M 1971

The distillery, which stands in a picturesque wooded glen just outside Rothes, was built in 1897, from stones quarried from an ancient river bed nearby, by a subsidiary of John Hopkins & Co. Ltd. That year was also Queen Victoria's Diamond Jubilee, and the proprietors were keen that their first casks should bear the historic date. As it happened, production only got under way during the last week of the year and only one barrel bore the magic date! Hopkins & Co. joined DCL in 1916, and Speyburn was licensed to John Robertson & Son.

In 1992, Speyburn was acquired by Inver House, which intends to develop the brand and market it as a single malt. Until now it has occasionally been available from the independent bottlers, but almost the entire production went for blending.

Tasting Notes: (1971) Pale gold in colour, Speyburn has a closed, dryish nose, with a trace of heather. It is medium-bodied, and smooth tasting. The flavour is malty, with heather-honey notes, but the overall impression is dry.

SPRINGBANK

Category: Campbeltown
Distiller: J. & A. Mitchell & Co. Ltd, Springbank Distillery, Campbeltown
Owner: as above
Expressions: 15, 21, 25 and 30 Years Old; C 1972

Springbank Distillery is still managed by the descendants of its founders, and is one of the few private distillers remaining in

Scotland. It produces a malt whisky which is acknowledged to be among the finest.

The Mull of Kintyre, where Campbeltown is situated (and the town itself) was a haven of illicit whisky distilling from remote times – indeed some authorities maintain that the art of distilling arrived here from Ireland in the 6th century – and it was one of the first centres of the commercial industry. Between the 1880s and the 1920s there were 34 working distilleries here, producing at their height nearly 2 million gallons (over 9 million litres) of whisky per annum. Today only Springbank and Glen Scotia still operate. (The third Campbeltown malt, **Longrow**, is made at Springbank Distillery from different malt.)

Springbank Distillery was built about 1828 by the Mitchell family, on the site of Archibald Mitchell's illicit operation. The Mitchells were originally farmers, and their descendants still own and control the distillery. The original buildings are still in use, and its processes are very traditional: floor maltings and boatskin larch washbacks, a unique wash still heated by both steam coils and oil fires, and employing a 'rummager' to prevent the yeast scorching. This curious feature – a length of chain on an arm, driven by a rotating arm which was originally turned by a water wheel – may contribute to the flavour of Springbank, since it continually exposes small areas of clean copper in the still. Another contributory factor is the distillery's employment of a 'doubling still' process (i.e. two low wines stills, rather than the more usual low wines and spirit still).

The spirit is matured in a mix of sherry and bourbon casks, and is manually filtered rather than chill-filtered. Since the 1970s the common practice is to chill-filter. The temperature of the spirit is lowered so that microscopic particles which might make the whisky cloudy when ice and water are added are suspended and may be filtered out. Unfortunately these particles are flavour congeners as well.

The distillery is one of only two in Scotland which bottles its whisky at source (the other being **Glenfiddich**).

Tasting notes: Springbank is a very distinguished whisky – described as *Premier Grand Cru Classé* by *The Times,* following a tasting in 1983. It is also very highly regarded by blenders, some of whom consider it indispensable for knitting together the many other components of a complex blend. It has a fresh, slightly salty nose, with some sweetness; a smooth body; an even, centre-of-the-palate flavour, holding a delicate savoury/sweet balance (coconut, toffee, edible seaweed, some peat) and a long, slightly briny finish.

Older expressions become raisiny and sherried, with traces of pepper, allspice and vanilla: SMWS describes it as "a black bun of a whisky"!

STRATHISLA

Category: Speyside (Strathisla)
Distiller: Strathisla-Glenlivet Distillery Co., Keith, Banffshire
Owner: The Seagram Co. Ltd, Montreal, Canada
Expressions: 12 Years Old; (G&M) 8 (and @ 57%), 15 (and @ 57%), 21 Years Old; 1948, 1949, 1954, 1955, 1958, 1960, 1963 1967

Flax dressing was an important industry in north-east Scotland in the early part of the 18th century, but by the latter half of the century the industry was in decline and George Taylor, a wealthy local businessman, decided to reinvest his money. In 1785 he took a lease from the Earl of Seafield for an area of land near Keith on Speyside, for the purpose of building a distillery.

Keith's connections with making alcohol are referred to as early as 1208, and the site itself was described in a charter of 1545 as having a *brassina*, or warehouse. The site had once belonged to Ogilvy of Milton, and the new distillery was named 'Milton' and opened in 1786: it is thus the oldest continuously operating distillery in Scotland.

The original still held only 40 gallons (180 litres) of wash, in order to take advantage of the lower rate of duty provided for by the Wash Act, and Taylor supplemented his output with another – illicit – still. He was discovered by the Excise, however, and fined £500, a huge sum in those days. Like most distillers he ran a farm as well, and he was an early innovator in feeding the draff from his still to his cattle and using the pot-ale as fertilizer.

In the 1820s Taylor suffered a riding accident and, unable to work, sold the distillery to a local saddler, from whom it passed to William Longmore, a banker and grain merchant, in the early 1830s. Longmore was an important figure on Speyside, having been instrumental in bringing the Great North of Scotland Railway to the district. This new link effectively changed the fortunes of local distillers, who were able to transport their product more easily, and accordingly to expand their markets south of the border.

Production at Milton continued for many years without hindrance until in 1876 and 1879 a fire and an explosion destroyed much of the machinery and caused considerable damage to the buildings. The equipment was replaced in the same year and a public company, William Longmore & Co. Ltd., was formed with Longmore's son-in-law, J. Geddes Brown, as managing partner.

After Longmore's death in 1881, a bottling plant was installed at Milton, and by the end of the century the whisky produced was called Strathisla and was well known locally and was being promoted further afield by Gordon & MacPhail of Elgin (see **MacPhail's**) who had an agreement with the distillery, allowing them a percentage of output, which they matured themselves.

Shortly after the outbreak of the Second World War a London financier, Jay Pomeroy, bought William Longmore & Co. and began sending the entire production of the distillery direct to London, cutting off supplies to local customers. The Customs and Excise became suspicious when they found that the companies buying the whisky were fictitious and, following a government inquiry, Pomeroy was discovered to be selling the whiskies, Strathisla included, under different names through the black market. He was charged and found guilty of tax evasion of £111,038.

Milton Distillery was in the hands of the receivers throughout the war, and in 1950 it was bought by Chivas Bros, whose managing director was James Barclay, one of the foremost figures of the whisky industry this century. He had been a director of George Ballantine & Son and had seen that company through its takeover by Seagram (see **Ballantine's**), the Canadian distillers. Seagram had also acquired Chivas Bros, to which company Barclay was appointed. Soon after this the distillery took the name of its product, Strathisla. Its whisky is hard to find, but worth looking for.

Tasting Notes: Nosed straight this is a rich, full-bodied malt, with toffee and nuts. When water is added, the nose is more sherried, with fruit-cake notes and some toasted cereal. It is smooth and well rounded to taste; sweet to start, dry to finish with some salty traces.

STRATHMILL

Category: Speyside (Strathisla)
Distiller: Justerini & Brooks Ltd
Owner: International Distillers & Vintners Ltd, 151 Marylebone Rd, London NW1
Expressions: independent bottlings only – C 1981

This distillery on the River Isla near Keith was originally built as a meal mill in 1823, converted into a distillery in 1891 and acquired by Gilbey's, the gin distillers, in 1895.

The Gilbey brothers were originally wine merchants from London in 1857 who turned their interests towards gin distilling and, having realized the market potential of Scotch whisky, began to buy distilleries. In 1962 the company merged with Unwin's which also owned the old-established wine merchants, Justerini & Brooks (see **J&B Rare**) to become International Distillers & Vintners Ltd.

The company now owns three distilleries, Glen Spey, Knockando and Strathmill, of which the latter two are licensed to Justerini & Brooks. Strathmill is not produced by the owners as a single malt although it is available in merchant bottlings.

Tasting Notes: The aroma is much richer than the pale colour would suggest; with water the nose becomes typically Speyside with some malty and feinty notes. The flavour starts sweet but immediately becomes sharp, even bitter, and the finish is extraordinarily hot and peppery, reminiscent of chillies.

TALISKER

Category: Island (Skye)
Distiller: John Walker & Sons Ltd
Owner: United Distillers
Expressions: 10 Years Old; G&M 1952, 1959; 1955 cask strength

Talisker is the only distillery on the Isle of Skye, set in the lee of Cnoc-nan-Speireag-Hawkhill. The distillery takes its name from a small farm some miles away near the village of Carbost on the shore of Loch Harport.

It was started in 1843 by Hugh and Kenneth MacAskill from Eigg. Hugh was a tacksman (senior tenant farmer, who leased land to others) and acquired the lease of Talisker House and estate from Macleod of Macleod. Having cleared the land of people to make room for sheep, the MacAskills built a distillery at Carbost.

After the brothers' deaths the distillery changed hands several times before being acquired by a partnership between Alexander Grigor Allan, Procurator Fiscal of Morayshire (who had an interest in Glenlossie Distillery) and Roderick Kemp, a wine and spirits merchant from Aberdeen. Substantial sums of money were invested in rebuilding and refitting the distillery and the product itself was by now well established. R. L. Stevenson mentioned it in a poem, 'The Scotsman's Return from Abroad' in 1880,

> *The King o' drinks, as I conceive it,*
> *Talisker, Islay or Glenlivet.*

In 1892, Kemp bought the **Macallan** Distillery on Speyside and Allan took over the entire ownership of Talisker which merged it with Dailuaine to form the Dailuaine-Talisker Distilleries Ltd. This company extended the premises at Talisker, built a pier, a tramway to link it to the distillery and houses to accommodate the employees and an excise officer.

In 1925 through a previous merger with some of the founding

members of the 'big five' the distillery became fully owned by DCL.

The distillery was partly rebuilt in 1960 after a fire and its own floor maltings were demolished in 1972. One of the only original features of the distillery is the presence of traditional condensers. Neil Wilson writes that "the modern, compact and efficient condensers seen in the majority of distilleries are absent at Talisker, instead the spirit passes down the lyne arms of the five stills to traditional worm tubs outside the stillhouse. Water carried along a lade from Carbost keeps the tubs brim full of cooling water."

Neil Gunn, the well-known Scottish novelist, writes: "At its best it can be superb but I have known it to adopt the uncertainties of the Skye weather."

Tasting Notes: Talisker has been called 'the lava of the Cuillins', exploding off the palate and slipping down like shreiving fire. Its flavour is distinctively peppery, oily and with a trace of Irish whiskey.

TAMDHU

Category: Speyside (Lower Spey)
Distiller: Tamdhu Distillery, Knockando, Banffshire
Owner: The Highland Distilleries Co. plc
Expressions: 10 Years Old; G&M 8 Years Old; 1957; C 1963

The opening of the Strathspey railway line from Boat of Garten to Craigellachie encouraged distilling along the upper Spey valley, and during the whisky boom of the 1890s no fewer than three distilleries were built in the parish of Knockando (Tamdhu, Knockando and Imperial). The site for Tamdhu (pronounced Tam-doo) was known locally as 'the smugglers' glen', and had been popular with illicit distillers on account of the excellence of its spring water.

The moving force behind Tamdhu's construction was one William Grant, a director of Highland Distilleries and the agent for the Caledonian Bank in Elgin. When it went into production in 1897, the distillery was one of the most modern in the UK. It still has its own Saladin maltings – today it is the only Speyside distillery to malt its own barley. By 1903 it was producing 135,000 proof gallons (over 600,000 litres) of spirit, but with the downturn in demand in 1906, this was halved. Recovery was strong after the war, but the Depression followed, and the distillery closed in 1928.

It remained closed for twenty years, but by the early 1970s was in such demand from blenders that it was doubled in size. It is an important ingredient in **The Famous Grouse** and sells well as as a single malt in France, Italy, Spain and Portugal and the USA.

Tasting Notes: Tamdhu is a mild, lightweight malt, with a clean Speyside character. The nose is sweetish, slightly biscuity and lightly malted, with a whiff of smoke; the flavour is very slightly toffee-like, but this develops into a dry peaty/smoky finish.

TAMNAVULIN

Category: Speyside (Upper Spey)
Distiller: Tamnavulin-Glenlivet Distillers Co. Ltd
Owner: The Invergordon Distillers Ltd, Leith, Edinburgh
Expressions: 10 Years Old; Stillman's Dram (extra long matured) will be produced from time to time.

Glenlivet is known as 'the longest glen in Scotland', so far spread are the distilleries which are entitled to attach the appellation: by the end of the last century the designation had become synonymous with Speyside. Although a latecomer to the tribe (the distillery was built in 1966) Tamnavulin is the only Glenlivet actually situated beside the fabled Livet Burn, although it draws its water from the surrounding hills.

The name is Gaelic for 'the mill on the hill': the carding mill referred to has been converted into an attractive visitor centre.

Tasting Notes: Unusually pale (no sherry wood is used in maturation); the lightest in body (not in taste) of the Glenlivets; sweetish floral nose, with traces of peat and cereal; also sweetish taste, with cut-grass freshness, floral notes, a trace of lemon.

TEANINICH

Category: North Highland
Distiller: R.H. Thomson & Co. (Distillers) Ltd
Owner: United Distillers
Expressions: 10 Years Old; G&M 1975/82

Teaninich Distillery was built by Captain Hugh Munro on his own land near Alness in Ross-shire in 1817. At this time, illicit distilling was endemic in the region, and most of the barley grown in the area was being used up by illegal producers. In spite of encouragement from the Excise, competition was fierce and several licensed distillers had to close. Munro told a parliamentary inquiry that he *"continued to struggle on"*. After the Excise Act of 1823, Teaninich (pronounced Chee-an-in-ick) was secured, and by 1830 Munro was producing thirty times the original output.

The distillery passed on to General John Munro who kept production going, and eventually Teaninich was acquired by Munro & Cameron (1898), spirit merchants and whisky brokers in Elgin, who invested a great deal of money in it.

In 1904 Innes Cameron became sole owner of Teaninich. He already had many interests in Highland distilleries, including Benrinnes, Linkwood and Tamdhu, and later in his life he became chairman of the Malt Distillers Association. He died in 1932 and a year later his trustees sold the distillery to Scottish Malt Distillers.

In 1970 a new stillhouse was constructed with extensive refurbishment. Apart from the war years and some silent periods Teaninich has remained in operation, supplying fillings for blending – exclusively until 1992, when United Distillers began to bottle a small amount at 10 years old as a single malt.

Tasting Notes: Pale, manzanilla colour. A pleasant, perfumed nose (barber's shop), faintly citric, slightly salty, estery, fresh and cheerful. The flavour is slightly reminiscent of Lapsang Suchong – a whiff of scented smoke. It is sweetish and slightly salty, with a hint of iodine. A perfect lunchtime whisky.

TOMATIN

Category: North Highland
Distiller: The Tomatin Distillery Co., Tomatin, Inverness-shire
Owner: Takara, Shuzo & Okura
Expressions: 10 and 25 Years Old (12 Years Old export only); C 1976; G&M 1964, 1968

Tomatin Distillery was built in 1897 by a consortium of Inverness businessmen, keen to take advantage of the phenomenal success the whisky industry was enjoying at this time. The chosen site was close to a 15th-century farmhouse called Old Lairds House, where drovers and travellers were wont to replenish their stocks of whisky at an illicit still before driving their beasts on to the southern markets. Close by is 'the hill of parting', where the clans were disbanded after their defeat at the Battle of Culloden in 1746. The distillery draws its water from Alt-na-frith, 'the free burn', which flows off the Monadhliath Mountains and down into the river Findhorn, passing through peat and over red granite – a passage which many claim makes for ideal distilling water.

Tomatin made steady progress until the war years, when grain shortages prevented distilleries working, and it was not until the 1950s that full production was resumed. Upgrading during the 1960s and 1970s made Tomatin one of the most modern, and certainly the largest malt distillery in Scotland, producing 5 million gallons (over 22 million litres) of proof spirit each year.

During the cutbacks of the 1980s, the Tomatin Distillery Company was forced into voluntary liquidation, but in 1986 it was bought in a joint venture between, Takara Shuzo Co. Ltd and Okura & Co. Ltd, two of Japan's most important trading companies, which had long been customers of Tomatin.

Not only does the company specialize in the production of a single malt but it also markets a 12-year-old de luxe blend and a standard blend, which are sold under the 'Big T' label.

Tasting Notes: A fresh aroma, lightly smoky, slightly caramel, with some oak wood. The flavour is smooth, but rather nondescript – neither sweet nor dry, with traces of ginger.

TOMINTOUL

Category: Speyside (Upper Spey)
Distiller: Whyte & Mackay Distillers Ltd, Dalmore House, 296 St Vincent St, Glasgow
Owner: as above
Expressions: 8 and 12 Years Old

The distillery was built in the 1960s by W. & S. Strong and Hay & MacLeod, two whisky broking firms from Glasgow, which later merged with Whyte & Mackay. Tomintoul (pronounced Tomintowel) has been available as a single malt since 1974.

Tasting Notes: A very light Speyside (perhaps the lightest in the district) – grassy, spirity, some floral notes. The flavour is sweetish, with maltiness and cereal overtones. Surprisingly long finish.

THE TORMORE

Category: Speyside (Upper Spey)
Distiller: The Tormore Distillery, Advie, Morayshire
Owner: Allied Distillers Ltd, 2 Glasgow Rd, Dumbarton
Expressions: 10 Years Old; 12 Years Old (France)

Tormore began production in 1959, and was the first new distillery to be built in the Highlands in the 20th century. It was commissioned by Long John International and designed by Sir Albert Richardson, a past president of the Royal Academy to be an architectural showpiece, complete with an ornamental lake and fountains: one writer has compared it, accurately, to a spa (the Whisky Heritage Centre in Edinburgh has a fine working model).

Some connoisseurs claimed that a newly constructed distillery would not be able to produce a traditional Highland malt. They were confounded when the first batches were bottled at 10 years old: not only is The Tormore a typical Speyside, it has a distinctive aftertaste. Its makers describe it as 'a contemporary malt', 'accessible' and 'approachable', and it enjoys particular success among younger malt-whisky drinkers, especially in Europe.

Tasting Notes: The nose is soft, with a trace of honey and some dryness; faintly smoky; the body is medium and firm; the mouth-feel is smooth – an intriguing balance of malty sweetness and smoky dryness; the finish is well-rounded.

TULLIBARDINE

Category: Highland (Perthshire)
Distiller: The Tullibardine Distillery Ltd, Blackford Perthshire
Owner: Invergordon Distillers Ltd, Edinburgh
Expressions: 10 Years Old; Stillman's Dram (extra long matured) will be produced from time to time; C 1964

Blackford is close to Gleneagles, on the northern slopes of the Ochil Hills in Perthshire, just above the Highland Line. From a very remote period it has been famous for its breweries: one produced a special brew by royal command for James IV's coronation in 1488. Tullibardine Distillery is on the site of the first public brewery in Scotland and draws its water from the same source in the Ochils as made the brewery famous.

The distillery was designed by the noted distillery builder, W. Delmé Evans, in 1949 and passed into Invergordon's ownership in 1972. It is small and compact, with four stills. Visitors are welcome, but by appointment only.

Tasting Notes: A soft, malty, slightly sherried nose, richer than one might expect from so southerly a distillery; medium body; full flavour, with an almost fruity richness, but only medium sweet; fragrant, Chardonnay finish.

DIRECTORY

BLENDED WHISKIES

Key

Category: There are no universally recognized categories of blended whisky. There are price differentials, however, and these tend to reflect a) the quantity of malt whisky in the blend and b) the age of the malts used. I have used: Vatted Malt, Liqueur Whisky, Standard Blend, Premium Blend and De Luxe Blend.

Licensee: In many cases the original owner/proprietor or creator of the blend will have been taken over by another company; in others the owning company will have licensed the brand to another. I have used the word 'Licensee' loosely to cover these possibilities.

Owner: Where there are chains of holding companies I have listed only the principal ones. United Distillers, whose name appears frequently, is owned by Guinness plc. The company's headquarters is Landmark House, Hammersmith Bridge Rd, London W6 9DP; its Registered Office is Distillers House, 33 Ellersly Rd, Edinburgh EH12 6JW.

Expressions: Where the brand is bottled in more than one category this is mentioned, e.g. Johnnie Walker Red, Black and Blue Labels are respectively Standard, Premium and De Luxe Blends.

The remarks in an entry reflect the amount of information brand-owners have been able to supply – not a great deal in some cases.

ABBOT'S CHOICE

Category: Standard Blend
Licensee: John McEwan & Co., Leith
Owner: United Distillers

(see **Chequers**) John McEwan was a successful farmer from Perthshire, who occasionally brought his animals to market in Edinburgh. The story goes that on one visit in the early 1860s he lost his dogs and entered a tavern to look for them. Here he got into conversation about blending whisky, and resolved to enter the industry himself. He bought **Linkwood** Distillery and several licensed premises, and created Abbot's Choice, a blend which was once very popular in Scotland (the name recollects the tradition that whisky distilling was brought to Scotland by monks).

McEwan & Co. was bought by DCL in 1933. The blend is now difficult to find.

AINSLIE'S

Category: Standard and De Luxe Blends
Licensee: Ainslie & Heilbron (Distillers) Ltd, 5 Oswald St, Glasgow
Owner: United Distillers

James Ainslie & Co. started as wine and spirit merchants in 1868. They became very successful and in 1896 bought up the **Clynelish** Distillery in Sutherland which had been built by the 1st Duke of Sutherland in 1816. After the terrible Sutherland Clearances many farmers had been moved to more fertile land on the coast and thus there was an ample supply of local grain for the distillery.

After a series of takeovers in the early part of this century and a merger with David Heilbron & Son, the company became a subsidiary of the DCL.

THE ANTIQUARY

Category: Standard Blend
Licensee: J. & W. Hardie, South Queensferry (subsidiary of Wm Sanderson)
Owner: United Distillers

The company was established in 1861, became a subsidiary of Wm Sanderson & Co. (see **VAT 69**) and joined DCL in 1953. The Antiquary (the name commemorates Sir Walter Scott's novel of the same name) was formerly a very successful de luxe whisky, packaged in a decanter-shaped bottle, and backed by national advertising and promotions.

Today it is a shadow of its former self and is only made from time to time.

ARGYLL

Category: Standard Blend; Single Malt
Owner: Beinn Buidhe Holdings Ltd, Argyll Estates Office, Inveraray, Argyll
Expressions: Malt bottlings at 12, 15 and 17 Years Old

These brands are only available from the shop at Inveraray Castle, home of the Duke of Argyll. I have not been able to ascertain where the malt whisky is distilled.

Inveraray Castle is one of Scotland's great houses. It was founded in 1746 to replace an older castle on a nearby site. The Dukes of Argyll are the chiefs of the mighty Clan Campbell.

AS WE GET IT

Category: Vatted Malt
Owner: J.G. Thomson & Co. Ltd, Glasgow
(parent: Bass plc)

As We Get It is bottled at cask strength (i.e. without the usual reduction to 40% or 43% ABV), so is usually sold at about 60% ABV (103° proof). The label states that it is distilled by Macallan-Glenlivet plc, Craigellachie, but the brand is apparently a vatting of several different malts. Each bottling is different from the last, so both the age and the strength of the finished product vary slightly.

As We Get It is only produced in small quantities, and is distributed only in Scotland owing to the limitation on the supply of fillings. As a result it is a something of a curiosity, sought out by enthusiasts.

AVONSIDE

Category: Premium Blend (8 Years Old)
Licensee: James Gordon & Co., Elgin
Owner: Gordon & MacPhail, George House, Boroughbriggs Rd, Elgin

(see **MacPhail's**) The river Avon (pronounced 'Arn') rises near Tomintoul Distillery, runs past Glenlivet Distillery and meets the Spey at Ballindalloch, close to Cragganmore Distillery. The Junction Pool, where the two rivers meet, is one of the Spey's most famous stretches.

BAILLIE NICOL JARVIE

Category: Premium Blend
Licensee: Nicol Anderson & Co., Ltd, Leith
Owner: Macdonald & Muir Ltd, 186 Commercial St, Leith

(see **Highland Queen**) Baillie Nicol Jarvie was a character in Sir Walter Scott's novel *Rob Roy*. While journeying from Glasgow to visit his infamous cousin, he was resting at an inn in Aberfoyle when he was set upon by a fierce-looking Highlander. Finding his sword was rusted into its sheath, the corpulent Baillie seized a red-hot poker and set the Highlander's plaid on fire! The Baillie's poker still hangs from a tree outside the Baillie Nicol Jarvie Hotel at Aberfoyle, and the incident is illustrated on the label of the blend which bears the Baillie's name.

The brand was introduced around the turn of the century, and has a charming period label.

BALLANTINE'S

Category: various blends
Proprietor: George Ballantine & Son Ltd
Owner: Allied Distillers, 2 Glasgow Rd, Dumbarton
Expressions: Premium (Finest); De Luxe (Founder's Reserve; Gold Seal (12 Years Old); 17 Years Old; 30 Years Old)

Ballantine's Finest consistently commands the third largest annual sales of Scotch whisky in the world, and is number one in Europe (78% share of the market). The 30 Years Old is probably the most expensive blended whisky in the world, and is available only in small quantities. The de luxe blends have established markets in the Far East, South East Asia, South America, and Europe: Ballantine's is a familiar name amongst whisky drinkers world-wide.

The eponymous George Ballantine (1807–91) was of Border farming stock, but served his apprenticeship with a grocer and spirit dealer, in which capacity he set up his own business in the Cowgate, Edinburgh, in 1827. In 1865 he delegated the running of his Edinburgh shop (by now situated on the more fashionable North Bridge, and was soon to move to most fashionable Princes Street), to his son while he opened a larger establishment in Glasgow (Argyll Street, then Union Street). Here he concentrated on the wine and spirit trade, bringing his second son, also named George, into the business. By the time he died a contemporary booklet described the firm as "*transacting an immense trade in supplying wines and spirits to families of distinction all over Scotland and in many parts of England and Ireland*". Two years later, in 1903, the firm was granted the Royal Warrant.

In 1919 the Ballantine family capitalized on its success and sold the business to the junior partners, James Barclay and R.A. McKinlay, who incorporated the company under the Ballantine name and turned their considerable energies to exports, particularly in the USA. Throughout the Prohibition era (1920–33) James Barclay's efforts to obtain distribution in the USA were tireless, and not without danger, but by the mid-1930s he had the best distribution network on the East Coast. David Niven, the actor, was an early salesman.

Increasingly large resources were required to compete in the growing world market, and these were provided by another of James Barclay's contacts, Hiram Walker Gooderham & Worts, a major Canadian distiller which acquired George Ballantine & Son Ltd in 1937. The new owner's first task was to secure supplies of malt and grain whiskies – to which end the company purchased Miltonduff and Glenburgie malt distilleries, and built their grain distillery at Dumbarton, the largest in Europe.

During the Second World War, and for some years after, supplies of grain for whisky production were rationed, but once rationing was lifted, heavy brand promotion in North America could proceed.

During the 1960s, the company turned its attention to Europe – at the time an unexplored market for Scotch – and by mid-decade it had secured a firm enough foothold on the Continent to resolve to gear the home trade operation to supporting the overseas business.

Between 1963 and 1975, Ballantine's sales in North America quadrupled (to 1.5 million cases), and during the same period Ballantine's Finest became the best-selling Scotch in the Eastern bloc. Hiram Walker (Scotland) Ltd won the Queen's Award for Export Achievement in 1968 and again in 1986 – by which time nearly two bottles of Ballantine's whisky were being sold somewhere in the world every second!

JOHN BARR

Category: Standard Blend
Licensee: John Walker & Co., Kilmarnock and London
Owner: United Distillers

Until the practice was banned by an EEC Commission Directive in December 1977, DCL's subsidiary companies operated a system of dual pricing for brands which sold well in export markets. Under the dual-pricing system a UK trade customer was charged a higher in-bond price if brands were bought for re-sale within the EEC than if they were bought for UK consumption (at that time a difference was £5 on a case). The reason for this was to compensate the appointed foreign distributors for the investment they had to make in promoting and distributing the brands within their markets, and competing with local spirit brands which often enjoyed more favourable taxes. Without the price difference it would also have been possible for UK trade customers to establish a profitable 'parallel exports' business, based upon the lower price at which they could buy whisky intended for the home market, thus removing incentives for foreign distributors and ultimately destroying the export markets themselves, both within and outwith the ECC.

Following the Directive, DCL promptly withdrew a number of their leading brands from the UK market, offering them for export only (notably **Johnnie Walker** Red Label and Haig **Dimple)** and increased the price on other brands so as to render them unattractive for parallel export (**VAT 69** and **Black & White**, for example). John Barr and The Buchanan Blend were introduced to replace Red Label. The former has never taken off and will probably disappear.

BAXTER'S BARLEY BREE

Category: Standard Blend
Licensee: James Watson & Co., Dundee
Owner: United Distillers

Founded in 1815, James Watson & Co. was acquired by the Buchanan-Dewar and Walker Group two years before they merged with DCL in 1925. The acquisition brought some 8 million gallons (over 36 million litres) of whisky in bond, together with Parkmore (defunct since 1930), **Ord** and **Pulteney** distilleries.

Watson's owned two blends, but their popularity declined after 1939; Baxter's Barley Bree is currently enjoying a revival, selling in South Africa, the Lebanon and Suriname, as well as in the UK – particularly through the Augustus Barnet chain, for which a 5-year-old variant is specially made.

I have been unable to discover who the eponymous 'Baxter' refers to; 'bree' is Scots for 'broth', 'sauce' or 'liquor', and was once a colloquialism for whisky.

JOHN BEGG

Category: Standard Blend
Licensee: John Begg, 75 Hope St, Glasgow
Owner: United Distillers

The eponymous John Begg took a long lease of 120 acres (48 ha) in the parish of Crathie on Deeside in 1845 and built a small distillery there, in the shadow of the mountain Lochnagar (3,791 feet/1,156 m), on a site which had been used for distilling since 1825 (see **Royal Lochnagar**).

Before he died in 1880 John Begg, realizing that the future of the whisky industry lay with blends, acquired a bonded warehouse, duty-paid cellar and a bottling line in Aberdeen, and proceeded to create and export John Begg Blue Cap and John Begg Gold Cap (a de luxe version, now extinct).

Promoted by the internationally famous slogan 'Take a Peg of John Begg' the brands prospered under the direction of his son Henry Farquharson Begg, and his son-in-law William Reid. The business became a limited company in 1902, and was sold to DCL in 1916.

Today the brand's main market is in Germany, with a substantial amount going to Madeira. A quantity is exported in bulk to the USA.

BELL'S

Category: Premium Blend
Licensee: Arthur Bell & Sons, Perth
Owner: United Distillers

In 1825 Thomas Sandeman, of the famous port family, opened a wine and spirit shop in the Kirkgate, Perth. In 1845 he employed Arthur Bell as his 'traveller', and in 1851 Bell became a partner in the firm.

The first quality blends of malt and grain whisky were appearing about this time (see **Usher's**) and Bell recognized that a drink which was lighter than a single malt and more flavoursome than grain whisky would have broad appeal. "*Several fine whiskies blended together please the palates of a greater number of people than one whisky unmixed*", he said, "*I have long adopted that practice and allowed the qualities of my goods to speak for themselves.*"

Bell's firm belief in the quality and potential of his blends led him to appoint an agent in London in 1863 – the first whisky company to do so – and he brought his sons, Arthur Kinmond and Robert, into the firm to look after the domestic and overseas markets respectively. He also interested himself in the whisky trade as a whole, successfully campaigning, among other things, for the introduction of standard bottle sizes for spirits.

By 1895 Bell's brands were selling in Australia, New Zealand, India, Ceylon, Italy and France, but it was only in 1904, four years after the death of Arthur senior, that the family name appeared on the label. A.K. Bell began to expand the business rapidly, first into Canada, then into almost every corner of the world with a potential market, including South Africa, where it quickly became the number one brand. At this time, the company adopted the slogan 'Afore Ye Go', which became known the world over, and which was officially registered as the company slogan in 1925.

In 1933 Bell's bought P. Mackenzie & Co., the owners of Blair Athol and Dufftown-Glenlivet Distilleries (see **The Real Mackenzie**, **Blair Athol**, **Dufftown**); in 1936 Inchgower Distillery was also purchased.

A.K. and Robert Bell both died in 1942, and this was the end of the family's connection with the company: William Govan Farquharson, who had joined the company in 1942, became chairman. He held this position until his death in 1973.

By 1970 Bell's Finest was brand leader in Scotland (with a 9.9% share of the UK market), and by 1980 a marketing effort which concentrated on the on-trade (pubs, etc.) had won a 22.9% share and was the best-selling Scotch in Britain. In 1980 Bell's lost its lead position of the Scottish market to Famous Grouse, but it retains its status in England. Growth in foreign markets was also steady, and this was recognized in 1983 by a Queen's Award for Export Achievement.

In 1985 Arthur Bell & Co. was acquired by The Guinness Group, and in 1987 Guinness took over DCL to form United Distillers, the world's largest (and most profitable) spirits company, reporting a turnover of £2,436 million in 1991, with profits of £749 million.

BEN AIGEN

Category: Standard Blend
Licensee: Strathnairn Whisky Ltd, Inverness
Owner: Gordon & MacPhail, George House, Boroughbriggs Rd, Elgin

(see **MacPhail's**) Ben Aigen, more usually spelt Benagen, is a mountain seven miles west of Fochabers, between Moray and Banffshire, immediately east of the river Spey.

BEN ALDER

Category: Standard Blend
Owner: Gordon & MacPhail, George House, Boroughbriggs Rd, Elgin

(see **MacPhail's**) Ben Alder (3,756 feet/1,145m) rises between Lochs Laggan and Ericht in Inverness-shire. Bonnie Prince Charlie lay concealed here between 2 and 12 September 1746, following his defeat at Culloden.

The brand was introduced in 1900, originally called Dew of Ben Alder.

BENEAGLES

Category: Standard Blend
Licensee: Waverly Vintners Ltd
Owner: Peter Thomson (Agencies) Ltd
Proprietor: Scottish & Newcastle Breweries plc

At one time the little yellow vans owned by Peter Thomson (Perth) Ltd and bearing the motif of Bencagles whisky were to be seen all over Scotland. Today, although Beneagles is still available it is no longer found in such quantities.

Peter Thomson started as a grocer and wine and spirit merchant in Perth in 1908. Drawing upon deep knowledge of Speyside malts and blending techniques, Thomson launched Beneagles in 1922, inspired by the newly built golfing resort of Gleneagles Hotel. The founder died in 1939 and ownership passed to his son David, who remained chairman until the company was sold in 1981. Following the Second World War efforts were concentrated on wholesale distribution and, by the 1970s, the firm's four retail shops had closed in favour of this area of the business.

The company enjoyed great success with a venture into miniature ceramic ornaments filled with whisky. In order to meet export requirements, which restricted the sale of miniatures in North America, larger, more impressive ceramics were created and the 'birds of prey' range of decanters is very highly sought after by collectors.

The business remained under family ownership until it was sold to Stakis plc in 1981. Two years later it was acquired by Waverly Vintners Ltd, the wine and spirit arm of Scottish & Newcastle Breweries, which sells Beneagles to the on-trade and through their tied houses. A little goes for export. The ceramics range is now owned by Whyte & Mackay. Beneagles is blended and bottled by The Invergordon Distillers.

BENMORE

Category: Standard Blend
Licensee: Benmore Distilleries, Glasgow
Owner: United Distillers

Benmore Distilleries formerly owned **Dallas Dhu,** near Forres, Benmore and Lochead Distilleries in Campbeltown (both now defunct) and Lochindaal on Islay (also defunct). Benmore was acquired by DCL in 1929: the brand sells in Belgium, and is exported in bulk to Australia. The name in Gaelic means 'the big hill'.

BEN ROLAND

Category: Premium Blend
Proprietor: Ben Roland Scotch Whisky Co., Birchwood House, Victoria Rd, Dartford, Kent (subsidiary of Unwin's Ltd)
Owner: Phillips Newman & Co. Ltd
Expressions: 5 Years Old

Ben Roland first appeared in a 1924 price list for Sordo Lopez & Son, wine shippers, and was registered in 1951. Sordo Lopez was owned by M.A. Wetz, whose grandson is currently managing director of Unwin's, for whom this is an 'own label' brand, sold through their shops in the south-east of England.

The blend employs Speyside and Highland malts of at least five years old and achieves a pleasant balance between sweet and dry.

BERRY'S BEST/BERRY'S ALL MALT

Category: Standard Blend; Vatted Malt
Owner: Berry Bros & Rudd, 3 St James's St, London SW1

(see **Cutty Sark**) Berry Bros has occupied the same premises near St James's Palace since the late 17th century. The firm was originally described as 'Italian warehousemen' – importers of such exotic groceries as tea, coffee and spices – and the sign which still hangs above their door is that of a coffee mill. This antique trademark decorates the labels of Berry's Best, a decent blend of 8-year-old (minimum) malts, predominantly from Speyside, and Berry's All Malt, which has a liberal dose of Islay malts, and considerable phenolic concentration.

BLACK & WHITE

Category: Standard Blend
Licensee: James Buchanan & Co., London
Owner: United Distillers

(see **Buchanan's**) When the redoubtable James Buchanan managed to persuade the Members Bar of the House of Commons to stock his whisky it quickly became the most popular blend. He changed its name first to House of Commons, then to Buchanan's Special, but everybody asked for it as 'Black and White', on account of the fact that its bottle was very dark and its label very white.

Realizing the opportunity that this offered, the name was changed again and reinforced by adopting black and white Scots terriers as its symbol (Buchanan's own idea). It quickly became one of the most popular brands in the world, and currently stands at about 12th best-seller, its main markets being South Africa, Canada and Italy.

BLACK BOTTLE

Category: Premium Blend
Licensee: Gordon Graham & Co. Ltd
Owner: Allied Distillers Ltd, 2 Glasgow Rd, Dumbarton

Black Bottle is probably the fastest-growing brand in the most discriminating of the world's whisky markets, Scotland. With good reason: it is a first-class blend – its makers claim that it has many of the attributes of a de luxe whisky (smooth, mellow, rich but not heavy, etc.), while selling at a premium price. Interestingly, the blend formula was altered and improved in the 1980s.

The brand was first registered in 1879 by Charles David and Gordon Graham, a company of tea importers and blenders in Aberdeen, for consumption by the partners and their friends. Initially it was known only in the north-east of Scotland (being especially favoured by the fishing community), but Aberdonians know what they like and took it with them around the world (see **Catto's**).

Gordon Graham & Co. as the company became known, abandoned tea to devote itself to its blended whisky. The company was taken over by the American giant, Schenley Industries Inc., in 1959 owners of **Long John** Distillers, **Kinclaith, Tormore** and **Glenugie** distilleries, and subsequently became part of Whitbread & Co. (1975), before being sold to Allied Lyons, along with Whitbread's other Scotch whisky companies.

Black Bottle's unique bottle-shape represents a pot still and dates from the 1890s. For many years the brand was advertised with the slogan 'Unchanged by Progress'; this has now been changed to 'A Wee Bit Out of the Ordinary'.

BLACK PRINCE

Category: Premium and De Luxe Blends
Owner: Burn Stewart Distillers plc, 65 Kelburn St, Barrhead, Glasgow
Expressions: Select; 12 and 17 Years Old (latter in ceramic pot)

Black Prince was first created before the Second World War by the Henkes Distillers Group of Holland, expressly for the US market. It was later acquired by Norden McCall Ltd of London, which later sold it to another Dutch company, Bols. Burn Stewart bought the brand in 1991, repackaged its three expressions, and is vigorously developing markets in the Far East. It is available in the UK and Europe, but is currently unusual (see **Burn Stewart**).

The Black Prince of Wales and Aquitaine (1330–76) was King Edward III's eldest son. He was called 'Black' on account of his dark armour. He distinguished himself in the battle of Crecy.

BUCHANAN'S

Category: De Luxe Blend
Licensee: James Buchanan & Co., London
Owner: United Distillers
Expressions: 12 Years Old

James Buchanan was born in Canada in 1849, of Scottish parents. He was brought back to Scotland in his first year, but his parents swiftly removed to Northern Ireland, and he did not return until he was 15 to become an office boy in a Glasgow shipping firm.

In 1879 Buchanan went to London as agent for Chas Mackinlay & Co. (see **Mackinlay's**), and within five years he had set up a business on his own account with capital borrowed from a friend and stocks from W.P. Lowrie (see **Lowrie's**). He first sold whisky by the barrel to wine merchants, and then set about creating a blend which would be acceptable to the English palate, to be sold by the bottle.

Having created The Buchanan Blend he seduced or cajoled a number of leading London hotels into stocking it. Within a year he had paid back the loan, and soon he was selling his blend, in its distinctive black and white livery, in both the Members' Bar of the House of Commons and the majority of London music halls. For the former outlet, the brand was renamed House of Commons, then Buchanan's Special, then **Black & White**.

In spite of being dogged by ill health, James Buchanan was a tireless worker and self-publicist. He was among the first to advertise his brands in the newspapers, adopting the symbol of black and white Scots terriers (his own idea). He also bought the Black Swan Distillery in Holborn, London, a famous coaching inn, and from here dispatched his whisky in a fleet of handsome drays, with uniformed coachmen (an operation which lasted until 1936). The company's first of several Royal Warrants was granted by Queen Victoria.

James Buchanan himself was something of a dandy – thin and aristocratic in appearance (his is the portrait on the brand's label) – and enjoyed the life of an English country gentleman. He loved horses – he had his own racing stables and twice he won the Derby. In 1920 he was made a baronet, and in 1922 was raised to the peerage as Lord Woolavington of Lavington. He was a leading philanthropist and was much mourned when he died in 1935, aged 86.

By the turn of the century, Buchanan's was firmly among the 'big three' (with **Dewar's** and **Walker's**). In 1915 the first two created Scotch Whisky Brands Ltd, (the name was changed four years later to Buchanan-Dewar Ltd) to protect their interests against DCL, but it was only a matter of time, and in 1923 the big three joined Distillers.

The brand's marketing proposition takes a leaf out of James Buchanan's own book and maintains that 'Buchanan's De Luxe is enjoyed by dynamic, successful people. It is a reward for success in business'!

Buchanan's De Luxe is currently 29th best-seller in the world, selling mainly in Mexico, Venezuela, Brazil, Aruba and Curacao (in volume terms 93% sells in Central and South America). **Dalwhinnie** is the blend's key malt whisky.

BULLOCH LADE

Category: Standard Blend
Licensee: Bulloch Lade & Co., Glasgow
Owner: United Distillers
Expressions: B & L Gold Label

Bulloch & Co. merged with Lade & Co. in the 1830s, and traded successfully until 1920, when the company went into voluntary liquidation and was taken over by a group of distillers and blenders led by DCL. Seven years later DCL bought the entire share capital and whisky stocks for half a million pounds.

The company owned **Caol Isla** Distillery between 1880 and 1920, and following the distillery's acquisition by DCL in 1927, it was again licensed to Bulloch Lade. Caol Isla is a constituent of B & L Gold Label, and the blend was apparently first produced at the distillery in 1857. Today a small amount is bottled in Scotland and sold in Canada, but the largest volume is shipped in bulk to the USA and New Zealand where it is bottled.

BURN STEWART

Category: De Luxe Blend
Proprietor: Burn Stewart Distillers plc, 65 Kelburn St, Barrhead, Glasgow
Expressions: 3 and 12 Years Old

Backed by venture capital and headed by a group of people with deep experience of the whisky industry, Burn Stewart was incorporated in 1988 as one of the few remaining independent whisky companies. The company's distilling base was achieved by the acquisition in 1991 of **Deanston** Distillery, and the same year it was granted the Queen's Award for Export Achievement and the British Venture Capital Association's prize for the Best Company Turnaround.

The brand, and company name, came from Burn Stewart & Co. Ltd, a well-established firm of blenders, exporters and brokers in Dumbarton and London, with a portfolio of five companies and about twenty brands.

Burn Stewart 12 Years Old has a noticeable trace of Islay in its flavour. The principal markets for. Burn Stewart are France, South Africa, Japan and Taiwan.

CAMPBELTOWN LOCH

Category: Premium Blend
Licensee: Eaglesome Ltd
Owner: J. & A. Mitchell & Co. Ltd, Campbeltown
Expressions: 10 Years Old

(see **Springbank**) J. & A. Mitchell & Co. is still a family company, and its blend Campbeltown Loch can be relied upon to have the excellent Springbank at its heart.

CATTO'S

Category: Premium and De Luxe Blends
Proprietor: James Catto & Co. Ltd
Owner: Inver House Distillers Ltd, Airdrie, Lanarkshire
Expressions: Rare Old Scottish Highland Whisky; 12 Years Old

James Catto established his firm of whisky blenders at Aberdeen in 1861 and soon built up a loyal local following. Before the end of the century this had become an international following through the enthusiasm of Aberdonian emigrants – in particular the support of two schoolfriends who founded famous shipping lines (P & O and White Star) and carried the whisky to destinations far and wide.

James Catto's son Robert opened up the English market, but was killed in France in 1916. After the First World War the company became part of Gilbeys, and recently it has been bought by **Inver House**.

CHAIRMAN'S

Category: Standard Blend
Owner: Eldridge, Pope & Co. plc, Weymouth Ave, Dorchester, Dorset

This is a comparatively new blend, created by the company's Wines & Spirits Director, Mr Naughtie, who is also a Master of Wine. The label is a picture of the current chairman's fireplace painted by Sir Hugh Casson, past President of the Royal Academy. (See also **Old Highland Blend**.)

CHEQUERS

Category: Standard Blend
Licensee: John McEwan & Co., Elgin
Owner: United Distillers

The brand-name refers to the *ex officio* country residence of the Prime Minister of the United Kingdom. John McEwan & Co. was established in 1863, and acquired Linkwood Distillery near Elgin through its membership of DCL, in 1932. Chequers is a big brand in Venezuela, Paraguay and Aruba.

CHIEFTAIN'S CHOICE

Category: A range of blends and malts
Licensee: Scottish Independent Distillers Co. Ltd
Owner: Peter J. Russell Group, Russell House, Dunnet Way, Broxburn
Expressions: At the time of writing, the range consists of 3 premium blends (8 Years Old, 12 Years Old, 18 Years Old), a vatted malt, 3 regional malts and 3 very old single malts (Speysides at 21 and 32 Years Old; a Highland at 26 Years Old and a Lowland at 30 Years Old)

Leonard Russell, father of the eponymous Peter J. (who is currently chairman of the Group), commenced business as a whisky broker in 1936 and soon expanded into blending and exporting. Today the Group sells annually over 10 million bottles of a year, worldwide and is one of the largest independent companies in the whisky industry.

The Group acquired the Scottish Independent Distillers Company Ltd in 1985. This company had been formed in 1928 by a number of independent blenders and distillers, with the intention of pooling their knowledge and skills to produce prestige whiskies.

The Chieftain's Choice range sells through specialist outlets in the UK, Japan, the USA and France.

CHIVAS REGAL

Category: De Luxe Blend
Licensee: Chivas Brothers
Owner: The Seagram Company Ltd, Montreal, Canada
Expressions: 12 Years Old

In 1801 William Edward established himself as a wine merchant and grocer at 49 Castle Street, Aberdeen. The small shop was close to the busy harbour where cargoes of tea, coffee, sugar, spices and dried fruits were continually being landed, as well as kegs of gin, brandy and rum. Edward's business grew steadily and before long he was looking for a partner.

A friend, the well-known Aberdeen advocate, Alexander

Chivas – suggested his young cousin James Chivas, who joined the firm in 1837. The same year the business was moved to a grander site at the head of King Street, where it remained for over one hundred years.

The Chivas family came from Tarves in Aberdeenshire and took their name from the ancient barony of Schivas. Four years after James Chivas joined the firm, William Edward died and Chivas formed a new partnership with another wine merchant, but this was not a success, and the relationship was dissolved in 1857.

The business prospered, however. Queen Victoria regularly had provisions sent down from Chivas' shop to her summer home at Balmoral, and granted the Royal Warrant to the firm in 1843. Its reputation travelled far and wide, and soon orders were arriving from all over Britain and abroad – the shop supplied whisky, among other items, to the Austrian Emperor.

In 1858 James Chivas took his brother John as a partner, and the firm became Chivas Bros. However John died five years later. Driven by James' energy, commercial flair and good taste, the firm continued to expand, both physically along King Street and economically. The range of services and goods offered included, for example, a staff agency for shooting parties, and a new department selling household goods. By the time of his death, in 1886 whisky had become a key part of the business.

Chivas Bros began to sell their own blend, Glen-Dee, in the early 1870s. It was eagerly bought by their existing customers, both locally and abroad: order books from the 1880s list princes and peers, admirals and generals, bishops and professors.

James was succeeded by his son, Alexander, but the latter died in 1893 of a 'quinsy throat' (followed by his wife, three days later), and control passed to his assistant Alexander Smith, who managed the firm on behalf of Chivas' trustees and brought one Charles Stewart Howard, an Edinburgh man, into the business.

Howard had worked for J. & G. Stewart & Co. and was experienced in the whisky trade. By this time the company had built up a good name abroad for its two export blends, Royal Glen-Dee and Royal Strathythan (the Queensland Licensed Victualler's Gazette of 1889 states "*in every well-conducted hotel Glen-Dee is as well known as Guinness or Pommery*"), and other brands were available locally. The retail side of the business continued, but was now secondary to the whisky. The firm had built up a good stock of well-matured malt whiskies and under Howard's guidance new blends were created and exported all over the world, especially to the new and burgeoning market in North America. In 1909 Chivas Regal was introduced to both Canada and the USA.

A fire at the King Street premises in 1929 destroyed much of the administrative and accounts departments, and the deaths of both Smith and Howard in 1935 resulted in Chivas Brothers becoming a limited liability company. In 1949 this company became a wholly owned subsidiary of Seagram's, the Canadian distilling giant. By this time Chivas Regal was one of the most successful brands in the world: currently it is within the top five best-selling brands in the world, and sells in over 150 countries.

In 1950 Chivas Bros Ltd/Seagram's bought **Strathisla** Distillery and seven years later began construction of a new distillery at **Glen Keith** incorporating parts of an old flour and meal mill – the first new malt whisky distillery built in Scotland since the Victorian era. Soon after the Keith Bond was built nearby to accommodate the output of both distilleries: at the time it was the largest complex of its kind in the world, and it is still among the biggest. In 1958, with growing stocks of whisky reducing the space available at Keith, it was decided to build a separate blending and bottling plant with further warehousing and since most of the company's exports went through Glasgow, a suitable site was found on Clydeside, at Paisley, which remains the company's base in Scotland. The original Chivas Bros retail and wholesale business in Aberdeen continued until 1981.

Some would argue that, along with J&B Rare, Chivas Regal is the only truly global brand of Scotch whisky. It sells in over 150 countries, is the top premium brand and is among the top five best-sellers in the world.

CLAN ARDROCH

Category: Standard Blend
Owner: Hall & Bramley Ltd, Aintree Building, Ormskirk Rd, Liverpool

(see **Glen Ghoil**)

CLAN CAMPBELL

Category: Standard and De Luxe Blends
Owner: Campbell Distillers, 924 Great West Rd, Brentford, Middlesex (a subsidiary of Pernod Ricard)
Expressions: Clan Campbell; Highlander (12 Year Old); Legendary (21 Year Old)

Clan Campbell is something of a phenomenon. Although it was launched only in 1984, it trebled its sales to 800,000 cases by 1991, and has won the accolade of being the fastest-growing brand of blended whisky in Europe.

From the outset, the company's marketing tactic was to invest heavily in France, with the help of its partner, Pernod Ricard. It is now number four in this market, and it also sells well in Italy, Spain, Belgium, Holland, Germany, Switzerland and Greece. A subsidiary company has been established in Australia to promote the brand in the southern hemisphere.

The House of Campbell (S. Campbell & Son Ltd) dates from 1879, and was originally based in Glasgow, then at Kilwinning, Ayrshire. The **Aberlour-Glenlivet** Distillery was bought in 1945, **Edradour** Distillery in 1982 and **Glenallachie** Distillery in 1989 (which effectively doubled the company's distilling capacity). It is safe to assume that all these malts play important roles within the Clan Campbell blends.

In late 1991 and early 1992 the company launched two de luxe expressions of Clan Campbell – a 12 Year Old and a 21 Year Old.

CLAN MACGREGOR

Category: Standard Blend
Licensee: J.G. Thomson & Co. Ltd, West George St, Glasgow
Owner: William Grant & Sons Ltd, The Glenfiddich Distillery, Dufftown

This secondary (i.e. price-competitive) brand was introduced by Grant's to North America in the 1970s: by 1990 it was selling over 500,000 cases in export markets, and it currently stands just within the top twenty best-sellers. Although it is available in the UK, it is principally an export whisky.

The warlike MacGregor clan fell foul of the politically powerful Clan Campbell and was outlawed in 1603: it became illegal to bear the name MacGregor and anyone was at liberty to murder a MacGregor, and to claim a reward. This brutal order was only repealed by Act of Parliament in 1774.

CLAN MURDOCK

Category: Standard Blend
Licensee: Murdoch McLennan, Edinburgh
Owner: Macdonald Martin Distilleries plc, 186 Commercial St, Leith

Murdoch McLennan was an agricultural experimenter as well as a whisky merchant, and specialized in ways of increasing his barley yield for the production of whisky (see **Highland Queen**, **James Martin's**).

CLAN ROY

Category: Standard Blend
Owner: Morrison Bowmore (Distillers) Ltd, Carlisle St, Glasgow

The markets for this blend are Spain, Portugal and North America (see **Rob Roy**).

CLANSMAN

Category: Standard Blend
Owner: Glen Catrine Bonded Warehouse Ltd, Laigh Rd, Catrine, Ayrshire

This blend is produced mainly for export to South America (see **Glen Catrine**).

(THE) CLAYMORE

Category: Standard Blend
Owner: Whyte & Mackay Group plc, St Vincent St, Glasgow (parent: American Brands Inc.)

The Claymore was launched by DCL during the summer of 1977 as a low-priced or 'secondary' brand, taking the company into a sector of the market it had hitherto shunned. The move was an attempt to secure market-share following the withdrawal of **Johnnie Walker** in the same year. The brand immediately became the leader in its sector, winning a 5.6% share of the market in the UK.

During the titanic take-over battle for DCL in 1985, one of the objections was the company's share of the UK market, and in order to avoid protracted investigation by the Office of Fair Trading, a number of brands were sold to **Whyte & Mackay**. The new owner has continued to develop Claymore's market, especially in the UK where it now ranks number four.

CLUB

Category: Premium Blend
Owner: Justerini & Brooks Ltd, St James's St, London

In the 1880s J&B became one of the first London wines and spirits merchants to buy up stocks of old whisky in Scotland in order to create a house blend of consistent quality. Their first brand was Club, which today is only available from J&B's shops in London and Edinburgh.

CLUNY

Category: Standard and De Luxe Blends
Licensee: John E. McPherson & Sons Ltd
Owner: The Invergordon Distillers Ltd, Leith, Edinburgh
Expressions: Standard Blend; 12 Years Old; 21 Years Old

John E. McPherson was an Edinburgh man and established his wines and spirits company at Newcastle upon Tyne in 1849. The brand takes its name from the Macphersons of Cluny, the chiefs of Clan Macpherson, one of whom escaped with Bonnie Prince Charlie after the battle of Culloden (1746), and was later hidden by his clan for nine years in a specially adapted cave, known as 'Cluny's Cage'.

In 1857, when the brand was introduced, the Macpherson of Cluny was John E. McPherson's cousin, and his arms – complete with supporters (two clansmen) and motto ('Touch Not The Cat Bot [*sic*] A Glove') adorn the label to this day. Clan Macpherson originated in Badenoch on Speyside.

Cluny quickly accumulated awards (and a Royal Warrant in 1931), but it is not sold in the UK today. Its main markets are in the USA, Canada, Australia, Sweden, Norway and Italy. In 1990 it stood at 31 in the league table of export brands.

COCKBURN'S HIGHLAND MALT

Category: Vatted Malt
Owner: Cockburn & Co. (Leith) Ltd, 19 Dublin St Lane South, Edinburgh

(see **The Dominie**)

CORNEY & BARROW

Category: Standard and De Luxe Blends
Owner: Corney & Barrow Ltd, 12 Helmet Row, London EC1
Expressions: Standard Blend; 12 Years Old De Luxe Blend

Established in 1780, Corney & Barrow claims to be one of the top UK specialist wine and spirit retailers and has been granted three Royal Warrants over the years. It has two shops in London, but most of its business is conducted by mail-order.

Between the wars, the firm held a controlling interest in James Catto & Co. (see **Catto's**), and once did its own blending and filling. A range of high-quality own-label whiskies was launched in Britain during the 1940s and several brands are now becoming established in the Japanese market. The whiskies are blended for Corney & Barrow by Peter J. Russell & Co., Edinburgh.

THE COUNTRY GENTLEMEN'S

Category: Standard Blend
Licensee: William Maxwell
Owner: The Country Gentlemen's Association, Hill Crest Mews,
London Rd, Baldock, Herts

This blend is available exclusively to members of the CGA, and to
customers of Hedley Wright & Co. Ltd (Bishop's Stortford) which
supplies it to the Association.

CRABBIE'S

Category: Standard Blend
Licensee: John Crabbie & Co., Leith
Owner: United Distillers

Crabbie & Co. was a family blending firm until it joined DCL, via
amalgamation with Macdonald Greenlees and others in 1922 (see
Old Parr). The firm traces its origins to 1801, and is especially
well known for its Green Ginger cordial (mixed with whisky to
make a Whisky Mac, a delicious cold weather drink).

At one time the firm held the licence for the historic – and
recently closed (1993) – Balmenach Distillery near Cromdale (see
Balmenach). United Distillers provide guided tours round
Crabbie's premises in Leith.

CRAWFORD'S 3 STAR

Category: Standard Blend
Licensee: (domestic market) Whyte & Mackay Brands, 310 St
Vincent St, Glasgow; (others) A. & A. Crawford, Edinburgh
Owner: United Distillers
Expressions: 3 Star; 5 Star (Premium Blend – currently not avail-
able)

The brothers Archibald and Aikman Crawford went into business
as whisky blenders and merchants at Leith in 1860. The company
was incorporated in 1942, by which time Crawford's 3 Star was a
leading brand in Scotland, and in 1944 its owners joined DCL.
In 1981 A. & A. Crawford & Associates Ltd was formed to han-
dle the Scottish domestic sales of ten of DCL's smaller companies.
The UK rights to the Crawford's brands were licensed to Whyte
& Mackay in 1986 (see **Whyte & Mackay**). 3 Star currently stands
at number five in the Scottish market (with a 30% market share)
and twelve on the UK best-selling list. It is exported to France,
Italy, the Netherlands, Japan, French Guiana, Costa Rica, Qatar
and South Africa.

The brand's label has apparently remained unaltered since 1900.

CRINAN CANAL WATER

Category: Premium Blend
Owner: Cockburn & Co. (Leith) Ltd, 19 Dublin St Lane South,
Edinburgh

The Crinan Canal was built in the late 18th century at the head of
the peninsula of Kintyre in Argyll, in order to allow direct access
from the Firth of Clyde to the Sea of the Hebrides, and thus to the

Atlantic. Before the canal was built, vessels had an extra 70 miles journey, around the treacherous Mull of Kintyre (see **The Dominie**).

CUMBRAE CASTLE

Category: Standard Blend
Proprietor: Macduff International Ltd, 299 West George St, Glasgow

This is a new brand recently launched by MacDuff International Ltd (see **MacDuff**). The islands of Little and Great Cumbrae are situated in the Firth of Clyde. The 'castle' is a ruined tower of indeterminate date, surrounded by a ditch and rampart, and was destroyed by Oliver Cromwell.

The brand takes its name, however, from a four-masted clipper which bore emigrants and pioneers from Scotland to the New World in the 19th century: the theme is that, in the export markets at which the brand is directed, it will provide a 'taste of home'!

CUSTODIAN

Category: Standard Blend
Licensee: Douglas Denham Ltd
Owner: Red Lion Blending Co. Ltd, North End Way, London NW3

This blend is chiefly exported to Venezuela (see **Diner's**).

CUTTY SARK

Category: Premium and De Luxe Blends
Owner: Berry Bros & Rudd Ltd, 3 St.James's St, London SW1
Expressions: Standard; 12 Years Old; 18 Years Old

No. 3 St James's Street has been occupied by the Berry family, or their close associates, since the 1690s. The firm remains essentially a family concern, the current chairman being Anthony Berry. The original business conducted from there was that of 'Italian warehousemen' (i.e. grocers and, later, wine merchants). The present building was erected in the 1730s, and the shop has changed very little since that time.

Cutty Sark originated over a luncheon in the 'parlour' of No. 3 St James's Street on 23 March 1923. Present were the partners – Anthony Berry's grandfather, Francis and great uncle, Walter, and Hugh Rudd – and the well-known Scottish artist, James McBey. Francis Berry wanted to augment the firm's existing list of blended Scotch whiskies with a new brand with a light character and colour (without the traditional addition of caramel colouring).

They required a name, and McBey suggested 'Cutty Sark' since the famous Dumbarton-built clipper ship had newly returned to England, after years of serving under the Portuguese flag. The *Cutty Sark* – which was the fastest ship of her day (and still holds the record for the run from Australia to England) – was herself named after the fleet-footed young witch in Robert Burns' great poem *Tam O'Shanter* (the name literally means 'short shirt'). McBey also volunteered to design the label, which remains exactly the same today as he drew it – right down to the hand-drawn lettering and the (unique) description 'Scots' whisky. Only the colour of the label is different: McBey wanted a shade of cream, but the printers accidentally used canary yellow. The mistake was so striking that it was retained.

Like several other firms, Berry Bros consolidated their 'off-shore' contacts in the Caribbean during the years of Prohibition, to build a springboard into the American market when the anti-drink laws were repealed. One of their 'agents' was Captain William McCoy, a rum-runner of proverbial integrity, whose name was to become synonymous with good whisky: 'The Real McCoy'. After 1933 the brand made rapid progress in the USA – even throughout the war years – and it remains one of the leaders in this market.

Today, Cutty Sark ranks among the top ten international Scotch whisky brands. It is brand leader in Greece and Portugal, and the fastest growing brand in Spain and Japan. In the UK it is available only through a limited number of outlets.

DALMENY

Category: Standard Blend
Owner: J. Townend & Sons (Hull) Ltd, 101 York St., Hull

This company of wine and spirit merchants, which has been well established in the north of England for over a century, acquired the business of J.J. Rippon in the 1930s, and with it the brand Dalmeny, which has been available since at least 1893.

Dalmeny House, on the southern shore of the Firth of Forth near Edinburgh, is the seat of the Earl of Rosebery.

PETER DAWSON

Category: Standard Blend
Licensee: Peter Dawson, Glasgow
Owner: United Distillers

Peter Dawson Ltd was a family company established in 1882, which owned distilleries at Auchnagie and Towiemore (both are now long extinct) and part owned **Balmenach** Distillery. The company was licensed to operate Ord Distillery (by John Dewar & Sons) until 1982 and sold **Ord** as a single malt.

Peter Dawson Ltd joined DCL in 1925, by which time the brand Peter Dawson was popular enough for the company to introduce special mallet-shaped bottled covered in 'blisters' as a protection against counterfeiting (see **VAT 69**).

Today the brand sells in such far-flung markets as Chile and Canada, Grenada and Norway, Belgium and Aruba.

DERBY SPECIAL

Category: Standard and De Luxe Blends
Owner: Kinross Whisky Co. Ltd, The Priory, Haywards Heath, Sussex
Expressions: 3, 5 and 12 Years Old

(see **Gold Blend**)

DEWAR'S WHITE LABEL

Category: Standard Blend
Licensee: John Dewar & Sons, Perth and London
Owner: United Distillers

Dewar's White Label has been, for many years, the best-selling Scotch in the United States, and is among the top five best-sellers world-wide.

The brand's story begins in 1828 when John Dewar, aged 23, walked the 25 miles from his home village of Moneydie to Perth to take up employment in a relative's wine and spirits shop. Nine years later he became a partner, but in 1846 he set up in business on his own, and opened a shop in the High Street of Perth, selling, among other items, his own blended whiskies. In the late 1860s Dewar began offering his blends in branded bottles, rather than by the keg or in plain stone jars, as was the usual custom. He was probably the first person to sell branded bottles.

John Dewar died in 1880, and was succeeded by his son John Alexander, who brought his brother, Thomas Robert, into the partnership five years later, when the latter reached the age of 21.

The Dewar brothers were men of outstanding ability, and began immediately to expand their business. Tommy went to London in 1885 to establish the firm's brands, and it has been said that he was probably more responsible than anyone else for the success of Scotch whisky in London. At the Brewer's Show in 1896 he employed pipers to draw attention to his wares and drown out any opposition! Still today, Dewar's retains the services of a piper for promotional purposes – echoing the image on the brand's label.

Before long Dewar's whiskies were in the bars of most of London's fashionable hotels, and in 1893 the firm was granted the Royal Warrant. Between 1892 and 1894 Tommy Dewar toured the world, visiting 26 countries and appointing 32 agents.

A New York office was opened in 1895, and bottling plants were built in London and Manchester in 1897 and 1898. In 1896 the firm commenced the construction of Aberfeldy Distillery to secure supplies of malt whisky (by 1923, the company also owned **Lochnagar**, **Ord**, **Pulteney**, **Aultmore**, **Parkmore** and **Benrinnes** distilleries).

John Alexander Dewar was very different from his extrovert brother. He became Treasurer of the City of Perth (for six years he was Lord Provost) and was a Liberal MP for Inverness-shire. He was made a baronet in 1907 (the first of the 'whisky barons') and was elevated to the peerage as Lord Forteviot in 1917.

Tommy Dewar became Baron Dewar of Homestall in Sussex in 1919, having been knighted in 1902. He was a Sheriff of the City of London and a Conservative Member of Parliament. Three times he was chairman of the Worshipful Company of Distillers.

The brothers died within a year of each other in 1929 and 1930. Peter Dewar (no relation) became chairman, but after 1946 the family again assumed the mantle of leadership, with John Arthur Dewar becoming Chairman and being succeeded by his cousin Evelyn Dewar, 3rd Lord Forteviot, whose son and heir is still a director.

Control of the company had long since passed into other hands, however. In 1915 Dewar's entered into 'close and permanent association' with James Buchanan & Co. Ltd, setting up Scotch Whisky Brands Ltd to pool profits and stocks (which included the largest holding of mature whisky in Scotland), and to draw on their joint resources under a management arrangement. Ten years later both companies joined DCL.

Dewar's benefited greatly from the lifting of Prohibition in the USA in 1933, and further dramatic growth continued throughout the 1950s, 60s and 70s (the company won six Queen's Awards for Export Achievement between 1966 and 1979). Today Dewar's White Label sells in 140 countries, its main markets being the USA, Greece, Venezuela, Spain, Aruba and Curacao and the Lebanon.

DIMPLE

Category: De Luxe Blend
Licensee: John Haig & Co., Markinch
Owner: United Distillers
Expressions: In North America this brand is sold as **Pinch**

(see **Haig**) The five sons of John Haig all learned distilling at Kilbagie in Kincardinshire, in the distillery of their uncle Robert Stein. The eldest son James, moved to Edinburgh aged 27, and with help from his uncle opened a distillery at Canonmills in 1782, and later at Sunbury and Lochrin. His sons continued to run the latter two, while their cousin, John, built Cameron Bridge Distillery, and later went on to develop a massive blending and bottling plant at Markinch close by. Dimple and the other Haig blends originated and are still made here.

John's son, John Alicius, established the firm of Haig & Haig Ltd in 1888 to market the family's products in the USA. Between 1909 and 1925 this company was controlled by Robertson & Baxter (see **Lang's**), before it became a subsidiary of John Haig & Co., and part of DCL. Haig & Co. was appointed purveyor to the House of Lords in 1906, and was granted a Royal Warrant by King Edward VII.

Following a ruling by the EEC Commission in 1977 concerning 'parallel exports' Dimple was withdrawn from the UK market for some years (see **John Barr**), but it has now been restored.

Dimple/Pinch's trademark has been its distinctive bottle, introduced in 1893 by George Ogilvy Haig. It has long been popular among sailors for displaying their 'ship-in-a-bottle' models, and among small boys for holding silver sixpences, when such were minted. It was the first-ever bottle to be patented in the USA, as late as 1958.

The other distinctive feature of the packaging is the wire net around the bottle. This was introduced to prevent the cork stopper from coming out during a sea voyage. The nets were specially made in France and applied by hand – expensive exercises, indicative of the value Haig's placed upon their de luxe blends. In 1987 Dimple won a gold medal at the International Wine & Spirits Competition.

DINER'S

Category: Standard and De Luxe Blends and Vatted Malt
Licensee: Douglas Denham Ltd
Owner: Red Lion Blending Co. Ltd, North End Way, London NW3
Expressions: 5, 8, 12, 21 Years Old (Blends); 15 Years Old (Vatted Malt)

The Red Lion Blending Company was established by Robert Mendelson and David Halgarten, two men well experienced in the wine and spirit trade. The two owners take an active role in the creation of the company's blends.

The company began as specialist bottlers and blenders for various companies around the world. The associate company, Douglas Denham Ltd is responsible for the range of own-label whiskies sold by Diners Club Inc. – the international credit-card company.

The 12 Years Old won prizes at the International Wine & Spirit Competition in 1979 and 1980. Red Lion Blending Company's main business is now bulk and case export.

DOCTOR'S SPECIAL

Category: Standard Blend
Licensee: Hiram Walker & Sons Ltd
Owner: Allied Distillers Ltd, 2 Glasgow Rd, Dumbarton

This brand was established by Robert McNish & Co. (see **Grand MacNish**) in the 1920s. It is only available in the Scandinavian market.

THE DOMINIE

Category: Premium Blend
Owner: Cockburn & Co. (Leith) Ltd, 11 Glenfinlas St, Edinburgh
Licensee: as above

Cockburn & Co. was established in 1796 in the prosperous port of Leith. Robert and John were the enterprising brothers who founded the business, although in the early days their names were less well known than that of their brother Henry, Lord Cockburn, the famous Scottish judge, and author of the *Memorials of My Time*. The two brothers prospered, and soon built up a large and prestigious client list. Upon his death in 1870, the inventory of Charles Dickens' cellar included "*17 dozen vey [sic] fine old whiskey Cockburn & Company, Leith*". Other clients included Sir Walter Scott, many aristocrats and even the Royal Household.

Cockburn's is better known for its port than for its whisky: one of the brothers went to Oporto and established this side of the business. The company was acquired by Drambuie in 1980, which sold it to The Wine Company (Scotland) Ltd in 1993. The latter had been set up to take over the Wine Emporium, Edinburgh (established 1986) and now trades under the distinguished name Cockburn's of Leith. The company plans to repackage and promote all Cockburn's whisky brands and to introduce their own single malt.

Dominie is the old Scots word for a minister or schoolmaster.

DRAMBUIE

Category: Whisky Liqueur
Owner: The Drambuie Liqueur Co. Ltd, 12 York Place, Edinburgh

After fleeing from his ruinous defeat at Culloden in 1746, Prince Charles Edward Stuart made his way to the isle of Skye, where he was sheltered by a loyal soldier, Captain John Mackinnon of Strathaird.

The Prince arrived at Mackinnon's house disguised as a maidservant, and spent the evening playing with his son, *"carrying him in his arms and singing to him, saying 'I hope this child may be a captain in my service yet'"*. The story goes that, on parting, the Prince had nothing to offer his host for his hospitality other than the recipe for a royal liqueur, Drambuie. The secret was kept by the family for many years – passed on down the generations and tasted only by close friends of the family.

Many years later (1906), Malcolm Mackinnon left Skye to work in Edinburgh, eventually ending up as sole proprietor of an established whisky firm, W. Macbeth & Son. Being in possession of the old family recipe for Drambuie he decided to prepare it for a wider market. With one of his employees, Sandy Cameron, he experimented with jelly bags and traditional copper pans and after two weeks the two men had filled a dozen bottles.

Initially the creation was not a success with conservative Edwardian drinkers – indeed in the first year only twelve cases were sold. But Mackinnon persevered. Skilful advertising paid off and during the Great War, Drambuie appeared in the officers' messes of Scottish regiments serving in France as an alternative to brandy. In 1916 the liqueur was ordered for the hallowed cellars of the House of Lords.

Malcolm Mackinnon died in 1945 and his widow, Gena, ran the company with her brother W.A. Davidson. After the Second World War demand for Drambuie grew steadily and a new processing plant was established at Kirknewton, outside Edinburgh.

Although many technical improvements have been introduced, it is confidently claimed that the liqueur is made to its original recipe, and it is now a household name all over the world.

The company increased its whisky interests by the acquisition in 1981 of the old Edinburgh wine and spirit merchants Cockburn & Co. (Leith) Ltd (see **The Dominie**).

DUNKELD ATHOLL BROSE

Category: Whisky Liqueur
Owner: Gordon & MacPhail, George House, Boroughbriggs Rd, Elgin

"Atholl Brose is a giant's drink" wrote Sir Robert Bruce Lockhart in his seminal book on whisky, published in 1951. However, he was not referring to the brand, for 'brose' has been drunk in the Highlands for centuries, and can be used to describe any drink.

There is, however, a curious tradition behind 'Atholl Brose'. Late in 1475 a sentence of death and forfeiture was passed on John, last Lord of the Isles. The Earls of Atholl and Crawford commanded a formidable sea-borne expedition into the Western Isles to enforce the sentence and the rebellious Lord took to the hills. The story goes that when the Earl of Atholl discovered where the fugitive was drawing water, he ordered that the well be filled with a mixture of whisky, honey, herbs and oatmeal, so as to encourage him to stay put while reinforcements were brought up. Alas, the last Lord of the Isles was beguiled, and 'Atholl Brose' was invented.

Described as 'a whisky liqueur of rare distinction', Dunkeld Atholl Brose is made to a secret recipe which dispenses with the oatmeal and uses only 12-year-old malt whisky. Gordon & MacPhail won a Silver Award in 1985 for it and Gold in 1987 at the International Wines & Spirits Competition: on the latter occasion it was named 'The Best Liqueur in the World'.

ALEXANDER DUNN

Category: Standard, Premium and De Luxe Blends; and Vatted Malt
Owner: Alexander Dunn & Co. (whisky blenders) Ltd, Bracknell, Berks
Expressions: 3 Years Old; 5 Years Old; 12 Years Old; 12 Years Old Vatted Malt

Alexander Dunn & Co. specializes in quality bottlings of wines and spirits as 'executive gifts' (see **Slaintheva**). This range was originally produced in 1987 for a French supermarket, and is now also available in Japan.

Since each expression is made to order, there is a certain amount of variation in strengths and contents.

EL VINO

Category: De Luxe Blend
Owner: El Vino Co. Ltd, Vintage House, 1 Hare Place, London EC4
Expressions: Connoisseur's Blend (7 Years Old)

El Vino wine bars have been a feature of the City of London since their foundation in 1879. They have always been wine and spirit merchants, and this distinguished blend was originally created for the company's founder, Sir Alfred Bower, in the 1880s. It was well known in London in the 1920s, when Sir Alfred was Lord Mayor and it was served at official functions.

The formula was lost after his death in 1948, and for a time the blend was unavailable. Happily, however, the original recipe was discovered in a notebook deep in Sir Alfred's desk by his grandson, David Mitchell, who is currently El Vino's Chairman.

Connoisseur's Blend is available from only one of El Vino's shops in the City, and also by mail order from the company's head office. The blend has a high malt content (about 50%), and is married in the sherry casks used to ship El Vino sherry.

THE FAMOUS GROUSE

Category: Premium Blend
Owner: Matthew Gloag & Sons, Bordeaux House, Perth

Matthew Gloag (d. 1860), the grandfather of the creator of The Famous Grouse, began life as a butler on a sporting estate near Perth. In 1797 he married the daughter of a grocer and wine merchant in Athole Street, and by 1820 had taken over the running of the business, supplying the gentry of Perthshire with provisions. When Queen Victoria visited the town in 1842, Gloag was invited to supply the wines.

Matthew's grandson, also named Matthew, worked in the wine and spirit trade in France (with Octave Calvet, of the famous family of wine négociants in Bordeaux) before returning to Perth in 1896 to take over the family business. The following year he created a new blend of house whisky, which he named The Grouse Brand, in the hope of attracting the many sportsmen who came through Perth during the shooting season. His daughter, Philippa, was responsible for the label which is still the brand's trademark. Early advertising described it as *"Mellow As A Night of Love ... One Grouse and you want No Other"*, and it proved so successful that within only a few years 'The Famous' was added, and 'Brand' dropped.

Today Matthew's great-grandson represents the family on the board – the sixth generation to do so.

By the 1920s, The Famous Grouse was dominating Gloag's business. Markets were opened up in the West Indies, and after the repeal of Prohibition in 1933 the brand was poised to sell in the USA. In 1936 a bonded warehouse and bottling plant was opened in Perth, and during the late 1930s further export markets were opened up.

The Gloag family still held all the equity in the company, but after the death of Matthew Frederick Gloag in 1970, followed within days by that of his wife, punitive death duties obliged them to sell the company to Robertson & Baxter and Highland Distilleries, from whom they had long bought the key fillings for The Famous Grouse – **Glen Rothes**, **Highland Park** and **Tamdhu**.

This provided the company with a much-needed injection of capital with which to build up stocks. At the same time, Retail Price Maintenance was abolished, which offered great opportunities to those companies which could afford to seize them.

The new owners immediately embarked on a marketing campaign for the brand which was so successful that Grouse became the fastest-growing brand in Britain, with its sales rising from 90,000 cases in 1970 to over one million cases in 1979. It has been brand leader in the discriminating Scottish market since 1980, and currently stands at number two in the UK. Its main export markets include France, Holland, Spain, Greece, the United States, South Africa, Australasia, Japan and Thailand.

FINDLATER'S FINEST

Category: Standard Blend
Licensee: Findlater Scotch Whisky Ltd (sole agent for Findlater, Mackie Todd & Co.)
Owner: The Invergordon Distillers Ltd, Leith, Edinburgh

Alexander Findlater went into business as a wine and spirit merchant in Dublin in 1823 at the age of 26. He had learned about Scotch from his father, an excise officer who had once worked with Robert Burns. The family came originally from the Moray Firth. Alexander's firm prospered and he established partnerships in various English cities, including Findlater Mackie Todd & Co. in London (in 1863).

The company holds the Royal Warrant as a supplier of wines and spirits, and its well-known product is bottled in dark green glass.

FINE OLD SPECIAL

Category: Standard Blend
Owner: Joseph Holt plc, Derby Brewery, Empire St, Cheetham, Manchester

The company was founded in 1849 and has been selling a blended whisky since very early in its history. This blend is available through the company's tied houses and free trade outlets within 20 miles of Greater Manchester.

FIRST LORD

Category: De Luxe Blend; Vatted Malt
Owner: Edwin Cheshire Ltd, Stansted, Essex
Expressions: a) 12 Years Old; b) Vatted Malt

Edwin Cheshire is a private company, and the device on the label of its brand depicts part of the coat of arms of the county of the same name – three sheaves of corn. The title 'First Lord' (now defunct) was that of the senior officer in the Royal Navy. The title persists in the First Lord of the Treasury (the British Prime Minister). The brands sell mainly in the export market.

FORTNUM & MASON (OWN LABEL)

Category: Premium and De Luxe Blends; Old Malt
Owner: Fortnum & Mason plc, Piccadilly, London W1
Expressions: 8 and 12 Years Old, and 'Choice Old' Blend; Linkwood 21 Years Old (see **Linkwood**)

Fortnum & Mason (est. 1707) is probably the most famous food store in the world, with a distinguished reputation for the high quality of its products. Fortnum & Mason's Choice Old has been available for many years, exclusively from the shop in Piccadilly.

FRASER MCDONALD

Category: Standard Blend
Licensee: Fraser McDonald Distillery Co. Ltd
Owner: Gibson International Ltd, 52–58 Weston St, London SE1

Fraser McDonald Distillery & Co. was one of the thirteen companies which joined together to form Amalgamated Distilled Products plc (see **Royal Culross**). I have been unable to obtain any information about this company or the brand.

FRASER'S SUPREME

Category: Standard Blend
Licensee: Strathnairn Whisky Ltd, Inverness
Owner: Gordon & MacPhail, George House, Boroughbriggs Rd, Elgin

(see **MacPhail's**)

GAIRLOCH

Category: Standard Blend
Owner: McMullen & Sons Ltd, 26 Old Cross, Hertford, Herts
Expressions: Superior Standard (4 and 5 Years Old)

McMullen & Sons is an established firm of independent brewers and wine and spirit merchants, who used to buy in single malts and blend Gairloch themselves. This is now done to their specifications by a blender in Scotland, who they consider to be 'the most knowledgeable sassanach in the industry', and who was responsible for training the Master Blender at Matthew Gloag & Co. (see **Famous Grouse**). First created in 1904, Gairloch is named after the port in Easter Ross on the loch of the same name. It mainly sells in the on-trade in the northern Home Counties.

A number of first-division malts are used in Gairloch, mainly from the Highland Distilleries/Robertson & Baxter stable, and including **Glengoyne**, **Glen Rothes**, **Highland Park**, **Tamdhu** and **Macallan** (all 3–4 Years Old).

GALE'S

Category: Standard Blend
Owner: George Gale & Co. Ltd, The Hampshire Brewery, Horndean, Hants
Expressions: 8 Years Old

George Gale & Co. traces its origins to the 1730s, and the purchase of the Ship and Bell Public House in Horndean, near Portsmouth. Today the company's principal activity is brewing, with a tied estate of 154 pubs and about 300 free-trade customers, mainly in Hampshire, West and East Sussex, Wiltshire, Surrey, Berkshire and the Isle of Wight. Their 'own name' whisky is sold through these outlets.

Gale's Blended Glenlivet, as it was originally named, was first created over 100 years ago, the title being allowed by verbal agreement with George & J.G. Smith (see **The Glenlivet**). When Glenlivet Distillery became part of Seagram's, it was thought wise to drop the appellation! Unlike many blend owners (and to their credit) George Gale & Co. is happy to declare the fillings for their blend: Glenlivet, Ben Nevis, Dufftown, Glen Grant, Bunnahbhain, Highland Park and Dalmore. Grains are: Strathclyde, Dumbarton, Cameron Brig and North British.

GAMEFAIR

Category: Vatted Malt
Owner: Hynard Hughes, Overton Rd, Leicester
Expressions: 10 Years Old

Hynard Hughes, wine merchants, was established in Leicester in 1926. It is still a family company, directed by Messrs M.W., J.M. and I.C. Hynard. The brand is popular locally.

GILLON'S

Category: Standard Blend
Licensee: John Gillon & Co., Glasgow and Stonehaven
Owner: United Distillers

The firm, established in 1817 by Sir John Gillon of Linlithgow, was acquired by Ainslie & Heilbron (see **Ainslie's**), became part of Macdonald, Greenlees & Co. (see **Old Parr**) and joined DCL in 1925. For many years Glenury Distillery was licensed to Gillon & Co. (see **Glenury Royal**). Italy is currently its only market.

GLAYVA

Category: Whisky Liqueur
Licensee: Glayva Liqueur Co.
Owner: The Invergordon Distillers Ltd, Salamander Place, Leith

This whisky liqueur is popular with ex-patriate Scots worldwide, and is available in most whisky markets, doing especially well in Australia, Canada, South Africa, New Zealand and Portugal.

It was introduced many years ago by Ronald Morrison & Co. Ltd, of Leith, a well-known firm of wine merchants and whisky blenders, and was the invention of Ronald Morrison himself and George Petrie, a flavour expert and rectifier, who spent months blending malt and grain whiskies with heather honey, herbs and botanicals (even some tangerine) before their Gaelic-speaking warehouseman pronounced the blend to be 'Gle Mhath' ('very good').

Glayva is the main sponsor of the world-famous Edinburgh Military Tattoo, and also supports curling throughout Scotland. It is a versatile drink, and may be enjoyed long or short (best over ice). It is also used successfully in cooking.

Tasting Notes: A delicate nose, sweet, full, mellow with a hint of tangerine. Extremely syrupy mouth-feel, with a rich, sweet, herbal, slightly tangerine flavour and a long, syrupy finish.

GLEN BAREN

Category: Vatted Malt
Owner: Kinross Whisky Co. Ltd, The Priory, Haywards Heath, Sussex
Expressions: 5 Years Old, 8 Years Old

(see **Gold Blend**)

GLEN CALDER

Category: Standard Blend
Owner: Gordon & MacPhail, George House, Boroughbriggs Rd, Elgin
Expressions: Also a 1949 bottling

(see **MacPhail's**) The name commemorates not a place but a person, Sir James Calder, MP in the 17th century for the Royal Burgh of Elgin. He built a mansion in North Street, Elgin, not far from Gordon & MacPhail's shop, which later acquired a reputation for being haunted.

GLEN CARREN

Category: Vatted Malt
Owner: Hall & Bramley Ltd, Aintree Building, Ormskirk Rd, Liverpool
Expressions: 10 Years Old

(see **Glen Ghoil**)

GLEN CATRINE

Category: Standard Blend
Owner: Glen Catrine Bonded Warehouse Ltd, Laigh Rd, Catrine, Ayrshire

This family-owned company has its origins in A. Bulloch & Co., established in 1856, a wine and spirit merchant based in Glasgow.

From the outset the company blended and bottled its own whisky brands, of which **High Commissioner** is the oldest. In 1973 the business was moved to a bonded warehouse in Catrine, Ayrshire, to allow for the expansion of the blending and bottling facilities.

In 1985 Loch Lomond Distillery was acquired from Inverhouse Distillers Ltd (see **Inchmurrin**). It resumed operation in 1987, and the company is completing the construction of an adjacent grain distillery, to commence production in autumn 1993. It will be the most technologically advanced of its kind to date.

The chairman of Glen Catrine is Alexander Bulloch, a direct descendant of the founder.

GLENCOE

Category: Vatted Malt
Licensee: R.N. MacDonald & Co. Ltd
Owner: Red Lion Blending Co. Ltd, North End Way, London NW3

(see **Diner's**) Glencoe is one of the most dramatic places in all of Scotland. Narrow and set about with high peaks, it is reputed to be the birthplace of Ossian, son of Fingal, the 3rd-century Scottish bard, whose work was 'discovered' by controversial literary figure James MacPherson in the late 18th century. It was also once the home of the MacDonalds of Glencoe, who suffered an attempted genocide in 1692. The fate of the Episcopalian/Jacobite cause was sealed when James II/VII went into exile in 1689, and the Presbyterian/Williamite governors of Scotland set about suborning the Episcopalian clans, among them Clan Donald.

King William offered a pardon to those chiefs who would take the oath of allegiance to him. However, the Campbell faction in the government — bitter enemies of the MacDonalds — had resolved to make an example of the MacDonalds of Glencoe. Even although their chief took the oath (five days late, owing to bad weather) two companies of Campbell militia were dispatched, led by Captain Robert Campbell of Glenlyon, with orders to exterminate the entire tribe of about 400 souls.

The Campbells arrived in February 1692, billeted themselves upon the MacDonalds for nearly two weeks and were received with customary Highland hospitality, then they rose up at dawn and set about their hosts as they slept. About 40 men and women were killed in their beds; the rest fled into the ferocious mountains, where many more perished in the snow. Massacres and bloody feuds were not uncommon in the Highlands. The particular horror of the Massacre of Glencoe lies in the breach of hospitality, traditionally inviolable in the Highlands, whatever the differences between host and guest. Still today there are MacDonalds who will not drink with Campbells, and the pub in Glencoe will not serve anyone who admits to the name.

GLENDARROCH

Category: De Luxe Blend
Owner: William Gillies & Co. Ltd, 53 Bothwell St, Glasgow
Expressions: 12 Years Old

'Darroch' is the Gaelic for an oak tree. I am unable to elicit any information about this company.

GLENDOWER

Category: Vatted Malt
Owner: Burn Stewart Distillers plc, 65 Kelburn St, Barrhead, Glasgow

An odd name for a whisky, this, since there is no Glen Dower in Scotland, and the name must refer to Owen Glendower (1359–1415), the last independent prince of Wales. Glendower was a national hero who campaigned against the English, and of whom it has been said that "Wales was never so close to being united and independent than under Owen's leadership". The market for the brand which bears his name is chiefly in France, Italy and Japan. (See also **Burn Stewart**.)

GLEN FLAGLER

Category: Vatted Malt
Owner: Inver House Distillers, Airdrie, Lanarkshire

Glen Flagler Lowland Malt Distillery was situated close to Moffat, near Airdrie, and its product was available as a single malt during the 1960s and 70s. The distillery was closed and dismantled in 1985. Inver House, its owner, still has stocks of Glen Flagler (the malt) but does not sell it as such, preferring to vat it with other malts and sell it as Glen Flagler Pure Malt Special Reserve. Thus is the name perpetuated.

GLEN GARRY

Category: Standard Blend
Licensee: John Hopkins & Co., Glasgow
Owner: United Distillers

In 1874 John Hopkins acquired the British agency for Otard cognac, one of the most famous names in the business. He immediately established a company to purvey this and to develop whisky brands, recruiting his brother and cousin to help him. Glen Garry was registered in April 1878 and won 'the highest award' at the Chicago Exhibition in 1892. In 1900 the firm's bonded warehouse complex in Glasgow was destroyed by fire (it was rebuilt and reopened the following year). John Hopkins retired from the business in 1911, and five years later the firm became a limited company. In 1916 the entire share capital was acquired by DCL, but it did not become part of the larger company until 1931 (see also **Oban**, **Tobermory**). Glen Garry is now sold exclusively in Spain.

GLEN GHOIL

Category: Standard Blend
Owner: Hall & Bramley Ltd, Aintree Building, Ormskirk Rd, Liverpool

In 1860 Charlton R. Hall, a prominent Liverpool businessman, set up as a wholesale wine and spirit merchant at 17 Dale Street, Liverpool. His son, Charlton R. Hall Jnr, succeeded his father and went into partnership with J.T Bramley. In 1892, the firm was referred to as "*one of the most noteworthy wine & spirit houses in the City*"; by 1900 it was trading under the name Charleton R. Hall

& Bramley, and the partners had secured the agency for Glen Grant, and were blending their own whisky, Glen Ghoil.

In 1922 two senior members of staff took over, and registered the company as Hall & Bramley Ltd. They opened a bonded warehouse at Henry Street, where they blended and bottled Scotch whisky, Irish whiskey and rum, and acquired the North of England agency for Gonzalez Byass (sherry) and Charles Heidsieck (champagne) which expanded the business considerably. In the 1960s the company diversified into French and German wines, requiring a move to larger premises beside the famous Aintree racecourse.

Today Hall & Bramley is the only long-established independent shipper in Liverpool and continues to blend and fill its own Scotch whisky. The company owns Golding Hoptroff Ltd which specializes in transportation for the wine and spirit trade.

GLEN GYLE

Category: Vatted Malt
Licensee: Fraser Macdonald Distillery Co. Ltd
Owner: Gibson International Ltd, 52–56 Weston St, London SE1
Expressions: 8 Years Old

(see **Royal Culross**) Vatted exclusively from Highland malts.

GLEN LYON

Category: Standard Blend
Licensee: Glen Lyon Blending Co., Glasgow
Owner: United Distillers

Originally a vatted malt, the blend sells in South Africa. The Glen Lyon Blending Company was a subsidiary of Macleay Duff.

GLEN NEVIS

Category: De Luxe Blend
Owner: Gibson International Ltd, 52–58 Weston St, London SE1
Expressions: 12 Years Old

(see **Royal Culross**)

GLEN NIVEN

Category: Standard Blend
Licensee: Douglas MacNiven & Co. Ltd, Leith
Owner: Macdonald Martin Distilleries plc, 186 Commercial St, Leith

(see **Highland Queen**, **James Martin's**) Glen Niven is available throughout the world in small quantities.

GLEN SHEE

Category: Standard Blend
Licensee: Findlater Mackie Todd & Co. Ltd, Merton Abbey, London SW1

Owner: Whitmore & Bayley
Expressions: 3 and 5 Years Old

(see **Findlater's Finest**) One of the Angus Glens, reaching north from Blairgowrie into the Grampian Mountains, Glen Shee means 'the glen of the fairies'. More prosaically, it has been a popular ski resort for over 20 years.

GLENSIDE

Category: Standard Blend
Owner: Thresher Ltd, Sefton House, Welwyn Garden City

In 1911, Glenside, a bay gelding with a pronounced blaze, was ridden to victory in the Grand National by one of the few amateur jockeys in the race, Jack Anthony. Glenside was the only horse to complete the race without mishap, a remarkable achievement since he was marked No. 13 and started at odds of 20–1! This blend is sold exclusively through the UK off-licence chain Thresher's.

GLEN STUART

Category: Standard Blend & Vatted Malt
Owner: W. Brown & Sons Ltd, 33 Townsend St, Glasgow
Expressions: 5 Years Old Blend; 5, 8, 12 Years Old Vatted Malts

Both the grandfther and great grandfather of William Brown had been spirits merchants in Glasgow, and when he set up his own company in 1976, his aim was to concentrate exclusively on export markets. The company is family owned and controlled (four of W. Brown's sons currently sit on the board), and as well as exporting Scotch whisky, it imports and bottles Jamaican rum, gin and vodka.

Several of Brown's brands were bought from The Stuart Whisky Company in the late 1970s, and have been registered for many years (included Glen Stuart, the company's leading brand); none of them is available in the home market.

GLENTROMIE

Category: Vatted Malt
Owner: Speyside Distillery Co. Ltd, 1 Park Circus, Glasgow
Expressions: 12 Years Old; 17 Years Old

The Speyside Distillery is situated on the banks of the river Tromie, near Kingussie (see **Speyside**) – hence the name of their vatted malt, which is largely composed of Highland malts and sells mainly in France, Japan and the USA.

GLEN URQUHART

Category: Standard Blend
Owner: Gordon & MacPhail, George House, Boroughbriggs Rd, Elgin

(see **MacPhail's**) Gordon & MacPhail is by far the world's largest specialist dealer in malt whisky. In the first year of trading (1895)

John Urquhart joined the firm. His youngest son, George (who joined the firm in 1933) and grandchildren now own and manage the company.

GOLD BLEND

Category: Standard Blend
Owner: Kinross Whisky Co. Ltd, The Priory, Haywards Heath, Sussex

Kinross is a family company, founded in 1970 by John Stoppani, his wife and sons, following research into export whisky markets. Gold Blend and their other brands are currently available in Europe, the Far East, parts of Africa, and Ecuador.

GOLD LABEL

Category: Standard Blend
Owner: Red Lion Blending Co. Ltd, North End Way, London NW3

The main markets for this whisky, the creation of which – like all the company's products – is personally supervised by the two owners of the company, are the Far East, South America, Europe and Japan (see **Diner's**).

GOLDEN CAP

Category: Standard Blend
Owner: J.C. & R.H. Palmer Ltd, The Old Brewery, Bridport, Dorset

The brand is named after the highest point on the south coast of England, Golden Cap cliff, and was first created in the 1930s by H.R.C. Palmer. J.C. & R.H. Palmer are brewers in the West Country and sell their brand through their tenanted public houses, to the free trade and through their own off-trade Wine Store, which is adjacent to the brewery. Golden Cap is available only in west Dorset, east Devon and south-east Somerset, in which parts it has a devoted following.

GOLDEN PIPER

Category: Standard Blend
Owner: Lombard Scotch Whisky Ltd, Ramsay, Isle of Man

(see **Lombard's**)

JAMES GORDON'S

Category: Premium Blend
Licensee: James Gordon & Co., Elgin
Owner: Gordon & MacPhail, George House, Boroughbriggs Rd, Elgin

(see **MacPhail's**) James Gordon went into partnership with John Alexander MacPhail in 1895 as 'Italian warehousemen'. Whisky blending and bottling was an important part of their business from early on, and the firm also had a broking side which dealt in mature whiskies: this was named James Gordon & Co.

GRAND MACNISH

Category: Standard and De Luxe Blends
Owner: MacDuff International Ltd, 299 West George St, Glasgow
Expressions: Standard Blend; De Luxe 12 Years Old

The Grand MacNish was created by Robert McNish (the name of the whisky was given an extra letter to make it easier to pronounce), a licensed grocer specializing in tea, tobacco and whisky, who established his business in York Street, Glasgow, in 1863.

It was his goal to create a blend which was lighter than usual but which had the appearance of a mature malt. Over forty different whiskies went into his recipe and the result was a product much lighter-bodied than single Highland malt, but with a full flavour.

Robert McNish died in 1904 and was succeeded by his two sons, John and George, who formed a limited company in 1908, moved to larger premises and laid down a large stock of maturing whisky. John, who had a flair for salesmanship and entertaining, moved to London; George remained in Glasgow to supervise production. He served in the Highland Light Infantry during the First World War, rising to the rank of colonel, and was awarded the CBE in 1919. On his return to civilian life he resumed his business activities, local government and charity work, becoming Deputy Lord Lieutenant for the City of Glasgow and a JP. He died in 1943 aged 77. Colonel McNish renamed his brand 'Grand' MacNish, simply because so many of his friends referred to it as 'grr-and' whisky! He also adopted the motto *Forti Nihil Difficile* ('to the strong nothing is difficult') which was included when the company's arms were registered in 1945.

In 1927 the company was sold to Canadian Industrial Alcohol Ltd of Montreal (which changed its name to Corby Distilleries Ltd in 1950), but remained based in Scotland: export sales of Grand MacNish, in North America and elsewhere, were boosted considerably by the sale.

In 1967 Corby authorized Hiram Walker (Scotland) to manage the brand (see **Ballantine's**), and during the reorganization which followed Hiram Walker's merger with Allied Vintners Grand MacNish was dropped, along with **Lauder's**. In 1991 both brands were sold to MacDuff International Ltd which has relaunched them in the North and Central American, French and South African markets, where they are already selling very well.

WILLIAM GRANT'S

Category: Standard Blend
Owner: William Grant & Sons Ltd, 206–208 West George St, Glasgow
Expressions: Family Reserve (Standard); 12 Years Old (Premium); Royal (12 Years Old, De Luxe); Superior Strength (100° proof); Classic (18 Years Old, De Luxe); 21 Years Old (Decanter, De Luxe)

William Grant & Sons has prospered in family ownership for five generations, and there are currently nine direct descendants of the founder in senior management positions in the company. The appropriately named Family Reserve (formerly Standfast) is among the top ten best-selling whiskies in the world; it is usually placed fourth in the UK market, and is the third most popular wine and spirit brand in world duty-free outlets. Over the past decade sales have grown by 57% (while total Scotch whisky sales have declined by 12%). It has been particularly successful in France, where sales rose from 3 million bottles in 1988 to nearly 8 million bottles in 1991, and is showing growth in markets as diverse as Spain, Portugal, Greece, Canada and South America.

The brand came about as a result of a crisis. William Grant and his nine children had established the **Glenfiddich** and **Balvenie** distilleries in the 1880s and 90s. Their principal customer was Pattison's of Leith, one of the largest blenders and wholesalers in the country, which unexpectedly collapsed in 1898. To avoid the same fate, the family decided to blend and market their own whisky, and named it with the Grant battle-cry 'Standfast'.

William Grant's son-in-law, Charles Gordon, became sales manager, and after 503 visits in Glasgow had only sold a single case! But his perseverence paid off gradually: In 1904 an office was opened in Blackburn, Lancashire; in 1905 another member of the family was dispatched to Canada and the USA with instructions to set up distribution networks; and in 1909 Charles Gordon embarked on a year-long tour of the Far East. By 1914 William Grant & Sons had established 60 agencies in 30 countries.

In 1957 the company sought a way to distinguish their product on the shelf, and came up with the now familiar triangular bottle. This helped to fix the brand in customers' memories, and the move was so successful that William Grant & Sons built their own grain distillery at Girvan in Ayrshire in 1963 - at the time, the largest and most technically advanced distillery in Europe - and another malt distillery on the same site (see **Ladyburn**). A fourth malt distillery was opened in 1990 at Kininvie, Dufftown.

GRIERSON'S NO. I

Category: Vatted Malt
Owner: Grierson's Ltd, 430 High Rd, Willesden, London NW10
Expressions: 12 Years Old

Grierson's is a well-known company of wine shippers and merchants, and a major supplier to the hotel and restaurant trade. The company was established in 1820 with a shop in Strand, London, and now has a product range of over 1,500 lines.

HAIG

Category: Standard and De Luxe Blends
Licensee: John Haig & Co., Clackmannan and London (Haig currently licensed to Whyte & Mackay in UK)
Owner: United Distillers
Expressions: Haig; Gold Label (see also **Pinch**, **Dimple**)

With good reason, the Haig family is described as 'the oldest name in Scotch whisky'. Connections with whisky distilling go back to at least 1655, when Robert Haig, a farmer at Throsk in Stirlingshire (and younger son of the ancient Bemersyde Haigs), was summoned before the Kirk Session for distilling on the Sabbath. It is supposed that he had been making whisky for his own domestic use since 1627, when he arrived at Throsk.

In 1751 Robert's great-great-grandson, John, married Margaret Stein, whose family had established successful distilleries at Kilbagie and Kennetpans in Clackmannanshire. John Haig died in 1773, leaving Margaret with five sons, all of whom were trained in their uncle's distilleries, and in time established their own distilleries in Edinburgh, Leith, Kincardine, Seggie (near Guardbridge in Fife) and Dublin.

By the 1770s Kilbagie was the largest distillery in Scotland, and by 1784 the Haig and Stein families were exporting 400,000 gallons (1.8 million litres) of whisky a year, mainly to London (where most of it was 'rectified' into gin) and mainly from grain imported from Europe (harvests had been poor in Scotland in the early 1780s, and the distilleries had even been attacked by mobs).

In 1824 a grandson of John Haig, also named John, built a grain distillery at Cameron Bridge in Fife, installing (in 1827) the recently invented Stein Patent Stills (see **Cameron Brig**). Production was immense, and led to amalgamation with other grain distillers to form DCL in 1877. John and one of his sons became directors of the new company; another son became company secretary.

John Haig & Co. had been producing blended whisky since the 1850s, and by John Haig's death in 1878, the company was producing annually over a million gallons (over 4.5 million litres). The blending side was transferred to Markinch, three miles from Cameron Bridge, and in 1894 John's youngest son, Captain Douglas Haig, joined the board.

Douglas Haig was to become Commander-in-Chief of the British Forces in France in 1916 and a Field Marshall. He was created Earl Haig after the War, became chairman of the family business in the 1920s, died in 1928 and was buried in Dryburgh Abbey – a privilege which had been enjoyed by the Haig family since the 13th century. Beside him is the tomb of Sir Walter Scott.

In spite of being one of the moving forces behind DCL, John Haig & Co. only merged with the larger company in 1919. By 1939, Haig was the best-selling whisky in the UK, supported by its well-known slogan 'Don't be vague, ask for Haig': today it ranks thirteenth in the UK and twentieth in the world. In 1986 the UK rights to the brand were sold to Whyte & Mackay, the rest of the world being controlled by United Distillers.

HANKEY BANNISTER

Category: Standard and De Luxe Blends
Licensee: Hankey Bannister & Co.
Owner: Inver House Distillers Ltd, Airdrie, Lanarkshire
Expressions: De Luxe at 12 Years Old

Hankey Bannister (wine and spirit merchants) was established in the fashionable West End of London in 1757. The company enjoyed royal and aristocratic patronage (customers included the Prince Regent, King William IV and the Dukes of Norfolk and Queensberry), and began marketing its own blended whisky in the 1890s. The old-established wines and spirits company Saccone & Speed, which bought the company in 1932, and which had long associations with the armed forces, extended the brand's cachet by introducing it into diplomatic circles, army messes and naval ward rooms. Today the brand is owned by Inver House, which has succeeded in doubling its market in recent years, selling large quantities in South Africa, France and Holland as well as in the UK (see **Inver House**).

HART'S

Category: Standard Blend
Owner: Donald Hart & Co. Ltd, 85 Springkell Ave, Glasgow
Expressions: 8 Years Old

This company was formed after Hart Bros (Vintners) (established in 1967) went into receivership in 1985. There is also an associate company, Hart Bros (1988) Ltd, which is used to market the exclusive 31 Years Old Bowmore Dynasty Decanter.

HARVEY'S SPECIAL

Category: Standard Blend
Licensee: John & Robert Harvey, Glasgow
Owner: United Distillers

John and Robert Harvey set up first as grocers and wine merchants, then as distillers (at Dundashill) in Glasgow in 1770. They began to blend their own whiskies about 100 years later, but were badly hit by the collapse of Pattison's of Leith in 1898, and applied to join DCL. At the time, DCL was engaged in other negotiations, so did not acquire Harvey's share capital until 1902, by which time Dundashill Distillery had closed. DCL did not reopen it, since at that time the industry was suffering from over-production.

Harvey's is blended for the USA (shipped in bulk) and for Israel (bottled in Scotland). Rare bottles can be found in the UK on-trade.

HEATHERDALE

Category: Standard Blend
Licensee: (in UK) Co-operative Wholesale Ltd, Baytree Land, Middleton, Manchester
Owner: (worldwide) Invergordon Distillers Ltd

A respectable 'own-label', blended and married for the CWS at Invergordon. CWS also has a 12 years old vatted malt, Glenfairn, which is made by Invergordon Distillers.

HEDGES & BUTLER ROYAL

Category: Standard and De Luxe Blends
Licensee: Hedges & Butler Ltd
Owner: Bass Export Ltd, Elmbank Chambers, 289 Bath St, Glasgow
Expressions: Standard and 12 Years Old

Hedges & Butler was established in 1667, as a firm of wine shippers and blenders and has enjoyed the patronage of the royal household since the reign of Charles II. Their services to royalty extend beyond Europe: the company can boast eleven past Royal Warrants, including that of the Emperor of Japan. Hedges & Butler began blending and exporting whisky after the First World War and the Royal range has had a good reputation as premium whisky for some years. The company is now a subsidiary of Bass plc, the major brewers. Royal De Luxe is not available in Britain although it is well established in the European export market.

HIGH COMMISSIONER

Category: Standard Blend
Owner: Glen Catrine Bonded Warehouse Ltd, Laigh Rd, Catrine, Ayrshire

This blend is the company's biggest brand selling in the UK market (see **Glen Catrine**).

HIGHLAND BLEND

Category: Premium Blend
Owner: Avery's of Bristol, 7 Park St, Bristol
Expressions: 15 Years Old

Bristol has always been one of England's major ports, and has long had trading links with Europe. The city's records show that in 1726 casks of wine captured from French ships were auctioned at an old coaching inn close to the harbour, and this inn subsequently became the premises of Avery's (1793): a hundred years later the firm was described as "*having a leading position in the trade of Bristol and a high reputation for quality*". Avery's great reputation was, and is, based upon their wines (principally from Bordeaux and Burgundy), sherries and madeiras. The first members of the family mentioned in the records were Joseph (who had been a customs officer) and his sons Joseph Clark and John.In 1923 Ronald Avery, John's grandson, joined the successful family business and set about expanding it, building up a tremendous stock of wines and creating the company's reputation as shippers and blenders. The company's very considerable wine-blending experience was also turned to whisky, although their most distinguished brands – Queen Elizabeth and Highland Blend – are now blended and bottled for them (owing to restrictions being placed upon independent bottlers in the early 1980s). Each of these blends retains an unusual old-fashioned quality: the only other blend I have encountered with this quality is **James Gordon's**. Ronald Avery died in 1976 and was succeeded by his son, John – one of the pioneers of New World wines – who has developed the company's agency side, and established the whisky brands in the export market, especially in Japan.

HIGHLAND CLAN

Category: Standard Blend
Owner: The Highland Bonding Co. Ltd
Licensee: The Seagram Co. Ltd, Montreal, Canada

(see **100 Pipers**)

HIGHLAND FUSILIER

Category: Vatted Malt
Owner: Gordon & MacPhail, George House, Boroughbriggs Rd, Elgin
Expressions: 5, 8, 15, 21 and 25 Years Old

(see **MacPhail's**) The Royal Highland Fusiliers regiment was formed in 1959 by the amalgamation of the Royal Scots Fusiliers (the 21st Fusiliers) and the Highland Light Infantry (the 71st and

74th Highlanders). Highland Fusilier was first created to mark the amalgamation. The 21st was the first Infantry Regiment of the Line to be raised in Scotland (in 1678); the 71st was the first Clan Regiment, raised in 1777 by John Mackenzie, Lord Macleod, and originally mustered in Elgin; the 74th was a Campbell regiment, raised in Argyll in 1788.

The brand won double Gold Awards at the International Wine & Spirits Competition in 1981, and a gold in 1982.

HIGHLAND GATHERING

Category: De Luxe Blend
Owner: Lombard Scotch Whisky Ltd, College St, Ramsey, Isle of Man
Expressions: Standard, 8, 12 15, 18, 21 and 25 Years Old (21 and 25 also available in porcelain decanters)

Highland Gathering was launched in September 1992 for world-wide distribution. The label features a painting of the same name by the 19th-century artist Louis Boswell Hurt, RA (1856–1929), in the collection of the Lombard-Chibnell family, the brand owners. As well as describing the gathering of Highland cows depicted in the painting, the brand name would like to imply the collection of whiskies which go into the blend.

HIGHLAND PEARL

Category: De Luxe Blend
Owner: Hall & Bramley Ltd, Aintree Building, Ormskirk Rd, Liverpool
Expressions: 12 Years Old

(see **Glen Ghoil**)

HIGHLAND QUEEN

Category: Premium Blend; De Luxe Blends
Licensee: Macdonald & Muir Ltd, Leith
Owner: Macdonald Martin Distilleries plc, 186 Commercial St, Leith
Expressions: Highland Queen Grand Reserve (15 Years Old); Highland Queen Supreme (21 Years Old)

Macdonald & Muir was founded in 1893 by Roderick Macdonald and Alexander Muir, at Leith, the port of Edinburgh. Roderick Macdonald's grandson is currently chairman of the company. Blending and bottling is done in the company's premises in Leith. Mary Queen of Scots landed at Leith in 1561 from France, recently widowed (she had been married to the Dauphin) and about to be crowned Queen of Scots.

To commemorate this event, the company named their leading blend Highland Queen (the label is decorated with a picture of the queen riding a white palfry), and with it pioneered the sale of Scotch in Mexico, Egypt, Scandinavia and parts of South America and the Far East. Today Highland Queen sells in 43 countries, and although not as common as it once was (and should be) in Scotland, it is very well thought of by connoisseurs (see **Glenmorangie**, **James Martin's**).

HIGHLAND STAG

Category: Standard Blend
Licensee: R.N. MacDonald & Co. Ltd
Owner: Red Lion Blending Co. Ltd, North End Way, London NW3

R.N. MacDonald & Co. was founded in 1970 by Major Andrew MacDonald, the great grandson of 'Long' John Macdonald – one of the best-known characters in the Scotch whisky industry, who established the **Ben Nevis** Distillery at Fort William. In 1982 the company was acquired by Highland Stag Whiskies. Highland Stag is marketed exclusively through Aldi supermarkets in England and is distributed in France by Champagne-Deutz (see **Diner's**).

HIGHLAND WOODCOCK

Category: Standard Blend
Owner: J.T. Davies & Sons Ltd, 7 Aberdeen Rd, Croydon, Surrey

J. T. Davies & Sons is a family business, established in 1875. Its eponymous founder died in 1913, when he was succeeded by his two sons. One of them, Alfred, built up the firm and then became personal private secretary to Lloyd George during the 1914–18 war. He was MP for Lincoln from 1918 to 1926, was knighted in 1933 and died in 1942. His sons, John and Anthony, joined the firm before the Second World War – John was killed in 1940 leading a Polish Hurricane squadron. At the end of the war Anthony returned to head the company and proceeded to expand the business to 80 wine shops (under the 'Davisons' name), a managed and tenanted public-house estate and a wholesale division serving the Greater London area. In 1985 Anthony's son Michael became managing director of the company and has continued to increase its profile, winning (in 1990 and 1992) the *Wine* magazine and *Sunday Telegraph* 'Wine Merchant of the Year' (Regional Chain) awards.

HOUSE OF LORDS

Category: De Luxe Blends
Licensee: William Whiteley & Co., Glenforres Glenlivet, Pitlochry
Owner: Campbell Distillers, 924 Great West Rd, Brentford, Middlesex (a subsidiary of Pernod Ricard)
Expressions: 8 and 12 Years Old

The company was founded in 1922 by William Whiteley, a Leith whisky blender who had inherited the family firm from his grandfather – the latter having set up business in the mid-19th century. Whiteley, known as 'the dean of distillers', was one of the characters of the industry in his day. He was highly respected as a blender and was ahead of his time as a marketing man (see **Edradour**). One of his ploys was to create a blend especially for the House of Lords, and then to market it overseas so successfully it was soon in demand in 94 countries. He also managed to persuade the College of Arms to grant his company a coat of arms which uses the griffons of Westminster as supporters.

Today these blends are only available in the UK in the House of Lords, but are available in the export market. They are especially popular in the USA.

HOUSE OF PEERS

Category: De Luxe Blend and Super-de Luxe Blend; Vatted Malt
Owner: Douglas Laing & Co. Ltd, Douglas House, 18 Lynedoch Crescent, Glasgow
Expressions: De Luxe; X.O. Extra Old; 12 Years Old; 22 Years Old (Vatted Malt)

Douglas Laing & Co. maintains that it is able to use unusually old malt fillings in its blends, yet still sell them at a manageable price, by using young (and therefore cheaper) grain fillings (see **King of Scots**). The brand has been marketed since 1947 and is presented in a traditional style of bottle, known as a 'mason's mallet' (**Old Parr** uses the same style, but it is dark green). The whiskies sold under the House of Peers label are similar in character, with the malt fillings becoming progressively older. Several of the malts in the 12 Years Old are considerably older than 12 years, and the blend is returned to oak barrels for marrying; the vatted malt draws constituents from Islay, Speyside and the Lowlands, each of them aged for at least 22 years.

100 PIPERS

Category: Standard Blend
Licensee: Joseph E. Seagram & Sons, Ltd
Owner: The Seagram Company Ltd, Montreal, Canada

Until the amalgamation of Guinness plc with Arthur Bell & Co., the Seagram Company was the largest producer of alcoholic beverages in the world.

The Seagram's were farmers and inn-keepers from Wiltshire who emigrated to Canada in the early 19th century. The next generation turned to grain-milling and distilling, and in 1857 Joseph Emm Seagram founded the family distilling business in Waterloo, Ontario. The founder has been described as "a pompous and flamboyant man, who modelled himself on Edward VII" (P. C. Newman), and his company soon became the largest distiller of Canadian rye whisky.

After Joseph Seagram's death, control of the company was divided between his family, and in 1928 his own shares were acquired by The Distillers Corporation Ltd of Canada. This company was headed by one of the great figures of the whisky industry, Samuel Bronfman.

Bronfman's first involvement with wines as spirits was as an inter-provincial, mail-order distributor – an arrangement whereby he bought quantities of wines and spirits direct from distillers and vintners, and sold them by mail order to individual homes. This system ended in the 1920s when the provincial governments took over the sale of alcohol in their areas, so Bronfman decided to build his own distillery at La Salle, a suburb of Montreal.

During the First World War Canadian distilleries were closed down and the only whisky available was Scotch. In order to retain this market after the war, Bronfman invited The Distillers Company Ltd of Scotland to buy shares in Distillers Corporation, and by this move he secured not only supplies of Scotch, but the licences to several popular brand names.

By 1928, when he bought Seagram's, Bronfman was convinced that Prohibition in the US would shortly end. He increased production at both La Salle and Waterloo, built warehouses and began to assemble a huge stock of maturing whiskies.

At this time DCL decided to concentrate their energies on Scottish distilling and exports and sold their shares back to Bronfman. A few years earlier Bronfman had travelled to Scotland to pursue his interests in Scotch whisky, and with the help of his friend James Barclay (see **Ballantine's**) he bought the Robert Brown Company and began to lay down stocks of Scotch.

In 1949 he bought Chivas Bros (see **Chivas Regal**), the producer of the world's most popular de luxe whisky, and Milton/Strathisla Distillery (see **Strathisla**). He also bought land at Keith, Paisley and Dalmuir on Clydeside. On these sites he built warehouses and blending and bottling plants: Paisley is now the Distillers Corporation – Seagram's headquarters in Scotland, and holds one of the largest stocks of Scotch whisky in the world.

In 1957 the Corporation built Glen Keith Distillery and Bond; Braes of Glenlivet followed in 1973 and Alt a'Bhainne in 1975. This portfolio of distinguished distilleries was completed with the acquisition of The Glenlivet Distilleries Ltd in 1978 (see **The Glenlivet**).

100 Pipers was first introduced in 1965 as a price competitive, popular blend, although it includes **Glenlivet**, **Glen Grant** and **Longmorn** among its fillings. It ranks among the top 20 world brands today. The name derives from the dreadful Scottish song of the same name, which begins:

'Wi' a hundred pipers an' a', an' a'...
We'll up an' gie 'em a blaw a blaw'.

It is available through Oddbins outlets (a subsidiary of Seagram's), and key markets include Latin America, Spain and the Far East.

HUNTLY

Category: Standard Blend
Licensee: Huntly Blending Company, Hurleford
Owner: United Distillers

Huntly Blending Company is a subsidiary of Slater, Rodger (see **Rodger's**). Huntly's markets are Hungary, the former Yugoslavia and the Lebanon.

IMMORTAL MEMORY

Category: Premium Blend (8 Years Old)
Owner: Gordon & MacPhail, George House, Boroughbriggs Rd, Elgin

(see **MacPhail's**) Immortal Memory was named Best Blended Whisky in the World at the International Wine & Spirit Competition in 1991. The name commemorates Robert Burns, who is toasted on Burns Night (25 January – the poet's birthday) with a speech entitled 'The Immortal Memory'.

IMPERIAL GOLD MEDAL

Category: Standard Blend
Owner: Cockburn & Co. (Leith) Ltd, 11 Glenfinlas St, Edinburgh

(see **The Dominie**)

INVER HOUSE (GREEN PLAID)

Category: Standard and De Luxe Blends
Owner: Inver House Distillers Ltd, Airdrie, Lanarkshire
Expressions: Standard Blend; 12 and 17 Years Old

Inver House Distillers Ltd was established in 1965 by the American spirits giant Publicker Industries Inc., and became independent through a management buy-out in January 1988. Since then the company has gone from strength to strength: in 1992 it received The Queen's Award for Industry (Export Achievement).

As well as owning Knockdhu, Glen Flagler and Speyburn malt distilleries, the company produces gin, vodka and a whisky liqueur. Inver House is light in colour and body – a typical export blend – it is within the top 30 international best-sellers, doing especially well in Spain, Greece, Holland and Mexico. It is not available in the home market.

ISLANDER

Category: Standard Blend
Licensee: Arthur Bell & Sons, Perth
Owner: United Distillers

(see **Bell's**) Islander was introduced in the late 1980s, with substantial advertising support. The blend uses a high proportion of Islay, Skye and Orkney malts, which imparts a slightly smoky flavour.

ISLAY LEGEND

Category: Standard Blend
Owner: Morrison Bowmore Distillers Ltd

This blend has a high malt content, mainly from the Bowmore Distillery on Islay and its main market is in France (see **Rob Roy**).

ISLAY MIST

Category: Vatted Malt
Owner: MacDuff International Ltd, 299 West George St, Glasgow
Expressions: De Luxe (no age statement) and 17 Years Old

Laphroaig Distillery on Islay was founded in 1815 by the Johnston family who retained ownership until 1962 (see **Laphroaig**). Islay Mist – a blend of Islay and Highland malt whiskies – was created by them in 1928 to mark the 21st birthday of the Laird of Islay House, Lord Margadale. It bears the seal of the Lord of the Isles (whose stronghold was in Islay) on its label, has a distinctive salty flavour reminiscent of Laphroaig and was originally blended at the distillery itself. The brand was acquired by MacDuff International in 1991 (see **MacDuff**).

ISLE OF SKYE

Category: Premium and De Luxe Blends
Licensee: Ian MacLeod & Co. Ltd, Russell House, Dunnet Way, Broxburn

Owner: Peter J. Russell & Co., Russell House, Dunnet Way, Broxburn
Expressions: Standard; 8 Years Old; 12 Years Old; 18 Years Old

The Isle of Skye is the heartland of Clan MacLeod, and the blend was originally created in Skye by Ian MacLeod (whose grandson is still a consultant to the company), about 100 years ago. The label depicts the entrance to Loch Scavaig on the south-west coast of the island, together with the bull-and-flag crest of the MacLeods. Ian MacLeod & Co. Ltd was incorporated in 1934.

The blend is made from Island and Speyside malts and allowed to marry for at least 6 months subsequent to blending. The flavour its creator was looking for was 'a taste of home' – hence the peaty notes, with oak overtones in the younger expressions. The Standard Blend is of 8-year-old malts and 4-year-old grains; the 18 Years Old has a delicious nutty, oaky aroma and has the full-bodied flavour one would expect of an elegant old whisky (see also **Chieftain's Choice**).

J&B JET

Category: Premium Blend
Owner: Justerini & Brooks Ltd, St James's St, London SW1

This is the latest brand to be launched by the well-known producers of **J&B Rare**. The company owns three Speyside distilleries and over 80% of the malt content is from that region.

J&B RARE AND RESERVE

Category: Premium Blend; De Luxe Blend
Owner: Justerini & Brooks Ltd, St James's St, London SW1
Expressions: 8 Years Old; 15 Years Old (Reserve)

Giacomo Justerini, from Bologna, established his business as a wine merchant in London in 1749, together with an Englishman, George Johnson. Eleven years later the firm was awarded what was to be the first of many Royal Warrants. In 1831 the company was bought by Alfred Brooks, and it has been known as 'Justerini & Brooks' ever since. In the 1880s it was among the first London companies to buy up stocks of old whisky in Scotland and create a superior blend (see **Club**).

When Prohibition was lifted in 1933 Justerini & Brooks set about the heavy promotion of J&B Rare in and around New York City. Market growth was interrupted by The Second World War, but by the late 1950s the brand had conquered America, where it is still a top-seller. With this secure base the company appointed distributors and agents throughout the world, and J&B Rare is today the no. two best seller in the world, available in over 150 markets and still growing. The company received the Queen's Award for Export Achievement in 1972, '73, '77, '85 and '89.

In the early 1950s J&B pooled its assets with another company to form United Wine Traders Ltd. Ten years later this company merged with W. & A. Gilbey Ltd to form International Distillers and Vintners (IDV) – a merger which greatly facilitated J&B Rare's promotion in export markets. In 1972 IDV was acquired by the hotel and catering giant Grand Metropolitan.

J&B Rare is blended from some 42 individual whiskies at Strathleven (the headquarters of J&B Scotland Ltd). The brand has a base of Speysides, including aged product from their own distilleries at Knockando, Auchroisk, Glen Spey and Strathmill, and this accounts for its delicate flavour. It also has a restrained smokiness, which indicates some light Islay malt. Very little caramel is added, so it has a distinctively pale colour.

THE JACOBITE

Category: Standard Blend
Licensee: Independent Cellars Ltd
Owner: Nurdin & Peacock Ltd, Bushey Rd, Raynes Park, London SW20

First created in 1983, to compete in the cut-price marketplace of British cash-and-carries. The Jacobite has built a strong position among independent retailers, supported by continual promotions. The owners believe that it now it stands at number eight in the UK best-sellers, being worth about £20 million at retail value.

The blend was created for Nurdin & Peacock by Invergordon and employs 47 malts. It sets out to be good value for money, with a distinctive character.

KING GEORGE IV

Category: Standard Blend
Licensee: The Distillers Agency, Edinburgh
Owner: United Distillers

Created by DCL in the early 1880s as an export brand, KG IV, as it became known, was registered and licensed to Distillers' export branch, which became the Distillers' Agency Ltd in 1924. It is the best-selling brand in Denmark, largely thanks to the efforts of its distributor, Hans Just & Co., which was founded in 1867 and has represented KG IV since 1899. The brand also sells in territories as far flung as French Guiana, South Africa and Suriname.

George IV's trip to Edinburgh in 1822 was the first visit to Scotland by a British monarch for nearly 200 years. The king was received with all the ceremony and pageantry that Sir Walter Scott – who was in charge of proceedings – could discover or invent. Much of the mythology of Highland custom and dress, accepted as ancient tradition (as it still is today), was in fact invented for the occasion.

The king was handed a glass of whisky as he landed (see **Glenlivet**), and enjoyed several more during his visit, and it is arguable that the attention drawn to 'things Scotch' by 'The King's Jaunt' made it easier, the following year, for the Duke of Gordon to persuade Parliament to appoint the Royal Commission which effectively laid the foundations for the modern whisky industry.

The portrait of King George IV on the label is from a painting by Sir Thomas Lawrence which hangs in the Pinacoteca Vaticana in Rome.

KING HENRY VIII

Category: Standard Blend
Licensee: Highland Blending Co.
Owner: H. Stenham Ltd, 117 Willifield Way, London NW11
Expressions: 5 and 12 Years Old

This is a one-man business, run entirely by Henry Stenham Esq., since 1953. He buys up stocks of blended whisky and exports it direct, mainly in bulk, which precludes the need for agents, advertising or broking fees (and thus keeps prices as low as is commercially possible). But it does not necessarily make for consistency. This blend and its sister (see **Queen Mary I**) can be found in supermarket chains around Europe.

KING JAMES VI

Category: Standard Blend
Licensee: Redford Bonding Co. Ltd
Owner: Forth Wines Ltd, Crawford Place, Milnathort, Kinross

Forth Wines is an independent wholesaler established in 1963. The company sells wines and spirits throughout the UK. King James VI is the firm's own-label brand; it also markets own-labels in other spirits, including gin and vodka.

James VI was the son of Mary, Queen of Scots, and became King James I of England in 1603. The label bears his portrait.

KING OF SCOTS

Category: De Luxe Blends
Owner: Douglas Laing & Co. Ltd, Douglas House, 18 Lynedoch Crescent, Glasgow
Expressions: 12, 17 and 25 Years Old; Rare Extra Old; Proclamation; Flagship; numbered edition

The brand name King of Scots was first registered in the 1880s, and was acquired by Douglas Laing & Co. in the 1950s. Its market was once almost exclusively in South America; its owners have now achieved a strong position for it in the Far East and the Pacific Rim.

Each of the expressions sold under the brand-name is variously packaged in ceramic and crystal decanters – this is considered to be one of the reasons for their success in these markets, and in the duty-free market, where they also do well. Another reason is the firm's blending policy. Only younger grain whiskies are used in the blends (which make no age statement) and the associated cost savings enable the firm to the purchase of some very old malts (up to 25 years), and to offer the brands at a competitive price against its major competitors.

Douglas Laing & Co. is an independent company, wholly owned and directed by members of the Laing family. Established in 1950, it has grown steadily since and was awarded the Queen's Award for Export Achievement in 1990.

KING ROBERT II

Category: Standard Blend; De Luxe Blend
Licensee: Wm Maxwell (Scotch Whisky) Ltd
Owner: Ian MacLeod & Co. Ltd, Russell House, Dunnet Way, Broxburn
Expressions: Standard Blend; 12 Years Old

King Robert II is part of a range of competitively priced spirits (including vodka and gin). It is a lighter blend of whiskies at four years, designed for large volume sales in export markets, principally the Middle East, but also in 25 other countries. The blend was first created in the 1950s, and the licensee company is part of the Peter J. Russell Group (see **Chieftain's Choice**).

King Robert II himself was Scotland's first Stewart king (1371–90) – *"tall and handsome, though the beauty of his face was marred by bloodshot eyes"* – the founder of the most ill-fated of any Royal House. Of 13 successors (down to Bonnie Prince Charlie in the late 18th century) only two died peacefully in their beds in their own kingdom – James VI (and I of England) and Charles II!

KING'S LEGEND

Category: Standard Blend
Licensee: Ainslie & Heilbron (Distillers) Ltd, 5 Oswald St, Glasgow
Owner: United Distillers

(see **Ainslie's**) Currently King's Legend's only current market is Norway, although it used to do well in Dubai and Réunion.

LAIRD O'COCKPEN

Category: De Luxe Blend
Licensee: Cockburn & Campbell Ltd, Cockpen House, Buckhold Rd, London SW18
Owner: United Distillers

Cockburn & Campbell was established in Edinburgh in the early 19th century by members of the Cockburn of Leith family (see **The Dominie**), and began blending whisky in the 1840s. The bonded warehouse on Duke Street in Leith had vaulted cellars well below street level which had an earthen floor and maintained an even temperature of 50°F (10°C) - conditions which greatly inhibit the loss of whisky during maturation. Indeed, HM Customs was sometimes surprised to find casks 'bung full', rather than reduced by several gallons, as would be expected.

The company was acquired by Young's Brewery, Wandsworth, in 1972. Cockburn & Campbell's whiskies were once well known in India, though today they are found only in the home market.

The 'Laird O'Cockpen' was Sir Alex Ramsay of Dalhousie, who was alive in the 14th century and who was known as one of the bravest warriors of his time, covering himself with glory at the night battle of Otterburn (1388). The brand was registered in 1913 and is bottled at 10 Years Old in a 60:40 malt to grain proportion.

LANGS

Category: Premium Blend; De Luxe Blend
Licensee: Lang Brothers Ltd
Owner: Robertson & Baxter Ltd, 106 West Nile St, Glasgow
Expressions: Langs Supreme; Langs Select (12 Years Old)

Alexander and Gavin Lang commenced business as whisky merchants and blenders in 1861, and their company remained under the control and direction of their successors until it was acquired by another independent firm, Robertson & Baxter, in 1965.

The brothers Lang bought **Glengoyne** Distillery in 1876, and this light Highland malt has formed the heart of their brands ever since. Langs Supreme is a blend of some 25 whiskies, and is married for nine months in oak casks; Langs Select has a high proportion of Speysides, and the youngest of the whiskies used in the blend is 12 years. Like its sister it is married in oak casks for at least nine months. The Langs Supreme main market is in the UK, where it is currently 17th best-seller. It also sells a respectable 125,000 cases a year in Europe and the Far East.

The company holds the Royal Warrant of HM Queen Elizabeth the Queen Mother.

LAUDER'S

Category: Standard Blend
Licensee: Archibald Lauder & Co., Glasgow
Owner: MacDuff International Ltd, 299 West George St, Glasgow

Lauder's is acknowledged to be a brand with a distinguished pedigree, but its history is obscure: the label maintains that the blend was 'established in 1837' and is 'a fine reminder of the Scotch Whisky of Old'. This date, of course, pre-dates the acknowledged origin of blended whisky as we understand it today (1853).

Be this as it may, Lauder's won gold medals at the Edinburgh International Exhibition in 1886, the Manchester Royal Jubilee Exhibition 1887, the Glasgow International Exhibition 1888, the Paris Exhibition 1889 and the Chicago World Columbian Exhibition 1893, and the brand, which was bought from Hiram Walker by MacDuff International in 1991 (see **Ballantine's**, **Grand MacNish**) has achieved strong positioning in the Swedish, Canadian, Latin American and Western European markets.

WILLIAM LAWSON'S

Category: Standard & De Luxe Blends
Owner: William Lawson Distillers Ltd, 288 Main St, Coatbridge, Lanarkshire

This blend was first created in 1849 by William Lawson, a whisky merchant and blender: today it is among the top twenty best-selling exports brands world-wide.

Lawson's initial business failed and remained in abeyance until after the Second World War when it was moved to Liverpool from where direct exports could be made. Subsequently the company moved back to Scotland where a blending and bottling complex was set up in Coatbridge, near Glasgow. Connections with the Martini & Rossi group gave the brand outlets all over Europe and it continues to grow in popularity.

The need to secure malt fillings for blending led the firm to buy Macduff Distillery near Banff on the Moray Firth (1972). The distillery's product is occasionally found in merchant bottlings under its name but is more generally available as **Glen Deveron**.

LISMORE

Category: Standard & De Luxe Blends
Owner: William Lundie & Co. Ltd, 11 Fitzroy Place, Glasgow
Expressions: 5, 8, 12, 15 and 18 Years Old

William Lundie has been a blending house since the 1920s (its founder began his career with David Sandeman in 1904 (see **VAT 69**). Lundie's is still an independent company and is managed by the third generation of the founder's family. The markets for Lismore are primarily in Europe and the Far East.

LOGAN'S DE LUXE

Category: De Luxe Blend
Licensee: White Horse Distillers, Edinburgh
Owner: United Distillers

(see **White Horse**) The blend was first created by J. L. Mackie & Co. in the 1890s, the 'Logan' being James Mackie's middle name. The blend was once very popular in Scotland, but is now difficult to find.

LOMBARD'S

Category: Standard Blend
Owner: Lombard Scotch Whisky Ltd, Claughbane Rd, Ramsay, Isle of Man

This is a small company of brokers, blenders and exporters – the only one based on the Isle of Man. The company is currently expanding its range of whiskies, but no information is available.

LONG JOHN

Category: Standard Blend
Licensee: Long John International Ltd
Owner: Allied Distillers Ltd, 2 Glasgow Rd, Dumbarton

Long John Macdonald – so called because of his height – established the first legal distillery in the Fort William area, **Ben Nevis**, in 1825. He had previously been a small farmer, but could trace his ancestry back to Somerled, King of the Isles, through the Macdonalds of Keppoch. His great-grandfather had fought for the Jacobite cause in the 1715 rising, and had rallied the Macdonalds of Keppoch to Bonnie Prince Charlie's banner in 1745. He was killed at Culloden the following year.

Long John's whisky was named Dew of Ben Nevis, and its reputation was made when Queen Victoria visited the distillery in 1848 on one of her Highland tours. *The Illustrated London News* reported: "*Mr Macdonald has presented a cask of whisky to Her Majesty and an order has been sent to the Treasury to permit the spirits to be moved to the cellars of Buckingham Palace free of duty. The cask is not to be opened until His Royal Highness the Prince of Wales attains his majority*" (i.e. 15 years later).

By the time he died in 1856, Long John was a famous figure in the Highlands. A contemporary traveller wrote: "*When a man goes to Caprera he, as a matter of course, brings a letter of introduction to Garibaldi. When I went to Fort William I, equally as a matter of course, brought a letter of introduction to Long John ... I presented my letter and was received with the hospitality and courteous grace so characteristic of the old Gael*" (Alexander Smith).

The distillery passed to Long John's son and later to his grandson, who sold the brand name to the London wines and spirits merchants W. H. Chaplin & Co., but retained the Ben Nevis Distillery. In 1981 the two happily came together again, when Long John International (at that time a subsidiary of Whitbread & Co. Ltd), acquired Ben Nevis (Fort William) Ltd. The current owners are Allied Distillers Ltd, the Scotch whisky division of Allied Lyons plc.

LOWRIE'S

Category: Standard Blend
Licensee: W. P. Lowrie & Co., Glasgow
Owner: United Distillers

W. P. Lowrie claimed to be the first to blend pot-still malt whisky with patent-still grain whisky, although this distinction is usually accorded to Andrew Usher (see **Usher's**).

Lowrie had been manager of **Port Ellen** Distillery in Islay, and started in business on his own account in 1869, as a whisky broker and agent. His company was apparently the first to be granted permission from the Customs and Excise to bottle in bond. It also had its own cooperage (the largest in the world at the time), its own case-making works, its own bottle manufactory and an extensive transport fleet.

To complete its requirements, W. P. Lowrie bought Convalmore Distillery (1904) and a substantial holding in **Glentauchers** Distillery. The latter was owned by Lowrie's friend, James Buchanan, and when Lowrie retired he invited Buchanan to chair the company. When Buchanan's joined DCL in 1906, Lowrie & Co. went too.

Lowrie's is not currently being shipped, although the brand is still available in some export markets.

WILLIAM LOW'S FINEST

Category: Standard Blend
Owner: William Low plc, Dryburgh Industrial Estate, Dundee

William Low & Co., was formed as a two-man partnership in 1868. The firm grew rapidly over the next 40 years and by 1914 a chain of 80 small grocers shops was spread throughout Scotland, with some outposts in England.

Between 1914 and the late 1950s the company pioneered several improvements in shop and hygiene standards, and from 1959 there was a rapid move towards self-service shops and, eventually, supermarkets.

In 1973 the company was publicly floated and two years later a separate chain of freezer shops trading as 'Lowfreeze' was launched.

By 1979 Wm Low had 45 supermarkets and 13 freezer shops. In 1980 a vigorous programme of expansion into larger supermarkets was begun and Laws Stores, a supermarket chain based near Newcastle-upon-Tyne, was acquired five years later.

Wm Low plc now trades from 65 premises. The company's own-label brand is sold exclusively through this supermarket chain in Scotland and the north of England. It is blended for the company by Peter Russell & Co., of Bathgate (see **Chieftain's Choice**).

MACANDREW'S

Category: Standard Blend
Licensee: Alistair Graham Ltd, Leith
Owner: Macdonald Martin Distilleries plc, 186 Commercial St, Leith

The brand was named after Lord Douglas MacAndrew, a colourful character who lived during the last century near Inverness. The label depicts him riding what appears to be a unicorn – he was a noted horseman – outside his home.

MACARTHUR'S

Category: Standard Blend
Licensee: J. MacArthur Jr & Co.
Owner: Inver House Distillers Ltd, Airdrie, Lanarkshire
Expressions: Standard; 12 Years Old

MacArthur's Select Scotch was first created in 1877, but it became prominent in the 1970s as a secondary brand – selling principally through supermarkets in the UK at a lower price than was normal, and causing a number of leading blenders to introduce similar 'fighting brands'. It is now available internationally, and does particularly well in France and Holland.

MCCALLUM'S PERFECTION

Category: Standard Blend
Licensee: D. & J. McCallum Ltd, Edinburgh
Owner: United Distillers

The brothers Duncan and John McCallum went into business together as innkeepers and wine and spirits merchants 1807, in Edinburgh. Their base of operations was a pub known as the 'Tattie Pit', which was soon expanded to include a shop and warehouse, and by 1914 they numbered among their customers many members of the Scottish aristocracy. Alas, their premises were utterly demolished in April 1916, during the only zeppelin bombing raid on Edinburgh of the First World War.

Long before this date the company had passed to the brothers' nephew (they had remained bachelors), Duncan McCallum Stewart who set about selling his brands overseas, rather than in the home market. McCallum's Perfection was introduced in 1911, and became a favourite in Australia (where the company established an office in Sydney) and in New Zealand. It is one of only two brands described as 'Scots' whisky (the other is **Cutty Sark**). McCallum's joined DCL in 1937. Perfection is available in the UK, but its principal market is in Thailand. Secondary markets are in New Zealand, Monserrat, St Kitts and Nevis.

> *Time was when every misty glen,*
> *From Cruachan to Cowal Shore,*
> *Saw clans that gathered for the fray,*
> *Their gathering cry 'McCallum Mhor'.*
>
> *These days are dead and gone now,*
> *But in Auckland, Sydney or Quebec,*
> *Where Scots forgather day by day,*
> *Their gathering cry is 'More McCallum'.*

SANDY MACDONALD

Category: Standard Blend
Licensee: Macdonald Greenlees, Edinburgh
Owner: United Distillers

(see **Old Parr**) Sandy Macdonald has a square, 'mallet'-shaped, bottle - reminiscent of its sister blend, Old Parr – with a 'cracked' pattern moulded in relief on its surface. This was originally introduced in the 1920s as a means of frustrating counterfeiters. The brand is big in Paraguay, Uruguay and Chile.

MCDONALD'S SPECIAL BLEND

Category: Standard Blend
Licensee: C. & J. McDonald, Perth
Owner: United Distillers

This company was a subsidiary of Arthur Bell & Co., and became part of United Distillers following the Guinness takeover of Bell's in 1986. The brand sells mainly in South Africa.

THE (STEWART) MACDUFF

Category: Standard Blend
Owner: MacDuff International Ltd, 299 West George St, Glasgow

MacDuff International Ltd was formed in 1991 by three of the Scotch whisky industry's senior executives. The company has acquired **Grand MacNish** and **Lauder's** from Allied Distillers, and has launched several new brands.

The MacDuff's claims to antiquity ('A family product handed down through generations') are based upon the pedigree of the MacDuff family – the premier clan in medieval Scotland – the chiefs of which were created Earls of Fife in 1056 and became hereditary crown-bearers to the Scottish monarchy. In fact the brand is named, as are so many great whisky brands, after its founder, the company's current managing director, Stewart MacDuff.

MCGIBBON'S

Category: De Luxe Blends
Owner: Douglas Laing & Co. Ltd, Douglas House, 18 Lynedoch Crescent, Glasgow
Expressions: Special Reserve (ceramic golf-club decanter) Premium Reserve (ceramic golf-bag decanter; numbered edition)

The McGibbon's range thrives on the association between Scotland's national drink and her national game, golf. The blends were originally presented in the company's own mallet-shaped bottles (see **House of Peers**): the golf-club range was introduced in the mid-1980s, and the golf-bag launched in 1990.

The range is available only through selected outlets in the Far East, and is very successfully distributed through duty-free shops, in which it currently rates 17th worldwide. The decanters are collectable, and often remain unopened by their proud owners.

Special Reserve was originally made exclusively for Frederick Douglas Laing's own enjoyment.

(THE ORIGINAL) MACKINLAY

Category: Standard, Premium and De Luxe Blends
Licensee: Charles Mackinlay & Co. Ltd
Owner: The Invergordon Distillers Ltd, Leith, Edinburgh
Expressions: 5, 12 and 21 Years Old

Charles Mackinlay set up business as a wine merchant in Leith in 1815. His son James joined the business after serving an apprenticeship with a firm of sherry shippers in London, and became chairman in 1867. James was succeeded in 1926 by his son, Charles, grandson, Ian (in 1934), and great-grandson, Donald, who is the current chairman of the company. He is one of the leading figures in the whisky industry today, and is World Grand Master of the Confrèrie de l'Ordre des Tastes Whisky Ecossais. The brand was first introduced in the mid-19th century, named simply Mackinlay's. It was one of the first to be supplied to the Houses of Parliament, and was carried to the South Pole by Sir Ernest Shackleton in 1907. In 1985 it was renamed The Original Mackinlay, and relaunched. Today, it is just outside the top ten most successful brands in the UK, and stands at no. 30 in world sales, its major markets being in Scandinavia, France, Portugal, Italy, Holland, Thailand and Japan.

Succeeding generations of the Mackinlay family have been closely involved in perpetuating the blend and maintaining its quality.

HOWARD MACLAREN

Category: De Luxe Blend
Owner: Gibson International Ltd, 52–58 Weston St, London SE1
(see **Royal Culross**)

SANDY MACNAB

Category: Standard Blend
Owner: Macnab Distilleries Ltd, Lochside Distillery, Montrose

After the Second World War, Joseph Hobbs bought the Ben Nevis Distillery, near Fort William, and installed a Coffey still alongside the traditional pot stills, in order to secure a reliable supply of both grain and malt whiskies for blending (see **Ben Nevis**). This had never been done before.

In 1957 he also bought Lochside Brewery, which he converted to a distillery and conducted the same dual still-type experiment (see **Lochside**). The blend produced by the company was named Sandy Macnab – apparently after the distillery manager – and a controlling company named Macnab Distilleries was set up to manage the production and sales of this new blend. (Incidentally, the 'loch' referred to in the distillery's name was long ago filled in.) Sandy MacNab inspired a lengthy poem, which starts:

> We are sitting tonight in the fire glow,
> Just you and I alone,

And finishes:

> And the woes of the world have vanished
> When I've pressed my lips to yours;
> And to feel your life-blood flowing
> To me is the best of cures.

> *You have given me inspiration*
> *For many a soulful rhyme –*
> *You're the Finest Old Scotch Whisky*
> *I've had for a long, long time.*

In 1973 Lochside was sold to Destillerias y Crianza del Whisky SA of Madrid, which quickly closed the grain production plant and, in 1992, ceased production altogether.

At the time of writing the distillery has been mothballed, and the staff have been paid off, apart from warehousemen: there is enough stock in bond to keep the warehouses busy for two or three years. Lochside's current manager, Charles Sharpe, worked with Hobbs in the early days and is confident that the distillery will find a buyer.

MAJOR GUNN'S

Category: Standard Blend
Licensee: Andrew MacLagan & Co. Ltd, Leith
Owner: Macdonald Martin Distillers plc, 186 Commercial St, Leith

The clan Gunn hail from Caithness and Sutherland, and trace their descent from Gunni, son of Olaf the Black, King of Man and the Isles (d. 1237). They were a warlike and ferocious tribe, *"well known for their superior fighting abilities, particularly over rough terrain … These skills and instincts were passed down from generation to generation to Major Gunn, who was a great leader of men and renowned for his quick thinking, fighting strategies and bravery."* (Major Gunn press release!)

JAMES MARTIN'S

Category: Premium and De Luxe Blends
Licensee: James Martin & Co., Leith
Owner: Macdonald Martin Distilleries plc, 186 Commercial St, Leith
Expressions: V.V.O. (8 Years Old); 12, 17 and 20 Years Old

James Martin was known as 'Sparry' on account of his prowess in the boxing ring. He went into business as a whisky merchant in 1878, in Edinburgh, and was a noted philanthropist in his home town.

V.V.O. – the initials either stand for 'Very Very Old' or 'Vatted Very Old' – was originally simply called Martin's V.V.O., but Martini Rosso, the vermouth manufacturer objected. The brand became famous when a shipload went down with the *SS Politician* off the island of Eriskay in the Outer Hebrides (4 February 1941) – the story was immortalized by Compton Mackenzie in *Whisky Galore* (see **SS Politician**).

Macdonald & Muir (see **Highland Queen**) acquired James Martin & Co. in the 1920s, and a holding company, Macdonald Martin Distilleries Ltd was set up in 1948. V.V.O. is one of the most popular whiskies in the USA, and is within the top 40 in the world. It is not available in the UK.

MILNER'S BROWN LABEL

Category: Standard Blend
Licensee: W. H. Milner Ltd

Owner: Marston, Thomson & Evershed plc, The Brewery, Shobhall Rd, Burton-on Trent

This is an own-label whisky sold exclusively through W. H. Milner Ltd, who are the wines and spirits sales division of the major brewer, Marston Thomson & Evershed. The brand is available through the company's 900 tied houses in England and Wales.

MILORD'S

Category: De Luxe (12 Years Old)
Owner: Macdonald Martin Distilleries plc, 186 Commercial St, Leith

Milord's was designed to appeal to the Venezuelan market, but now sells mainly in Denmark! It is not available in the UK (see **Highland Queen, James Martin's**).

THE MONARCH

Category: Premium Blend (10 Years Old)
Owner: Lambert Bros (Edinburgh) Ltd, 9–11 Frederick St, Edinburgh

Lambert Bros was established in 1849 and is still owned and directed by the descendants of the founder. The shop in the Georgian New Town of Edinburgh holds one of the largest stocks of whisky in the world. The Monarch was first created in 1894, by the current managing director's great-grandfather. The label depicts a 'royal' stag, and the name derives from 'The Monarch of the Glen', implying that this is 'a king among whiskies'. It was a favourite in the Allied messes in France during the First World War, and since then has been successfully exported to Europe and the Far East.

(SIR IAIN'S SPECIAL) MONCREIFFE

Category: De Luxe Blend
Licensee: Moncreiffe & Co. plc
Owner: Gibson International Ltd
Expressions: 8 and 15 Years Old

Sir Iain Moncreiffe of that Ilk, 11th Baronet and 23rd Laird of Moncreiffe in Perthshire, Albany Herald, CVO, QC, died in 1985. He was one of the most colourful Scots of his generation, and was also well known in the south, where he was once described as "the most clubbable man in London … And he used them all as a vehicle for his kindness."
Moncreiffe "8" was launched by Sir Iain in 1983, supplied by the distinguished London wines and spirits merchants, Dolamore Ltd (which was originally available only through such fashionable outlets as Annabel's Night Club and The Ritz, and of course in Sir Iain's many London clubs), but it is now available through Peter Dominic's off-sales premises.

MONSTER'S CHOICE

Category: Standard Blend
Licensee: Strathnairn Whisky Ltd, Inverness

Owner: Gordon & MacPhail, George House, Boroughbriggs Rd, Elgin

(see **MacPhail's**) This curiously-named whisky is in fact of some antiquity – it was registered at the turn of the century. The attractive label has recently been redesigned, and states that the blend is 'Nessie's Favourite Dram'!

MUIRHEAD'S

Category: Standard Blend
Licensee: Charles Muirhead & Son, Edinburgh
Owner: Macdonald Martin Distilleries, 186 Commercial St, Leith

Charles Muirhead & Son was a well-known Edinburgh wine and spirit merchant and shipping company, established in 1824 to import wines from France. The firm's interests extended to whisky after it acquired another wine shipper in the 1920s, and Muirhead's Blue Seal, to give the brand its full title was introduced then, first only in Edinburgh, then in Northern Scotland when Muirhead became a specialist supplier of wines and spirits to country estates. Today it sells worldwide.

OLD ANGUS

Category: Standard Blend
Licensee: R. H. Thomson & Co., Edinburgh
Owner: United Distillers

An old-established company which once held the licence for Teaninich Distillery at Alness on the Cromarty Firth (see **Teaninich**), it became part of Macdonald Greenlees & Co. in the 1890s (see **Old Parr**), and of DCL in 1925.

Old Angus, the company's sole surviving brand, sells principally in Uruguay and South Africa.

OLD COURT

Category: Standard Blend
Owner: Gibson International Ltd, 52–58 Weston St, London SE1
Expressions: 8 and 12 Years Old

This blend is marketed exclusively in the Far East. The scene on the label derives from a woodcut depicting King James I of Scotland holding court in Edinburgh in 1424, and comes from an early copy of Holinshed's *Chronicles,* now in the British Museum (see **Royal Culross**).

OLD DECANTER

Category: De Luxe Blend
Owner: Cockburn & Co. (Leith) Ltd, 19 Dublin St Lane South, Edinburgh
Expressions: 12 Years Old

(see **The Dominie**)

OLD ELGIN

Category: Vatted Malt
Owner: Gordon & MacPhail, George House, Boroughbriggs Rd, Elgin
Expressions: 8 and 15 Years Old; 1938, 1939, 1940, 1947, 1949

(see **MacPhail's, Pride of Strathspey**) Elgin, the 'capital' of Speyside, was once the main bottling centre for the 30-odd distilleries in the region. G&M has the largest stocks of old whiskies in the world, and is uniquely able to produce vattings of very aged whiskies. Old Elgin employs Speyside whiskies exclusively.

OLD GLASGOW

Category: Standard Blend
Licensee: Donald Hart & Co. Ltd, 85 Springkell Ave, Glasgow

(see **Harts**)

OLD GLOMORE

Category: Standard Blend
Owner: James Williams (Narberth) Ltd, Dyfed, Wales

Established in 1830 this firm has been blending and bottling its own brand, by hand, ever since. The whisky will only be found in Pembrokeshire.

OLD HIGHLAND BLEND

Category: Standard Blend
Owner: Eldridge, Pope & Co. plc, Weymouth Ave, Dorchester, Dorset

The company was founded in 1833 and is now one of the largest regional brewers in England. It has been blending and bottling its own whisky since 1907. Old Highland Blend is said to have a higher than usual malt content – a familiar claim, but supported and made credible by the fact that the malt fillings are listed on the label. The current Director of Wines & Spirits, Mr Naughtie, is a Master of Wine and takes personal responsibility for blending.

OLD INVERNESS

Category: Standard Blend
Owner: J. G. Thomson & Co. (parent: Bass plc)

This blend first appeared in 1961 in the retail outlets of HD Wines (Inverness) Ltd. The brand is now owned and distributed by J. G. Thomson mainly in the north and north-east of Scotland, but increasingly in the Central Belt.

OLD MATURED

Category: Standard Blend
Licensee: Daniel Crawford & Sons, Leith
Owner: United Distillers

A firm of whisky merchants in Glasgow, Daniel Crawford & Sons came into being in 1850. Its offices were moved to Leith by DCL (1972). Old Matured was once a big name in Europe, New Zealand, Mauritius and Bahrain; today its main market is Greece.

OLD MULL

(see **Whyte & Mackay**, **The Claymore**).

OLD ORKNEY

Category: Premium Blend
Owner: Gordon & MacPhail, George House, Boroughbriggs Rd, Elgin

(see **MacPhail's**) 'Double O', as this whisky is sometimes known, has the epithet 'The Island's Peedie Dram' on its label: '*Peedie*' means 'little' in Orkney. The brand name has a distinguished provenance, once being used to describe the product of Stromness Distillery in Orkney (founded 1818; closed 1928).

OLD PARR

Category: De Luxe Blends
Licensee: Macdonald Greenlees, Edinburgh
Owner: United Distillers
Expressions: 12 Years Old; Superior; Tribute (Japan and duty-free only); Elizabethan (Japan and duty-free only)

In 1635 John Taylor, 'The Water Poet', published a pamphlet entitled: "*The Olde, Old, Very Olde Man or Thomas Parr, the Sonne of John Parr of Winnington in the Parish of Alderbury in the County of Shropshire, who was borne in 1483 in the Reigne of King Edward the 4th and is now living in the Strand, being aged 152 yeares and odd monthes, 1635.*" Old Parr became a celebrity when he was discovered and brought to London by the Earl Marshal of England, the Earl of Arundel. He was presented at Court to Charles I; the King said "you have lived longer than other men, what have you done more than other men?" He replied, "I did penance when I was an hundred years old."

The penance was for an illicit amour! Parr had married in his eightieth year, and some twenty years later he fell for another, but was discovered. He was obliged to be 'purged by standing in a sheet' in the parish church. He married again in his 120th year – "*Catharine Milton, his second wife, whom he got with child; and was, after that era of his life, employed in threshing, and other husbandry work*"! He was painted by Van Dyke and Rubens and died in November 1635, to be buried in Westminster Abbey on the King's order.

Promotional material for the brand makes this connection: "Just as Thomas Parr lived through the reigns of ten English monarchs, so Old Parr represents timeless quality in an ever changing world … Its makers were inspired by a man whose prestige and enduring quality stood for everything their brand represents"!

The brand is one of the world's largest selling de luxe whiskies, and is number one in the important Japanese market. Tradition has it that it was introduced to Japan over a hundred years ago by the Foreign Minister, Tomoni Iwakura.

Old Parr De Luxe Scotch Whisky was first created in 1871 by James and Samuel Greenlees, brothers from Ayrshire. It immediately did well in London – where it was described as having an almost 'total monopoly on supply', but, somewhat surprisingly, this success did not survive long and the brand soon became an export whisky, early consignments going to Canada and Brazil.

Greenlees & Co. was bought by Sir James Calder and merged with Alexander & Macdonald (see **Sandy Macdonald**) about 1900. It became part of DCL in 1925. Glendullan Distillery was licensed to the company, but the heart of **Old Parr** has always been Cragganmore (see **Glendullan**, **Cragganmore**).

OLD ROYAL

Category: De Luxe Blend
Owner: Burn Stewart Distillers plc, 65 Kelburn St, Barrhead, Glasgow
Expressions: 21 Years Old

(see **Burn Stewart**)

OLD ST ANDREWS

Category: Standard, Premium and De Luxe Blends
Owner: Old St Andrews Ltd, 153 Main Rd, Biggin Hill, Westerham, Kent
Expressions: 4, 8 and 12 Years Old

Old St Andrews Ltd was established in 1970 as an export marketing exercise. 26% of the shares were held by **Tomatin** Distillery, the remainder by the Haswell family, which still directs the company and which bought out Tomatin's holding in 1985.

From the outset the idea was to make a clear association between whisky and golf. An early ploy packaged half-gallon bottles in miniature leather golf bags and mounted them on diminutive caddie carts (this presentation is still available, although the bags now contain 70cl bottles). In 1991 the company launched a new presentation in miniature 5cl plastic barrels, coloured lighter or darker according to the age of the whisky it contains and boxed in packs of three or six. Such has been the success of this presentation, that it was followed in 1992 by 70cl barrels containing an 8 year-old malt and a 12 year-old blend. Some 90% of Old St Andrews market is export, principally Japan and the Far East.

OLD SMUGGLER

Category: Standard Blend
Licensee: J & G Stodart Ltd, Dumbarton
Owner: Allied Distillers Ltd, 2 Glasgow Rd, Dumbarton

In 1835 James and George Stodart, brothers from a wealthy Glasgow family, began a whisky-blending business. They named their leading brand Old Smuggler – a reference to the quality of the illicit distillers' product which, pre-1822, was generally acknowledged as being better than that produced legally. The brothers Stodart are reputed to have been the first to 'marry' their blend (which was probably a vatted malt in its early manifestation) in sherry butts.

In 1931 J. & G. Stodart Ltd was acquired by Hiram Walker-Gooderham & Worts Ltd, the giant Canadian distilling company – in anticipation of the repeal of the Prohibition laws in the USA. In 1936 Hiram Walker also acquired a share in **Ballantine's**, which had already established good distribution in the United States, and in order to secure stocks of malt whisky, bought two distilleries – Glenburgie-Glenlivet and Miltonduff-Glenlivet (the former was licensed to Stodart's and the latter to Ballantine's) and built what was at the time the largest grain distillery in Scotland.

These moves resulted in both Old Smuggler and Ballantine's becoming two of the most popular blends in America, and they remain so to this day. Old Smuggler is also well established in Europe, with a significant position in the German market.

OV 8

Category: De Luxe Blend
Owner: Cockburn & Co. (Leith) Ltd, 19 Dublin St Lane South, Edinburgh
Expressions: 8 Years Old

(see **The Dominie**).

PASSPORT

Category: Standard Blend
Licensee: William Longmore & Co.
Owner: The Seagram Company Ltd, Montreal, Canada

(see **100 Pipers**, **Chivas Regal**) Although unknown in the UK market, Passport is one of the top 20 whisky brands worldwide, well known in Europe and with key markets in the United States, Mexico, Brazil, Spain, Portugal and Korea.It was introduced in 1968, and, with Seagram's acquisition of The Glenlivet Group, now makes use of such distinguished malts as **The Glenlivet**, **Glen Grant**, **Longmorn** and **Caperdonich**. The malts are vatted in the Highlands and blended with grain whisky at Paisley.

PEATLING'S

Category: Standard Blend
Licensee: Thos Peatling & Co., Bury St Edmunds
Owner: Greene King plc, Westgate Brewery, Bury St Edmunds

Thomas Peatling, from Bury St Edmunds, started a wine and spirits business partnership with a Mr Hepplewhite in 1826 at Wisbech, Cambridgeshire. By 1830 Smith, Brown & Peatling had established branches in Bedford and St Ives. Later Brown dropped out and the company became Thos Peatling & Sons.

At the beginning of this century, Peatling's acquired an old business in King's Lynn, and in 1911 took over the spacious cellars of Aplin Robinson & Percival, which enabled the firm to become agents for the well-known brewers, Greene King & Sons of Bury St Edmunds, with whom they amalgamated in 1934.

Greene King was founded in Bury St Edmunds by Benjamin Greene in 1799. His descendants, and those of the King family, are still involved in the company. Peatling's was introduced in 1955, blended for the company by Macdonald & Muir (see

Glenmorangie). At this time the firm was trading as Peatling & Cawdron, but reverted to Thos Peatling in 1988.

PIG'S NOSE

Category: Standard Blend
Licensee: Sheep Dip Whisky Co., Oldbury on Severn, Bristol
Owner: The Invergordon Distillers Ltd, Leith

Pig's Nose was introduced in 1977 by M. J. Dowdeswell Esq., the owner of a free house at Oldbury on Severn, as a companion brand to his remarkably successful **Sheep Dip**. It took over two years to come up with a name as memorable as its running mate, and the explanation is supplied on the label:"'tis said that our Scotch is as soft and smooth as a pig's nose.' Anyone selling this brand is invited to become a member of the Pig's Nose Club!

PINCH

Category: De Luxe Blend
Licensee: John Haig & Co.
Owner: United Distillers

This is the name Haig's Dimple has long been sold under in the United States (see **Haig** and **Dimple**).

POIT DHUBH

Category: Vatted Malt
Licensee: Praban na Linne Ltd, Isle Ornsay, Isle of Skye
Owner: Sir Iain Noble, Bt, OBE.
Expressions: 12 and 21 Years Old

(see **Te Bheag nan Eilean**) A blend of Island and Speyside malts, Poit Dhubh (pronounced 'Pot-Doo') is bottled without chill-filtering, so retains the finer oils and esters of pure spirit, but may turn slightly cloudy in the glass.

The brand was introduced in 1978 to support the local economy and promote the Gaelic language. In parallel, Sir Iain Noble, its owner and inspiration, established a college at Eilean Iarmain to teach business studies through the medium of Gaelic. This has been a great success in training people for careers in the West Highlands and Islands, rather than them having to emigrate. For his services to the Gaelic language and the people of the Hebrides, Sir Iain was awarded the OBE in 1979.

Poit Dhubh literally means 'black pot', and was the term used to describe the illicit still of the smuggler. The brand has won a loyal following in Scotland, especially in the Islands, and also in France, Switzerland and Canada.

PINWINNIE

Category: De Luxe
Owner: Inver House Distillers Ltd, Airdrie, Lanarkshire

(see **Inver House**)

JOHN PLAYER SPECIAL

Category: Premium Blend; De Luxe Blends
Licensee: Douglas Laing & Co. Ltd, Douglas House, 18 Lynedoch Crescent, Glasgow
Owner: Langside Distillers
Expressions: Fine Old; 12 Years Old; Special Rare

It is unusual for an international company of the size of John Player to allow its name to be used by a small independent whisky company – the product bearing the name must have been deemed of sufficient quality before the licence was granted.

Like the other Douglas Laing brands (see **McGibbons**; **King of Scots**) John Player Special's principal market is in the Far East and the Pacific Rim – it is among the top 10 duty-free bands in Taiwan. Each of these expressions benefits from the company's policy of including a proportion of very old malt whiskies in the blend, indeed, Special Rare includes malts from Islay, Speyside and the Lowlands of up to 25 Years Old, and employs more than 25 different malts in the blend. Each bottle of this blend is numbered, to ensure quality control and to remind of its rarity.

PRIDE OF ISLAY, PRIDE OF THE LOW-LANDS, PRIDE OF ORKNEY, PRIDE OF STRATHSPEY

Category: Vatted Malts
Owner: Gordon & MacPhail, George House, Boroughbriggs Rd, Elgin
Expressions: all at 12 Years Old; Strathspey at 25 Years Old, 1950, 1946, 1940, 1938

Gordon & MacPhail opened its shop in Elgin in 1895, and has great experience in vatting malts and blending malt and grain whiskies (see **MacPhail's**).

It has been said of the firm's distinguished range of vatted malts that: "all are skilfully put together and combine to give something which is often superior to some of the single malts which go to make them up." The constituent malts are selected to demonstrate the classic characteristics of each region.

PUTACHIESIDE

Category: De Luxe Blend
Licensee: William Cadenhead Ltd, Aberdeen
Owner: J. & A. Mitchell & Co. Ltd, Campbeltown
Expressions: 12 Years Old

William Cadenhead & Co. was founded in Aberdeen in 1842, and became a limited company in 1972. The original business was that of importers, bottlers and wholesalers of a wide range of wines and spirits, but for the past 50 years the stress has been on bottling and wholesaling Demerara rum and old malt whiskies. Cadenhead's claims to be the only company in the world which holds extensive stocks of old Demerara rum matured in oak; the company's bottlings of rare malts often provide the only chance to taste some superb whiskies, and are well represented elsewhere in this book.

Putachieside, the company's de luxe blend, is difficult to find, although it has been on their list for a hundred years.

QUEEN DIANA

Category: Standard, Premium and De Luxe Blends
Owner: Glen Murray Blending Co. Ltd, 2 Gayton Rd, Harrow, Middlesex
Expressions: 3, 15 and 21 Years Old

Created first in 1971, Queen Diana sells mainly in export markets.

QUEEN ELIZABETH

Category: 1) Standard Blend; 2) De Luxe Blend
Licensee: 1)Burn Brae (Blenders), Perth; 2) Avery's of Bristol
Owner: 1)United Distillers 2) Avery's of Bristol, 7 Park St, Bristol

So far as I can ascertain, this is the only case of two brands having the same name. The first is a plain secondary blend, made for Abu Dhabi and South Africa (though it used to sell in Eastern Europe); the second a very distinguished de luxe blend (see **Avery's**).

Burn Brae (Blenders) was a subsidiary of Arthur Bell & Sons, and became part of United Distillers following the Guinness takeover of that company in 1986.

QUEEN MARY I

Category: Standard Blend
Licensee: Premier Scotch Whisky Co.
Owner: H. Stenham Ltd, 117 Willifield Way, London NW11
Expressions: 5 and 12 Years Old

(see **King Henry VIII**)

QUEEN'S CHOICE

Category: Standard Blend
Licensee: C. & J. Macdonald, Perth
Owner: United Distillers

This company was a subsidiary of Arthur Bell & Sons, and became part of United Distillers following the Guinness takeover of that company in 1986. The brand sells mainly in Spain.

THE REAL MACKAY

Category: Standard Blend
Owner: Mackay & Co. Ltd, St Peter Port, Guernsey

Alexander Mackay, a Scot, established himself as a wine merchant on Guernsey in 1909. He had bought an existing business and quickly added whisky to the stock for sale. The Real Mackay is blended by Long John Distillers Ltd and is available only in the Channel Islands.

THE REAL MACKENZIE

Category: Standard Blend
Licensee: Peter Mackenzie & Co., Perth
Owner: United Distillers

Peter Mackenzie & Co. was originally an Edinburgh distilling company, with its roots in the 1820s. The company owned Blair Athol and Dufftown-Glenlivet distilleries, and its brand The Real Mackenzie was produced in 8-, 12- and 20-year-old expressions: the brand-name may be as old as 1826. It sells in the UK and its main markets are in Greece and South Africa.

The company was bought by Arthur Bell & Sons (see **Bell's**) in 1933 – an event which has been described as 'Bell's coming of age as an all round whisky operation'.

RELIANCE

Category: Standard Blend
Licensee: Forbes, Farquharson & Co., Perth
Owner: United Distillers

This company was a subsidiary of Arthur Bell & Sons, and became part of United Distillers following the Guinness takeover of that company in 1986. The brand sells mainly in South Africa.

ROB ROY

Category: De Luxe Blend
Owner: Morrison Bowmore Distillers Ltd, Springburn Bond, Carlisle St, Glasgow

The company was incorporated in 1951 as Stanley P. Morrison Ltd, Whisky Brokers. Morrison, a well-respected whisky broker in Glasgow, founded the company with James Howat, a young accountant who was succeeded Morrison as chairman on the latter's death in 1971.

The business grew steadily and in the 1960s acquired several companies – including the Bowmore Distillery Co., on Islay, the Roseburn Bonding Co. and Tannochside Bonding Co. – by which time Morrison's operations embraced distilling, blending and broking. In the early 1970s two more distilleries were purchased – **Auchentoshan** and **Glengarioch**.

In 1989 the son of the founder, Brian Morrison, became chairman and the name of the company was changed to reflect the importance of its major malt whisky, Bowmore. Now, with a wide portfolio of single malts and blended whiskies Morrison Bowmore is building up contacts in whisky markets worldwide. Rob Roy's principal markets are in the UK, France, Holland and Japan.

RODGER'S

Category: Standard Blend
Licensee: Slater, Rodger & Co., Hurleford
Owner: United Distillers
Expressions: Rodger's Old Scots Brand, Rodger's Special

Thomas H. Slater set up as a dealer in tea and groceries in Glasgow in 1834, and as early as 1856 could boast customers in Australia, India, South Africa, the West Indies, Canada and the United States.

In 1865 he joined forces with George Smeaton Rodger, and by 1888 they were shipping their own whisky brands to 70 different countries. Ten years later the company formed an association with

John Walker & Co. (see **Johnnie Walker**), and Alexander Walker, chairman of that company, joined the board. Slater Walker was taken over by Walkers in 1911, whence it became part of DCL.

Rodger's Old Scots now sells in Israel and the Middle East, and Rodger's Special is well established in Paraguay.

ROYAL & ANCIENT

(see **Laird o'Cockpen**)

ROYAL BLEND

Category: Standard Blend
Licensee: Wm Sanderson & Son, South Queensferry
Owner: United Distillers

In 1925, William Sanderson & Son Ltd dropped all its brands except the leader, **VAT 69**. In recent years, the company's tradition of tailoring blends to individual customers or markets has been imitated by United Distillers (see **Sanderson's Gold**). Royal Blend is a case in point, made especially for Israel.

ROYAL CULROSS

Category: Vatted Malt
Licensee: Glen Scotia Distillery Ltd
Owner: Gibson International Ltd, 52–58 Weston St, London SE1
Expressions: 8 Years Old

Gibson International is the successor to Barton International, formerly Barton Distilling (Scotland) Ltd, which became a subsidiary of the Amalgamated Distilled Products plc in 1982, when the latter acquired the American company Barton Brands Inc. Royal Culross was formerly owned by the principal whisky company in the ADP group, A. Gillies & Co. (which had acquired it through purchase of **Glen Scotia**, Campbeltown's 'other' distillery, in 1955). In short, it is a brand of some pedigree.

So pretty is Culross, in Fife, that it was the first village to be taken on for wholesale preservation by the Historic Buildings Division of the Scottish Office (in the 1950s). It is a charming, if somewhat over-preserved, 16th/17th-century port, and was a merchant community whose wealth was founded on salt and coal. It is also the birthplace of St Kentigern, the 6th-century founder of Glasgow Cathedral, who was, according to tradition, born on the beach there. Culross was made a Royal Burgh by James VI in about 1590.

The Royal Culross label bears the 'Royal Warrant of the Hammermen of Culross', and a certificate from the 'Provost, Magistrates and Councillors' of the tiny town, granted in 1972.

ROYAL EDINBURGH

Category: Standard Blend
Licensee: Marblehead Trading Company (until 1992)
Owner: United Distillers

Royal Edinburgh was invented by the distilling company, Ainslie & Heilbron (see **Ainslie's**), and became its most famous brand, selling especially well in Australia (it was imported in bulk) and in Belgium (where its name has now been changed simply to Ainslie's). The brand is now sold exclusively in the UK, under licence: it is not certain what plans United Distillers has for it.

ROYAL ESCORT

Category: De Luxe Blend
Owner: Gibson International Ltd, 52–58 Weston St, London SE1
Expressions: 12 Years Old

The Third Jacobite Rising, known as the '45, began with several victories for the Highland army led by Bonnie Prince Charlie, notably at the battle of Prestonpans, fought outside Edinburgh on 21 September 1745, and ended with the rout of the superior Hanoverian army under General Sir John Cope. The Jacobites had entered Edinburgh four days earlier, but after so convincing a victory, nobody could resist them, and the label of this whisky depicts the Prince's triumphant entry into Edinburgh after the battle, surrounded by his 'royal escort' (see **Royal Culross**).

ROYAL FINDHORN

Category: Standard Blend
Owner: Gordon & MacPhail, George House, Boroughbriggs Rd, Elgin
Expressions: 5 Years Old

(see **MacPhail's**) The river Findhorn rises south of Inverness, not far from the ancient homelands of clan MacPhail. Like the Spey it is renowned for its salmon fishing.

ROYAL GAME

Category: Standard Blend
Owner: Winerite Ltd, Gelderd Rd, Leeds
Expressions: Highland Game (at 37.5% ABV) is also available in the super-budget sector

Winerite was started in 1973 by Gerry Atkinson, who has a small licensed grocery in Leeds: today it is the largest independent importer and distributor in the UK, with an annual turnover in excess of £150 million. The end of Retail Price Maintenance in the early 1970s allowed the business to expand into the wholesale market. The company's policy has always been to offer 'value for money': products are bought in bulk, and a range of own brand wines and spirits is continually being enlarged. Royal Game is the company's main whisky brand and is available to their retail customers.

ROYAL HOUSEHOLD

Category: Premium Blend
Licensee: James Buchanan & Sons, Glasgow and London
Owner: United Distillers

It used to be said that this blend was available only in two places: Buckingham Palace and the tiny Rodel Hotel, on the Isle of Harris in the Outer Hebrides. It is not drunk by the Royal Household today, but it was still available at the ancient, if somewhat derelict Rodel Hotel when I last enjoyed its excellent hospitality.

Many stories have grown up about this odd conjunction. The truth is that during the 1920s the Lord Chamberlain invited a number of whisky blenders to submit samples to be licensed exclusively for the use of the Royal Household. The winner was a little-known, but high-quality blend submitted by James Buchanan & Co. (see **Buchanan's**), but the company felt honour-bound to respect the interests of the blend's existing purveyors. One of these was Jock McCallum, who owned an hotel in Stornoway. A deal was struck allowing the existing suppliers to continue to offer the blend – re-christened Royal Household – for as long as they, or their descendants, owned their outlets. McCallum had already bought the Rodel Hotel, so he was given a dispensation to sell it there on the same terms. His grandson still owns the hotel, but has problems obtaining supplies of the preferred blend: it is not available in the home market today – only in Japan!

ROYAL SALUTE

Category: Premium Blend
Licensee: Chivas Brothers Ltd, Aberdeen
Owner: The Seagram Company Ltd, Montreal, Canada
Expressions: 21 Years Old

A royal salute is a 21-gun tribute to a member of the Royal Family on a special occasion, such as the Queen's birthday. Royal Salute was introduced in 1953 to commemorate the Coronation in the same year.

Originally it was made available only in the American market – presented in a ceramic decanter made from Royal Doulton china and wrapped in a velvet bag. Today the flagon is supplied by the Wade potteries, and the brand is available in over 100 countries (see **100 Pipers**, **Chivas Regal**).

SAINSBURY'S (OWN LABEL)

Category: Standard and Premium Blends; Vatted and Single Malts
Owner: J. Sainsbury plc, Stamford House, Stamford St, London SE1
Expressions: 3 and 5 Years Old Blends; Vatted Islay Malt; 12 Year Old Speyside ('from one of the Glenlivet distilleries')

Sainsbury's was established in 1869 and today owns 232 supermarkets throughout the UK. The company has been offering price-competitive, own-label whiskies for at least 30 years, and their consistency and high quality make them worthy of inclusion in a book such as this. Sainsbury's whiskies are supplied by the Peter J. Russell Group (see **Chieftain's Choice**).

ST. JAMES'S

Category: De Luxe Blend
Owner: Berry Bros & Rudd, 3, St James's, London SW1
Expression: 12 Year Old De Luxe Blend

(see **Cutty Sark**) The Berry family, or their relatives and close associates have occupied the same premises in the fashionable St James's district of London since the 17th century. The label of St James's depicts St James's Palace, built by Henry VIII for Anne Boleyn, now occupied by the Lord Chamberlain's Department.

SANDERSON'S GOLD

Category: Standard Blend
Licensee: Wm Sanderson & Sons, South Queensferry
Owner: United Distillers

Sanderson's Gold was first introduced in 1991, and is blended specifically for the West African market. It continues Sanderson's tradition of tailoring brands to individual tastes (see **VAT 69**) – in this case a light whisky appropriate to a tropical climate.

SCOTIA ROYALE

Category: De Luxe Blend
Licensee: Glen Scotia Distillery Ltd
Owner: Gibson International Ltd, 52–58 Weston St, London SE1
Expressions: 12 Years Old De Luxe Blend

(see **Glen Scotia** and **Royal Culross**) Ancient legend maintains that the Scots were originally Greeks who sailed via Egypt and Spain to Ireland, and thence came to Kintyre. Before they arrived in Ireland, their leader married an Egyptian princess, Scotia – from whom the race took its name. Scotia Royale has been prominent in the Far East for some years, particularly in Japan, South Korea and Taiwan. The brand is now making good progress in Europe.

SCOTTISH LEADER

Category: Standard Blend
Owner: Burn Stewart Distillers plc, Barrhead, Glasgow

(see **Burn Stewart**) Scottish Leader is targeted at the supermarket customer, and is the company's fastest growing brand.

SCOTS POET

(see **Findlater's Finest**). The poet is, of course, Robert Burns.

JOCK SCOTT

Category: Standard and De Luxe Blends
Licensee: Findlater, Mackie Todd & Co. Ltd, Merton Abbey, London SW19
Owner: Whitmore & Bayley
Expressions: 3, 5, 8 and 12 Years Old

(see **Findlater's Finest**) Jock Scott was introduced in the 1930s and is named after the well-known salmon fly, which was especially popular on the river Tweed before the war. The labels of all expressions except the 12 Years Old depict salmon fishermen.

SHEEP DIP

Category: Vatted Malt
Licensee: Sheep Dip Whisky Co., Oldbury on Severn, Bristol
Owner: The Invergordon Distillers Ltd, Leith
Expressions: 8 Years Old

M. J. Dowdeswell, a Gloucestershire gentleman farmer and owner of a free house in Oldbury on Severn, introduced this blend in 1974 for his customers, mainly local farmers – indeed, the label even proclaims: 'This whisky is much enjoyed by the villagers of Oldbury on Severn'. Its popularity and availability has grown steadily ever since, however, following early orders from major stores like Harrod's.

According to local sources, Sheep Dip (pronounced 'Ship Dip') has always been the name given to whisky in this part of England, although one cannot help but wonder about the possible tax advantages to a farmer putting several gallons of Sheep Dip through his books... Sheep Dip and its sister brand, **Pig's Nose**, were bought by The Invergordon Distillers Ltd. It is available in Canada, Italy, New Zealand, Australia, the UK and Eire.

SLAINTHEVA

Category: De Luxe Blend
Owner: Alexander Dunn & Co. Ltd, Bracknell, Berks
Expressions: 12 Years Old

Slaintheva – the name derives from the Gaelic toast, more usually spelled 'Slainte Mha' – 'good health' – was first created in 1959It won a gold medal for quality and excellence at the 19th World Selection of Wines, Spirits and Liqueurs in Amsterdam, 1981. It is sold in the UK, Japan and Europe as an 'executive gift', each bottle being individually inscribed with the recipient's name. As well as the usual 75cl, it is bottled as a 'kingnum' (their registered name for a 1.75 litre flagon) (see also **Alexander Dunn**).

SOMETHING SPECIAL

(see **100 Pipers**)

SPEY CAST

Category: De Luxe Blend
Licensee: James Gordon & Co., Elgin
Owner: Gordon & MacPhail, George House, Boroughbriggs Rd, Elgin
Expressions: 12 Years Old

(see **MacPhail's**) Spey Cast was first created by the distinguished blender John Urquhart, whose sons and grandchildren still own and manage Gordon & MacPhail. Its name derives from that most elegant of all methods of casting a salmon fly, evolved to cope with the Spey's steep banks and overhanging trees. The label, which was designed in the 1920s, depicts a be-tweeded angler nonchalantly casting: the decorative loops and arabesques make the cast look impossibly difficult! Spey Cast won a double Gold Award at the International Wine & Spirit Competition in 1982.

SPEYSIDE

Category: Premium and De Luxe Blends
Owner: Speyside Distillery Co. Ltd, 1 Park Circus, Glasgow
Expressions: 'Rare'; 8, 12, 15, 17 and 21 Years Old

The company was incorporated in 1955 by the Christie family to market a range of blended whiskies, and a vatted malt (see **Glentromie**). In 1990 the company opened the 'new' Speyside Distillery, near Kingussie, close to the site of a distillery of the same name which had been established in 1895 and which has long been out of production.

The company has high hopes for its product (the first batch of which is still in the early stages of its maturation at the time of writing), and in keeping with their quality policy they have built the new distillery entirely in stone: it is almost entirely the work of one man – dry-stane dyker Alex Fairlie of Reswallie.

SS POLITICIAN

Category: De Luxe Blend (limited edition)
Owner: SS Politician plc
Licensee: Douglas Laing & Co. Ltd, Douglas House, 18 Lynedoch Crescent, Glasgow

The *SS Politician* sank off the island of Eriskay in the Outer Hebrides in February 1941. Her principal cargo was whisky – 50,000 cases, it is said – and the tale was immortalized by Sir Compton Mackenzie in his (much-filmed) book *Whisky Galore*.

In 1989 a company was established to salvage what remained of the cargo, and in 1990 a small number of intact bottles were raised from the wreck. The whisky they contained was distilled in 1938 and bottled at proof strength. Its years on the sea bed had done it no harm at all. Rather than offer the small stock of bottles for sale individually at huge prices, it was decided to blend the whisky with appropriately aged malts and grains and make it available to a wider, though still extremely limited, market.

Before the war, whisky was coloured more than it is today. This fact, combined with the age of the malt fillings which have gone into this unusual blend, creates an unusually dark whisky (see **King of Scots**).

STAG'S BREATH LIQUEUR

Category: Whisky Liqueur
Owner: Meikle's of Scotland, Newtonmore, Baddenoch

"*Then he went to a locker and produced a bottle of Stag's Breath, a brand which had been particularly favoured by the inhabitants of the two Toddays in the good old days of plenty.* 'Stack's Press', *murmured Jockey, transfixed by the beauty of the sight before his eyes ...*" (from *Whisky Galore* by Compton Mackenzie (see *SS Politician*)).

The Meikle family of Newtonmore, in the ancient Lordship of Baddenoch in Upper Speyside, first created their whisky liqueur in the early 1980s, and introduced it to the market in 1989 after careful refinement.

The liqueur is a clever commingling of Speyside whiskies and fermented heather honey-comb, blended to be lighter and drier that traditional whisky liqueurs.

STEWART'S CREAM OF THE BARLEY

Category: Standard Blend
Licensee: Alexander Stewart & Son of Dundee Ltd
Owner: Allied Distillers Ltd, 2 Glasgow Rd, Dumbarton

Alexander Stewart founded his company in 1831 at the Glengarry Inn in Castle Street, Dundee, and quickly won a reputation for his whisky, first locally, then throughout Scotland. Until relatively recently, the blend went under the name Century Hyatt Cream of the Barley. Stewart's became part of the Allied Lyons Group in 1969, and the brand was repackaged in an unusual bottle (somewhere between a cut glass decanter and an aftershave flask) in 1989. It is currently placed number four in Scotland and is winning ground in the UK mid-price sector. It is also available in Ireland, France, Italy, the Netherlands, Norway and Canada.

STRATHBEG

Category: Standard Blend
Owner: MacDuff International Ltd, 299 West George St, Glasgow

Strathbeg is a loch, about two and a half miles long, in north-east Aberdeenshire. It lies parallel to the coast and is separated from the sea by a ridge of sand about half a mile broad. It formerly had a tidal communication with the sea, but in 1720 a strong east wind blew a mass of sand into the channel, stopping the communication and forming a lagoon. Apparently there was once a hamlet here named Cox Haven – a community of half a dozen families all bearing the name 'Cox'. History does not relate where they came from – one source maintains, curiously, that their true name was 'Kuchs', that they were refugees from religious persecution in the Low Countries, and that they held ritualistic ceremonies connected with 'fresh-water' dolphins that had been stranded in Loch Strathbeg at the time it was cut off from the sea.

Strathbeg is a new blend created by MacDuff International to compliment their range of Scotch whiskies (see **MacDuff**).

STRATHFILLAN

Category: Standard Blend
Owner: Forth Wines Ltd, Crawford Place, Milnathort, Kinross

(see **King James VI**) This brand is mainly found in the UK market although a foothold has been achieved in markets abroad.

Strathfillan is near Killin in Perthshire. Fillan was a Celtic saint, whose relics (notably his staff and arm-bone) were very influential in the Highlands, before the rites of the Celtic Church were superseded by Roman ways.

(J.M. & CO.) SUPERIOR MOUNTAIN DEW

Category: Standard Blend
Owner: Malpas Stallard Ltd, 9 Copenhagen St, Worcester

Josiah Stallard of Worcester is one of the oldest wine merchants in the country, having records dating back to 1642. Josiah Malpas & Co. now purveys the blend.

SWORDS

Category: Standard Blend
Licensee: James Sword & Son Ltd
Owner: Morrison Bowmore Distillers Ltd, Carlisle St, Glasgow

Sword & Son was formed in 1814, a traditional small blending house in Glasgow. It was acquired by Stanley P. Morrison & Co. in 1983. Its main markets are Spain and Portugal (see **Rob Roy**).

TEACHER'S

Category: Premium and De Luxe Blends
Licensee: Wm Teacher & Sons
Owner: Allied Distillers Ltd, 2 Glasgow Rd, Dumbarton
Expressions: Premium (Highland Cream); De Luxe (Royal Highland, 12 Years Old)

In 1830, William Teacher was employed in a small grocery business in Anderston, Glasgow. He married the owner's daughter, and persuaded the firm to take out a liquor licence. By 1851 he was listed as a wholesale wine and spirits merchant, and had expanded into take-home retail shops and 'dram shops' – basic public houses, where customers could drink on the premises. By the time he was joined in the business by his sons, Adam and William, he was the single largest licence-holder in Glasgow, with 18 shops.

The art of creating blends of consistent quality was still in its infancy. The Teacher sons showed great aptitude in this field and the quality of their blends not only made their dram shops popular, it led to requests from other retailers for supplies of blended whisky. Bulk sales developed throughout the 1870s, the firm – by now named Wm Teacher & Sons – offering a range of its own blends as well as blending to individual specifications. The blend which was to make the family fortunes, Teacher's Highland Cream, was registered in 1884: today it is the third most successful brand in Britain and among the top 20 best-sellers worldwide, with annual sales in excess of 2 million cases. The de luxe expression, Royal Highland, was first created in 1968.

The need to secure adequate supplies of malt fillings led the company to build its own distillery, **Ardmore**, at Kennethmount in Aberdeenshire, in 1897/98. In 1960 Teacher's acquired the maker of the other main component in the blend, **Glendronach** Distillery. Highland Cream is guaranteed to contain at least 45% malt whisky, and is credited with being the first brand to position itself as a 'premium' blend – between 'standard' and de luxe'.

In 1913, William Manera Bergius, a nephew of Adam Teacher, devised and patented the now familiar replaceable cork (i.e. a cork with a wooden cap, which did not require a corkscrew): Highland Cream was described as 'the self-opening bottle', and it was advertised with the slogan 'Bury the Corkscrew'.

Until it became part of Allied Lyons in 1976, Teacher's was the largest independent Scotch whisky company still under the control of its founder's descendants, and members of the family continue to be involved. An earlier attempt by DCL to acquire the company in 1921 – principally to obtain the company's considerable stocks of whisky, husbanded during the Great War by a self-rationing scheme – had failed.

Even in the 1920s, Teacher's advertised Highland Cream as 'The Whisky of the Good Old Days': its distinctive flavour is rich and well-rounded, it has good depth of body, a smooth mouth-feel and a clean finish. Its makers describe it as appealing to the experienced whisky drinker.

TE BHEAG NAN EILEAN

Category: Standard Blend
Licensee: Praban na Linne Ltd, Isle Ornsay, Isle of Skye
Owner: Sir Iain Noble, Bt, OBE

Te Bheag nan Eilean (pronounced 'Chay Vek nan Eelan') means 'the little lady of the islands'. 'Te Bheag' is a familiar term of affection – 'the wee one' – and it also puns on the Gaelic for a large Scotch – 'Te Mhor'. The brand was first created in 1976, with the label partly in English, but a local bard remarked that "this whisky is greatly improved in flavour by having Gaelic on the label", so now the packaging is entirely in Gaelic!

The brand's producer is based at Isle Ornsay on the Isle of Skye, the home of the owner, Sir Iain Noble. Isle Ornsay (Eilean Iarmain, to give the place its correct, Gaelic, name) was formerly an important fishing harbour, until the railway reached Mallaig on the mainland, and it is still a popular anchorage. A fishing boat is depicted on the Te Bheag's label.

The brand was launched by Sir Iain Noble expressly to strengthen the local economy and to promote the Gaelic language. It has been most successful, and is highly regarded in Scotland, especially in its natural marketplace, the Western Isles. It is also becoming popular in France (half the output now goes to Paris) and Canada. It is supplied to the British embassies in Washington and Paris (see also **Poit Dhubh**).

TRIBUTE

Category: Standard & De Luxe Blends
Owner: William Lundie & Co. Ltd, 11 Fitzroy Place, Glasgow
Expressions: 5 and 15 Years Old

This small family-run broking company was founded in 1932 by Robert Donald Lundie, who had begun his career working for David Sandeman, the famous port shipper (see **VAT 69**).

Lundie's original company was sold off some years later and other members of the company launched a new company. This pattern repeated itself several times and the present chairman is Bruce Lundie, who chiefly exports his brands to the Far East, North America and Europe.

UBIQUE

(see **MacPhail's**)

USHER'S GREEN STRIPE

Category: Standard Blend
Licensee: Andrew Usher & Co., Edinburgh
Owner: United Distillers
Expressions: Also sold as Cordon Vert and Old Vatted Scotch (O.V.S)

Andrew Usher II is generally credited with being the first blender of malt and grain whiskies, in 1853. His father, Andrew Usher I, was born in the Borders in 1782, and set up as a wine and spirits merchant in Edinburgh in 1813. In 1840 he obtained the exclusive agency for The Glenlivet – the best-known malt whisky of the day, and the first distillery to have taken out a licence. He was aware of the improvement that maturation made to whisky – most was drunk as 'new make', immature spirit, in those days – and built large bonded warehouses to hold his maturing stocks.

Usher also began to experiment with blending whiskies. Crude and random blends been made by spirits merchants since at least the 1820s: Usher's contribution was to adopt a scientific approach to creating something which was better than the sum of its parts, and which could be repeated. In this he was influenced by French brandy-makers. To begin with he mixed malts only, 'vatting' Glenlivet and other malts, and creating among others a successful blend called, not surprisingly, Old Vatted Glenlivet. In 1844 he began to sell his whiskies in London, and about this time his sons, Andrew and John, who were themselves both wine merchants, joined him in the business.

In 1853 the first of several measures was taken to equalize excise duty between England and Scotland. This was to Scotland's disadvantage, resulting in whisky rising in price in the south, but it may have inspired Andrew Usher II to begin experimenting with blending pot-still malts with cheaper patent-still grain whiskies, since the first 'modern' blended whisky dates from this year.

In 1860 the firm purchased Glen Sciennes Lowland malt distillery (renamed Edinburgh Distillery), and 25 years later the need to secure supplies of grain whisky led Andrew Usher II to become the driving force behind the foundation of the North British Distillery Co – for many years the largest distillery in Scotland.

When blended whisky began to supersede brandy in popularity, in the early 1880s, the Ushers were ready to take the initiative. They rapidly developed their export trade, which had been growing steadily since the mid 1850s, and by 1910 it was recorded in the *Illustrated London News* that: "they are represented by leading firms all over the world, and their organisation is so complete that in every important centre in practically every country, the foremost houses are closely identified with Messrs Usher's interests."

Both the Usher brothers were great benefactors of the City of Edinburgh. Andrew endowed 'the finest concert hall in Great Britain', the Usher Hall (with £100,000, in 1896); John built the Usher Institute for Public Health – a medical research laboratory – for the University, and was created a baronet in 1900.

In 1919 Andrew Usher & Co. Ltd was acquired by DCL, through its subsidiary, the distinguished firm of J. & G. Stewart Ltd (see **Stewart's Finest Old Vatted**). Green Stripe's main market today is in South America, and it is the leading brand in Venezuela (which imports it in bulk). It also goes to the USA (in bulk), to Canada, France and South Africa.

VAT 69

Category: Standard Blend
Licensee: Wm Sanderson & Son, South Queensferry
Owner: United Distillers

Leith-born William Sanderson set up as a "manufacturer (i.e. blender) of wines and cordials" in 1863, aged 24. He was one of the first to sell his own blends of malt and grain whiskies. 'VAT 69' is not the Pope's telephone number, as is often suggested by dullards: the true story is that Sanderson created 100 different blends and in July 1882 he invited a group of knowledgeable friends and colleagues from the whisky trade to sample them and name their favourite. The unanimous choice was sample ('vatting') number 69, and the lack of name stuck.

In 1914 quantities of the blend accompanied Sir Ernest Shackleton on the Imperial Trans-Antarctic Expedition – Sir Ernest promising that it would be *"used for medicinal emergencies and for feast days in the Antarctic."* Again in 1921, stocks accompanied Shackleton's third expedition, and this time he wrote: "it has been used on the trip on Saturday nights when the naval toast of 'sweethearts and wives' is drunk, and has been greatly appreciated by the members of the expedition".

The business was run by the founder's son and grandson until 1935 when it merged with Booth's, the London gin distillers. This partnership was short-lived, however, since both companies joined DCL two years later. For the last ten years VAT 69 has remained about tenth in the list of best-selling whiskies in the world. It deserves a revival in the UK.

JOHNNIE WALKER

Category: Standard, Premium and De Luxe Blends
Licensee: John Walker & Sons, Kilmarnock and London
Owner: United Distillers
Expressions: Red Label; Black Label; Blue Label (duty free); Swing; Swing Superior (Taiwan); Premier (SE Asia & duty free); Gold (Japan); Honour (Asia Pacific)

Johnnie Walker Red Label is the world's best-selling Scotch, some 6.5 million cases a year are drunk; Johnnie Walker Black Label is the world's best selling premium whisky.

The story begins in a small grocer's shop in Kilmarnock, opened in 1820 by the eponymous John Walker, and selling wines and spirits. By 1850 the shop was offering its customers a house blend named Walker's Kilmarnock Whisky.

The business prospered, and with the opening of the London–Glasgow railway, which passed through Kilmarnock, Walker's blend began to be appreciated furth of Ayrshire.Then, in 1852, the shop's entire stock was destroyed by a flood. The family faced ruin, but it happened that John had a very talented son, Alexander, who joined the firm (1856) and persuaded his father to expand into wholesale trading.

Within six years, 100,000 gallons (over 450,000 litres) of Walker's Kilmarnock were being sold a year. The firm supplied 'merchant adventurers' – ships sailing out of Glasgow, which carried assorted cargoes all over the world, selling the goods and keeping a percentage of the profit – and made early inroads into the London market, where an office was opened in 1880. By 1890 there were also offices in Birmingham, Manchester and in Australia, where the brand won the top awards at exhibitions in Sydney (1880), Melbourne (1881), Adelaide (1887), Dunedin (1890) and Brisbane (1897). In 1893 the firm bought **Cardhu** Distillery.

Alexander's sons joined him, the youngest, Alec (later Sir Alexander) becoming chairman on his father's death in 1889, the other two, John and George Paterson Walker, travelling extensively to set up distribution agencies across the world: the former died in Australia in the early 1890s.

It was only in 1909, once these foundations had been laid, that the firm introduced the Johnnie Walker Black and Red Label brands. George Paterson Walker saw the need to develop a lighter blend, in line with changing tastes, particularly abroad. The idea of commemorating their grandfather was Alec Walker's, and a well-known commercial artist of the day, Tom Browne, was commissioned to produce a portrait. The original intention had been to name the brands Very Special Old Highland and Extra Special Old Highland, and it was only when the portrait turned out so successfully that the names were changed. The famous slogan 'Born 1820 – still going strong' was contributed by James Stevenson, a director, as was the square bottle and slanted label packaging.

Stevenson was a superb administrator, and during the First World War he and Alec Walker showed great ability in the Ministry of Munitions, where they supervised the production of ammunition. Walker was knighted for his services; Stevenson was made a baronet, and in 1924 he was elevated to the peerage.

Walker's went public in 1923 and joined DCL in 1925. The brand continued to grow world-wide, winning famous supporters along the way – including Sir Winston Churchill who was no doubt inspired by his favourite Scotch to write the famous minute shortly after the end of the Second World War, warning against depriving the Scotch whisky industry of its barley supplies. In 1977 Red Label had to be withdrawn from the domestic market, due to EEC rules (see **John Barr**), but is now available once again.

WHITE & GOLD

Category: Standard Blend
Licensee: Alistair Graham Ltd, Leith
Owner: Macdonald Martin plc, 186 Commercial St, Leith

(see **Highland Queen**, **James Martin's**) Alistair Graham was an early blender and reputed to be an obsessive experimenter who travelled the length and breadth of Scotland visiting distilleries and buying fillings.

WHITE HORSE

Category: Standard Blend
Licensee: White Horse Distillers, Edinburgh
Owner: United Distillers

It is said that White Horse was first created in 1883, in Islay, by the owners of **Lagavulin**, J. L. Mackie & Co. The distillery is now owned by its famous creature. J. L. Mackie was one of the few heads of whisky firms in the 1880s to have learned distilling (at Lagavulin), and he named his brand after a tavern in the Cowgate of Edinburgh. The inn had served as an informal officer's mess during Bonnie Prince Charlie's occupation of Edinburgh in 1745; twenty years on Dr Johnson arrived there off the London stage coach to be met by James Boswell, who hurried him away …

The name is interesting. A white horse was the heraldic crest of the House of Hanover, so the pub sign may well have been adopted to display political loyalty. Tradition has it, however, that the hostelry was named for a real horse, owned by the publican, which won a race on Leith Sands, saving its owner from bankruptcy.

J. L. Mackie was succeeded in 1900 by his nephew Peter, a man described as "one third genius, one third megalomaniac and one third eccentric". He was known as 'restless Peter' and met all counsels of caution with the words "nothing is impossible" – the phrase became a by-word within the company. He was an acknowledged authority on shooting, and wrote the seminal *The Keeper's Book*. He was an ardent Conservative (although he was made a baronet by a Liberal Prime Minister in 1920), and he was the outspoken champion of several good causes, not least that of allowing whisky to mature.

By the outbreak of the Great War, White Horse was the favourite of many army messes and had achieved a strong position in both the home and export markets. In 1926 the firm was the first to introduce the screw cap – an innovation which took the marketplace by storm and doubled sales of the brand in six months.

Today White Horse sells about 2 million cases per annum in 100 countries throughout the world, and rates within the top ten best-sellers. It is currently rated no.1 in the important Japanese market, and its other main markets are South Africa (where it was formerly no.1), Chile and Portugal. It is rated no. 2 in the UK mid-market, but its sales are almost all through the off-trade.

WHYTE & MACKAY

Category: Standard & De Luxe Blends
Owner: Whyte & Mackay Group plc, 310 St Vincent St, Glasgow (parent: American Brands Inc.)
Expressions: Special Reserve, 12 and 21 Years Old

Charles Mackay went into business with James Whyte in 1882, as bonded warehousemen and whisky merchants, but their firm was founded upon an early venture, Allan & Poynter (1844), of which Mackay had been manager. Whyte & Mackay's Special Reserve was launched soon after the firm was renamed.

It became a private limited company at the end of the First World War and was restructured in 1926, with one of Whyte's sons as a director and another joining the board a few years later. During the 1930s the company developed a strong export market, particularly in North America, South Africa and New Zealand and after the war it concentrated on the UK market with considerable success.

In 1960 this company merged with Mackenzie Bros, owners of **Dalmore** Distillery, and three years later acquired its English distributors, Jarvis Halliday & Co. The same year, Whyte & Mackay pioneered a plastic screw-cap which doubled as a measure or small cup, and introduced the 40 oz bottle size which has since become standard in bars. Such moves, combined with soccer and golf promotions and widespread advertising to make it the best-selling brand in the massive Glasgow market – a position it still holds.

In 1972 the company was taken over by Sir Hugh Fraser's Scottish & Universal Investments, which bought Fettercairn and Tomintoul Distilleries the same year. Following rulings against DCL in 1986, Whyte & Mackay acquired world-wide ownership of **The Claymore**, **John Barr**, **Stewart's Finest Old**, **Jamie Stuart** and **Old Mull**, and UK domestic rights to **Haig**, **The Real Mackenzie**, **The Buchanan Blend** and **Crawford's 3** and **5 Star**. In 1988, the established bottling and blending company William Muir (Bond 9) Ltd of Leith, was also acquired. This remains a separate profit centre.

In 1990 Whyte & Mackay Ltd was bought by Gallaher Ltd, a wholly owned subsidiary of American Brands Inc which had long been the company's US agents through another subsidiary, Jim Beam Brands.

Whyte & Mackay Special Reserve incorporates about 35 malts and employs the admirable, but now uncommon, practice of vatting the malts and grains separately in sherry butts for some months before they are blended. The blend itself is then returned to cask for a second period of marrying – a fact which for almost two decades the company's advertising made much of, and which it maintains contributes to the whisky's 'smooth taste and texture'. It is among the world's top 15 best selling brands, and consistently ranks number five in export markets.

WILLIAM & MARY

Category: Premium Blend
Owner: Edwin Cheshire Ltd, Stansted, Essex
Expressions: 5 Years Old

This brand was first produced in 1988 to mark the tercentenary of the accession to the throne of the Dutch Stadtholder, William of Orange, and his queen, Mary Stuart. The label depicts the Dutch and British flags (see also **First Lord**).

YELLOW LABEL

Category: Standard Blend
Licensee: John Robertson & Son
Owner: United Distillers

The firm originated in Dundee in 1827, and moved to Leith upon joining DCL in 1915. Yellow Label is available in small quantities in the UK, and is exported to Spain.

YE WHISKY OF YE MONKS

Category: Standard Blend
Licensee: Donald Fisher & Co., Edinburgh
Owner: United Distillers
Expressions: Ye Monks (also standard blend)

Ye Whisky of Ye Monks was registered in 1898. The name makes reference to the belief that whisky was introduced to Scotland by Irish monks (in Ireland it is believed that art of distilling was brought by St Patrick, himself from southern Scotland!).

According to a history of the firm, Ye Monks owes its origin to the Anglo-Indian President of the Wine Committee of an exclusive club in India, who had been deputed to select a whisky which would satisfy the discerning tastes of the members. The vatting selected "embraced the makes of nearly a score of distilleries, and the components and ages have been strictly adhered to ever since".

Donald Fisher, who died in 1915, has been described as 'one of the pioneers of the Scotch whisky trade'. His success was based upon his understanding of the value of using mature whisky in blending – he accumulated huge stocks of mature whisky – long before the Immature Spirits Act required a minimum three years maturation – and it was said that his whiskies were "contained in sherry casks imported direct from the bodegas in Spain where they have contained fine old soleras and which give exceeding mellowness which is characteristic of Donald Fisher's whiskies".

His company was purchased by DCL in 1936. Ye Monks was packaged in hand-made stone jars, and this became its trademark. It was originally a de luxe blend, known throughout the world, and sold for export only (mainly in South and Central America, where it is still a major brand). The company was awarded the Queen's Award for Export Achievement in 1982.

APPENDICES

A WHISKY FLAVOUR CHECKLIST

The following notes are applicable to mature spirit (not new spirit) and are merely indications of the likely aromas which might be encountered in each flavour group. It goes without saying that not all the flavour groups will be present in every brand of malt whisky. I am beholden to staff at Pentlands Scotch Whisky Research Ltd (who were responsible for defining the flavour terminology of Scotch whisky) for their help in compiling this checklist.

1) Appearance
colour; clarity

2) Aroma
Intensity of Aroma (1-5)
Nose Feel (*pungency, prickle, burn, etc.*)
Aroma Groups (run through the following groups and sub-groups and try to break down the aromas present in the sample):

Estery Notes
fragrant (*carnations, roses*); fruit fruits (*pear-drops, apples*); solvent (*nail varnish, ethyl alcohol*); dried fruit (*raisins, dried figs, Christmas pudding*)

Sweet Associated Notes
honey, vanilla, custard powder, toffee, sherry, chocolate

Green (Aldehydic) Notes
floral (*green tomatoes, flowering currant*); leafy (*mown grass*); hay-like (dry hay, mown hay, herbs)

Cereal/Feinty Notes
toasted (*malty, toast, digestive biscuits*); cooked mash, cooked vegetables; husky (*chaff-like, tobacco*)

Phenolic Notes
medicinal (*TCP, iodine, carbolic, seaweed, etc.*); peaty (smoky, dry, creosote, mossy, tar, etc.)

Woody Notes
new wood (*resinous, pencil shavings, pine*); developed extract (*burnt rubber, paraffin, rum*); defective wood (*sour, musty*)

Oil Associated Notes
nutty (*marzipan, coconut*); buttery, fatty (*soapy*); rancid

Other Aromas (*including off-notes*)

3) Taste
Total intensity of flavour (1-5)
First impression of flavour
Integrated flavour complex (whisky identity)

Mouth-feel (*warming, astringent, viscous*)
Primary Taste (*sweet, sour, salty, bitter*)

Fruity/estery character
Peaty/smoky character
Sweet-associated character

4) Finish (1 min. after swallowing)
Character
Linger

VISITING DISTILLERIES

Just as a touring holiday in France would be incomplete without a visit to a vineyard or château, visits to distilleries have become an essential part of a holiday in Scotland. They are rewarding experiences: the distilleries are often picturesque and their situations delightful; the tours are often free of charge and conclude with a free tasting. And, since every distillery is different, the comparisons are fascinating and tours can be planned around distilleries. Visiting distilleries is a relatively recent phenomenon, associated with the massive growth in interest in malt whisky during the last decade. Many distilleries are now equipped with extensive facilities for visitors: often with a bar, coffee shop and gift shop; several with lecture theatres, video presentations, and full-blown restaurants. Others have no formal facilities, but all the distilleries listed below welcome visitors and are happy to provide guided tours. Most are open between 10am and 4pm, but there are sometimes variations between summer and winter opening times, and some visits are by appointment only. It is wise to telephone in advance.

ABERFELDY DISTILLERY, Aberfeldy, Perthshire ((0887) 20330

ABERLOUR-GLENLIVET DISTILLERY, Aberlour, Banffshire (0340) 871204

BALBLAIR DISTILLERY, Edderton, Tain, Ross-shire (086282) 273

BEN NEVIS DISTILLERY, Lochy Bridge, Fort William (0397) 700200

BLADNOCH DISTILLERY, Wigtown, Wigtownshire (09884) 2235

BLAIR ATHOLL DISTILLERY, Pitlochry, Perthshire (0796) 2234

BOWMORE DISTILLERY, Bowmore, Isle of Islay (0496) 81671

BRUICHLADDICH DISTILLERY, Bruichladdich, Isle of Islay (0496) 85221

BUNNAHABHAIN DISTILLERY, Bunnahabhain, Isle of Islay (0496) 84646

CAOL ILA DISTILLERY, Caol Ila, by Port Askaig, Isle of Islay (049684) 207

CARDHU DISTILLERY, Knockando, Aberlour, Banffshire (03406) 204

CLYNELISH DISTILLERY, Brora, Banffshire (0408) 21444

DALMORE DISTILLERY, Alness, Ross-shire (0349) 882362

DALWHINNIE DISTILLERY, Dalwhinnie, Inverness-shire (05282) 264

EDRADOUR DISTILLERY, Pitlochry, Perthshire (0796) 2095

FETTERCAIRN DISTILLERY, Fettercairn, Laurencekirk, Kincardineshire (05614) 34020

GLENDRONACH DISTILLERY, Forgue, Huntly, Aberdeenshire (046682) 202

GLENFARCLAS DISTILLERY, Ballindalloch, Banffshire (08072) 245

GLENFIDDICH DISTILLERY, Dufftown, Banffshire (0340) 20373

GLENGOYNE DISTILLERY, Dumgoyne, nr Killearn, Stirlingshire (041) 332 6361

GLEN GRANT DISTILLERY, Rothes, Morayshire (03403) 413

GLENKINCHIE DISTILLERY, Pencaitland, East Lothian (0875) 340451

THE GLENLIVET DISTILLERY, Glenlivet, Ballindalloch, Banffshire (08073) 427

GLENMORANGIE DISTILLERY, Tain, Ross-shire (086289) 2043

GLEN SCOTIA DISTILLERY, High Street, Campbeltown, Argyll (0586) 52288

GLENTURRET DISTILLERY, Glenturret, Crieff, Perthshire (0764) 2424

HIGHLAND PARK DISTILLERY, Holm Road, Kirkwall, Orkney (0856) 4619

JURA DISTILLERY, Craighouse, Isle of Jura (0496) 82240

LAGAVULIN DISTILLERY, by Port Ellen, Isle of Islay (0496) 84207

LAPHROAIG DISTILLERY, Port Ellen, Isle of Islay (0496) 2418

MACALLAN-GLENLIVET DISTILLERY, Craigellachie, Banff-shire (0340) 871471

MACDUFF DISTILLERY, Banff, Banffshire (02612) 2612
OBAN DISTILLERY, Stafford Street, Oban (0631) 64262
ORD DISTILLERY, Muir of Ord, Ross-shire (0463) 870421
PULTENEY DISTILLERY, Huddart Street, Wick, Caithness (0955) 2371
ROYAL LOCHNAGAR, Crathie, Ballater, Aberdeenshire (03397) 42273
STRATHISLA DISTILLERY, Keith, Banffshire (05422) 7471
STRATHMILL DISTILLERY, Keith, Banffshire (05422) 2295
TALISKER DISTILLERY, Carbost, Isle of Skye (047 842) 203
TAMDHU DISTILLERY, Knockando, Aberlour, Banffshire (03406) 221
TAMNAVULIN DISTILLERY,Tomnavoulin, Ballindalloch, Banffshire ((08073) 442
TOBERMORY DISTILLERY, Main Street, Tobermory, Isle of Mull (0688) 2119
TOMATIN DISTILLERY, Tomatin, Inverness-shire (08082) 234
TULLIBARDINE DISTILLERY, Blackford, Perthshire (076482) 252

Bottling Plants
DEWAR'S, Inveralmond Perth (0738) 21401
JOHN WALKER & SONS, Hill Street, Kilmarnock (0563) 23401

Visitor Centres
CAIRNGORM WHISKY CENTRE, Rothiemurchas, near Aviemore (0479) 810574. Video presentation; tasting room; displays on making whisky; small museum of distillery relics.

DALLAS DHU DISTILLERY, Forres, Morayshire (0309) 76548
A well preserved traditional distillery, now no longer working.

THE SCOTCH WHISKY HERITAGE CENTRE, Castlehill, Royal Mile, Edinburgh (031) 220 0441
The Centre is close to Edinburgh Castle, and the 'experience' includes time-travel in an motorized half-barrel past various tableaux depicting key events in the history of Scotch whisky (commentary in English, Dutch, French, German, Italian, Japanese and Spanish). There is also an A/V presentation, a model of Tormore Distillery and lectures on making whisky and blending. A shop sells a variety of malts.

The Malt Whisky Trail
A signposted tour on Speyside guides the visitor to eight distilleries with well-established facilities. The trail is about 70 miles long, and member distilleries are:Cardhu, Glenfarclas, Glenfiddich, Glen Grant, The Glenlivet, Strathisla, Tamdhu and Tamnavulin.

WHISKY SOCIETIES

THE SCOTCH WHISKY ASSOCIATION
(20 Atholl Crescent, Edinburgh EH3 8HF)
Established in 1942 by the leading companies in the industry to protect and promote the interests of the Scotch whisky industry world-wide.

The SWA has a Secretariat of 28 full-time staff, operating from offices in Edinburgh and London, headed by the Director General and Secretary, Colonel H.F.O. Bewsher. It is governed and its activities determined by a Council of 18, drawn from the member companies – most of the leading companies in the industry are represented. The Council is supported by several Committees and Working Parties which examine and progress specific areas and issues.

THE KEEPERS OF THE QUAICH
(Burke Lodge, 20 London End, Beaconsfield, Bucks HP9 2JH)
Although of relatively recent foundation (1988), The Keepers of the Quaich is the most prestigious and exclusive whisky society in the world. It was established by some of the Scotch whisky industry's leading companies (United Distillers, Allied Distillers, Justerini & Brooks, Highland Distilleries and Chivas/Glenlivet) to honour those who have contributed significantly to the prestige and success of Scotch whisky world-wide, and to advance the standing and reputation of the Scotch whisky industry and the hospitable traditions of Scotland.

The Society has just over 500 members in 38 countries (only about half the membership is British); its current Grand Master is Sir Iain Tennant, and its patrons include the Dukes of Atholl and Argyll, and the Earls of Erroll, Elgin & Kincardine and Mansfield. Its headquarters are at Blair Castle, the magnificent seat of the Duke of Atholl, where splendid banquets are held bi-annually.

THE SCOTCH MALT WHISKY SOCIETY
(The Vaults, 87 St Giles Street, Leith, Edinburgh EH6 6BZ)
SMWS grew out of the enthusiasm for cask strength malt whisky of a handful of connoisseurs in Edinburgh. It was formally established in 1983, and now has a world-wide membership of over 20,000. The Society selects casks and bottles their contents without chill filtering or reduction, so that the individual characteristics of the cask and the whisky can be appreciated. The distillery and the number of the cask is identified on each bottle. Although available bottlings vary from time to time, the Society has bottled a range of ages from over 100 distilleries. Members have the use of splendid accommodation at the Vaults, Leith (the old port of Edinburgh); there is a quarterly Newsletter and seasonal 'Bottlings' catalogue, listing those whiskies which are currently available (usually 20–30 at a time).

THE ADELPHI DISTILLERY LTD
(3 Gloucester Lane, Edinburgh EH3 6ED)
The Adelphi Distillery, Glasgow, was founded in 1820 and demolished in 1960. At the turn of the century it was owned by Alexander Walker (no relation) and his grandson, James Walker, revived the name in 1993 for a mail-order whisky company. The Adelphi sets out to buy and bottle casks of mature malts at unusual ages from unusual distilleries and to bring these bottlings to the attention of its customers. There is no fee to join this 'club'.

THE CASK STRENGTH SCOTCH MALT WHISKY SOCIETY OF TOKYO
(c/o Scots Imports, World Import Mart 6F1, 1–3–3 Higashi Ikebukuro, Toshima-ku, Tokyo 170)
Formed in 1993 under the patronage of the British Ambassador to Japan. Its Honorary President is whisky writer Wallace Milroy.

THE WHISKY CONNOISSEUR CLUB
(Thistle Mill, Biggar, Midlothian ML12 6LP)
Recently founded by Arthur J.A. Bell (no relation), the Club's tasting panel selects about 40 whiskies every two months – mainly single cask malt bottlings, with some unusual blends and liqueurs; half bottles and miniatures also. These are offered to its members, with tasting notes and distillery histories.

WORLD SALES

The following tables are compiled from information supplied by HM Customs and Excise and from individual whisky companies. I am also indebted to analysis which has been carried out by The Scotch Whisky Association (Statistical Report 1992), Charterhouse Tilney (*The Scotch Whisky Industry Review 1992* (by Alan S. Gray) and Impact International.

World Consumption of Scotch Whisky
(Pure alcohol, millions of litres)

	Exports	UK	Total Sales
1980	249.92	50.16	303.78
1981	244.24	47.71	295.83
1982	251.28	44.75	300.23
1983	227.84	44.48	276.82
1984	231.29	43.36	279.54
1985	225.89	46.15	277.19
1986	236.19	45.64	287.33
1987	240.17	44.60	290.75
1988	245.94	45.18	296.12
1989	242.49	43.03	290.52
1990	238.30	41.34	285.29
1991	227.75	38.26	270.01
1992	231.27	35.79	267.06

Scotch Whisky Production
(Pure alcohol, millions of litres)

31 Dec.	Malt	Grain	Total
1990	192.82	235.94	428.76
1991	186.26	230.53	416.80
1992	166.50	216.98	383.50

Top Twenty Markets, 1991/2
(Pure alcohol, millions of litres)

		1991	1992
1	USA	40.88	38.41
2	UK	38.26	35.78
3	France	25.68	28.68
4	Spain	18.80	22.39
5	Japan	18.02	18.55
6	Germany	9.18	9.05
7	Greece	8.19	8.62
8	Australia	6.85	6.96
9	Italy	8.62	6.70
10	Venezuela	4.36	6.25
11	South Africa	5.62	5.95
12	Portugal	5.28	5.25
13	Thailand	5.47	4.80
14	Korea	5.19	4.60
15	Netherlands	3.66	4.19
16	Canada	3.58	3.20
17	Belgo–Lux	4.30	3.14
18	Brazil	4.60	3.11
19	Mexico	2.54	2.88
20	Paraguay	3.20	2.69

Notes:
1) The major growth markets (1981–92) have been Thailand, Korea, Spain and Portugal.

2) Most of Australia's whisky is bought in bulk (63% in 1991).

3) In 1992 51% of sales to Japan were bulk malt whisky.

4) Italy buys over 99% of its whisky Bottled in Scotland (BIS) – as opposed to bulk; about 25% of sales are single malts (representing 27% of the world's sales of single malts).

5) Spain and Portugal have been particularly buoyant markets since their entry to the EC in 1986.

Best-Sellers

a) Top Ten Malt Whiskies

At the time printing, the most recent figures available relate to 1991: the first six positions were unchanged from 1990.

	World Sales	UK Sales	Export Sales
1	Glenfiddich	Glenfiddich	Glenfiddich
2	Glen Grant	Glenmorangie	Glen Grant
3	The Glenlivet	Macallan	The Glenlivet
4	Glenmorangie	The Glenlivet	Glenmorangie
5	Macallan	Laphroaig	Macallan
6	Cardhu	Isle of Jura	Aberlour
	Aberlour		
7	Cragganmore	Highland Park	Cardhu
			Cragganmore
8	Knockando	Knockando	Knockando
		Singleton of Auchroisk	Springbank
9	Springbank	Bowmore	Bowmore
10	Isle of Jura	Lagavulin	Lagavulin

Notes:

The no. 1, Glenfiddich, sold in the region of 800,000 cases world-wide in 1991; no. 2, Glen Grant, sold 500,000 cases; Isle of Jura at no. 10 sold 32,000 cases. In the UK Glenfiddich sold approx. 125,000 cases; Lagavulin at no. 10 sold 7,300 cases (20,700 in export markets).

b) Top Twenty Blended Whiskies

At the time of printing, the most recent figures available relate to 1991. There were few changes from 1990: VAT 69, Muirhead's and The Glenlivet appeared on the UK list for the first time.

	World Sales	UK Sales	Export Sales
1	Johnnie Walker Red	Bell's	Johnnie Walker Red
2	J&B Rare	Famous Grouse	J&B Rare
3	Ballantine's	Teacher's	Ballantine's
4	Bell's	Claymore	Chivas Regal
5	Chivas Regal	Whyte & Mackay	Dewar's
6	Dewar's	Grant's	Johnnie Walker Black
7	Johnnie Walker Blk	White Horse	Grant's
8	Grant's	Stewarts Cream of the Barley	Cutty Sark
9	Famous Grouse	(Glenfiddich)	Bell's
10	Cutty Sark	VAT 69	White Horse
11	Teacher's	Haig	Black & White
12	White Horse	Crawford's 3*	William Lawson's
13	VAT 69	Johnnie Walker Black	VAT 69
14	Black & White	Mackinlay's	Clan Campbell
15	Whyte & Mackay	(Glenmorangie)	Teacher's
16	William Lawson's	Chivas Regal}	Long John

World Sales	UK Sales	Export Sales
	Langs Supreme}	
	100 Pipers }	
17 Claymore	J&B Rare	Old Parr
		(Glenfiddich) }
18 Clan Campbell	(The Glenlivet)	Scoresby Rare }
19 (Glenfiddich)	Clan Campbell	Famous Grouse
20 Long John	Muirhead's	Clan Macgregor

Notes:

World Sales – Johnnie Walker Red Label sold an estimated 6,512, 000 cases in 1991;

J&B Rare 6,045,000, Ballantine's 4,785,000. Band 1) brands sold over 3 million cases, Band 2) over 2 million cases, Band 3) over 1 million cases, Band 4) under 1 million cases (Long John at number 20 sold 740,000).

UK Sales – Bell's sold an estimated 2,210,000 cases in 1991; Famous Grouse 1,380,000; Teacher's 925,000. Thereafter, Band A) is more than 500,000 cases sold, Band B) is more than 100,000 cases, Band C) is more than 25,000 (Muirhead's at number 20 sold 26,000 cases).

Export Sales – Johnnie Walker Red Label sold an estimated 6,495,000 cases in export markets in 1991; J&B Rare 6,000,000, Ballantine's 4,775,000.

Band 1) is over 3 million cases, Band 2) over 2 million cases, Band 3) over 1 million cases, Band 4) over 700,000, Band 5) over 600,000. Clan Macgregor sold an estimated 510,000 cases in export markets.

Bulk Blends – The tables above relate only to blends bottled in Scotland. Some brands – notably Crawford's 3,★ 100 Pipers and Passport – are shipped in bulk to certain markets (especially South America, Korea and Germany) for reasons of tax, and sell in large quantities at a competitive price.

COLLECTING WHISKIES

Note: *I am indebted to Christie's Scotland for much of the information in this section, and in particular to Martin Green, their Whisky Specialist.*

Most of the 'classic' whisky writers of the 1930s, 40s and 50s recount stories of the occasional very old whiskies they have been privileged to sample, some of them bottled in the 19th century. In more prosaic times, these old whiskies are rarely drunk, but they are more avidly collected today than ever before, and proudly displayed by their owners. Which is not to say they are not drinkable. On the contrary, Michael Jackson, the contemporary whisky-writer, pronounced samples salvaged from the wartime wreck SS *Politician* (see entry) to be excellent. I have tasted blended whisky which was bottled during the war and found it like old brandy. It is said that, unlike wine, whisky does not continue to mature in bottle, but it does change – I believe for the better. There is something miraculous about a comestible surviving from another age.

Some of the best collections of Scotch whisky are found abroad – one of the finest, some 2,185 different brands and expressions, belongs to the President of the Brazilian Whisky Collector's Association. The reason for this is that many export brands are unavailable in the home market. Some of the best collections in the UK are owned by the distilleries and brand owners themselves, and they are always keen to acquire bottles for their archives.

The attraction of old bottles of whisky depends upon: a) rarity, b) originality of bottle shape and design, c) attractiveness of label. Features that indicate age, which collectors look for, include:

Stoppers

These give one of the clearest indications of age. The earliest form of seal was melted wax, applied after the cork had been driven in. Often the wax was embossed with the producer or brand name or badge. By the 1890s, lead or alloy capsules were used to protect the cork, and these too were often embossed. Some early bottles were fitted with a glass stopper rather than a cork: a slight indentation around the neck, beneath the capsule, shows where the edge of the stopper meets the neck of the bottle. The replaceable cork (one fitted with a wooden rim) was invented by William Menera Bergius in 1913, and first used by Teachers, for **Highland Cream** – with the slogan 'bury the corkscrew'. In the early 1920s spring caps made of metal were adopted by some companies. The metal screw cap was first introduced in 1926 by **White Horse**.

Bottles

Early bottles were hand blown or made in three pieces and formed while the glass was molten. Look for tiny bubbles and imperfections in the glass, which is usually clear, dark blue or dark green in colour. Often these hand-made bottles are not conventionally shaped, and some will not stand completely upright.

Labels

The condition and legibility of the label is highly important from the collectors' point of view. Look for date, name of bottler, company name, crest and logo, as well as brand name. Some labels are very colourful, and exquisitely designed, sometimes with fanciful (often Highland) subjects; others, including many 19th century malt bottlings are plain and restrained. Where the bottle is a single malt, look for the name of the distillery. 'Liqueur Scotch Whisky', 'Rare Old Scotch Whisky', 'Fine Old Scotch Whisky', etc., indicate that the whisky was moderately mature when bottled. Where blends are concerned, look for the words 'Rare' or 'Fine Old Blended': some of the malts used in such blends may have spent between 5 and 25 years in cask prior to blending.

A SELECTION OF RECENT AUCTION PRICES

Many distilleries release special commemorative bottlings from time to time, aimed at the collector and the connoisseur (this book lists many such releases). Because the quantity bottled is necessarily limited, these vintages or expressions immediately have rarity value, and some quickly find their way into auction houses, of which Christie's is pre-eminent. Here is a selection of current auction estimates, based upon results of recent Christie's sales:

	Price per bottle
Aberlour 25 Years Old (1964)	£60–80
Auchentoshan 1966	£30–50
Balblair 1957	£50–70
Balvenie 50 Years Old (1937)	£1,000–1,200
Ben Nevis 1881	£1,250–1,350
Bowmore 1956	£90–130
Bowmore 1963	£60–80
Bruichladdich 21 Years Old (1965)	£40–50
Bunnahabhain 28 Years Old (1947)	£500–700
Dalintober 40 Years Old (1868)	£2,300–2,500
Dallas Dhu 64 Years Old (1921)	£2,800–3,000
Dalmore 50 Years Old (1928)	£950–1,200
Dew of Ben Nevis 1882	£1,350–1,550
Fettercairn 30 Years Old (1955)	£150–200

	Price per bottle
Glenfiddich 1936	£650–750
Glen Grant 1895	£1,560–1,760
Glen Grant 59 Years Old (1891)	£2,000–2,500
Glen Grant 42 Years Old	£150–200
Glen Grant 1936	£130–180
Glen Grant 1948	£90–130
Glen Grant 1949	£200–260
Glen Grant 1952	£80–120
Glenlivet 1938	£90–110
Glenlivet 1939	£50–100
Glenlivet 1940	£90–110
Glenlivet 1946	£90–130
Glenlivet Special Export Reserve 34 Years Old (1944)	£250–300
Glenlivet 21 Years Old (1963)	£100–170
Glenmorangie 22 Years Old (1963)	£90–120
Glenrothes 42 Years Old (1932)	£400–500
Glenturret 1965	£90–130
Lagavulin 30 Years Old (1881)	£3,000–3,200
Longmorn 1939	£400–420
Linkwood 44 Years Old (1938)	£150–180
Macallan 60 Years Old (1926)	£6,000–6,500
Macallan 50 Years Old (1928)	£1,600–2,000
Macallan 40 Years Old	£500–600
Macallan 1937	£300–400
Macallan 1938	£400–550
Macallan 1940	£500–600
Macallan 1945	£550–650
Macallan 1947	£250–280
Macallan 1950	£250–350
Macallan 1951	£250–300
Macallan 1954	£150–200
Macallan 1955	£100–130
Macallan 1959	£90–110
Macallan 25 Years Old (1958)	£90–130
Macallan 1961	£70–90
Macallan 1963	£60–80
Macallan 1964	£50–70
Macallan 1965	£50–70
Old Elgin 46 Years Old (1938)	£150–180
Old Orkney (circa 1915)	£850–950
Pride of Strathspey 1938	£90–110
Pride of Strathspey 1940	£80–100
Rosebank 1938	£400–500
Royal Lochnagar 30 Years Old (1952)	£80–120
Springbank 50 Years Old (1919)	£1,200–1,600
Strathisla 1939	£70–90
Talisker 1947	£130–150
Talisker 1956	£60–80
Talisker 1957	£90–110
Talisker 1970	£50–60
White Horse 1926	£500–600
White Horse 1935	£450–550
White Horse 1940	£200–260
White Horse 1941	£150–180
White Horse 1944	£180–220
White Horse 1951	£180–200
White Horse 1952	£80–100
White Horse 1957	£90–110

BIBLIOGRAPHY

(* indicates leading titles)

Barnard, Alfred, The Whisky Distilleries of the United Kingdom (London 1887; repr. Newton Abbot, 1969; Edinburgh 1987)*

Birnie, William, The Distillation of Highland Malt Whisky (Private, 1937 and 1964)

Brander, Michael, The Original Scotch (London, 1974)

— A Guide to Scotch Whisky (Edinburgh, 1975)

— The Essential Guide to Scotch Whisky (Edinburgh, 1990)

Bronfman, Samuel, From Little Acorns, The Story of Distillers Corporation – Seagrams Limited (Private, 1970)

Bruce-Lockhart, Sir Robert, Scotch (London, 1951)*

Cooper, Derek, A Taste of Scotch (London, 1989)

— The Little Book of Malt Whiskies (Belfast, 1992)

Daiches, David, Scotch Whisky (London, 1969) *

— A Wee Dram; Drinking Scenes from Scottish Literature (London, 1990)

Distillers Company Limited, DCL and Scotch Whisky (London, 1961; numerous editions)

Dunnet, Alastair, The Land of Scotch(Edinburgh, 1953)

Grindal, Richard, The Spirit of Whisky (London, 1992)

Gunn, Neil, Whisky and Scotland (London, 1935, rep. 1990) *

Hills, Philip et al., Scots on Scotch (Edinburgh, 1991)

House, Jack, Pride of Perth: The Story of Arthur Bell & Co .(London, 1976)

Jackson, Michael, The World Guide to Whisky (London, 1987)*

— The Malt Whisky Companion (London, 1989)*

Laver, James, The House of Haig (Perth, 1958)

Macdonald, Aeneas,Whisky (Edinburgh, 1930)

McDowall, R.J.S., The Whiskies of Scotland (London, 1967)*

MacLean, Charles, Scottish Toasts (Belfast, 1993)

MacNeill, F. Marian, The Scots Cellar, Its Traditions and Lore (Edinburgh, 1956)

Mantle, Jonathan, The Ballantine's Story (London, 1991)

Milroy, Wallace, The Malt Whisky Almanac (Moffat, 1986; 5th edn, 1992)*

Morrice, Philip, Scotch, The Schweppes Guide to (London, 1983)*

— The Whisky Distilleries of Scotland and Ireland (London, 1987)

Moss, Michael S. and Hume, John R., The Making of Scotch Whisky – A History of the Scotch Whisky Distilling Industry (Edinburgh, 1981)*

Nettleton, J.A., The Manufacture of Scotch Whisky and Plain Spirit (Aberdeen, 1913)

Robb, J.Marshall, Scotch Whisky, A Guide (Edinburgh, 1950)*

Ross, James, Whisky (London, 1970)

Scotch Whisky Association, Scotch Whisky, Questions and Answers (Edinburgh 1957, numerous reprints – latest 1992)

Skipworth, Mark, The Scotch Whisky Book (London, 1987)

Sillet, S.W., Illicit Scotch (Aberdeen, 1965)

Smith-Grant, Captain W., Glenlivet: The Annals of the Distillery (Private, 1924, repr. 1959)

Spiller, Brian, Cardhu, The World of Malt Whisky (London, 1985)

— D.C.L. Distillery Histories (London, 1981)*

Wilson, Neil, Scotch and Water: Islay, Jura, Mull, Skye (Lockerbie, 1985)*

Wilson Ross, Scotch Made Easy (London, 1959)

— Scotch, The Formative Years (London, 1970)*

— Scotch, Its History and Romance (Newton Abbot, 1973)